Reasoning about God

Reasoning about God is an introduction to philosophy of religion, meeting college students where they are with their own doubts and questions. Each chapter begins with a passage from a fictional student, who raises intellectual problems against God, which is followed by the author's informed and easy-to-understand analysis. This debate structure allows student readers to clearly see the clash of ideas, gets them involved in the issues, and encourages their critical thinking (since students are pushed to find flaws in the ideas). It emulates the structure the author followed successfully in his *Ethics: A Contemporary Introduction*, which is now in its third edition and has been translated five times into other languages. This structure works well in philosophy of religion, even better than it does in ethics.

Key Features of *Reasoning about God*

- Written clearly and concisely, making difficult issues easy to understand.
- Makes a strong case for belief in God, based on various factors – including arguments about fine-tuning, Kalam, and near-death experiences – as well as approaches that are more instinctual or emotional. A major theme of the book is "There are many paths to God."
- Includes material on both traditional topics of philosophy of religion (like the problem of evil) and other related topics of interest (like whether religion is harmful, life after death, the variety of world religions, and the meaning of life).
- Explores how science connects to God's existence, arguing that recent science is friendlier toward religion than older science.
- Written by a Christian author whose defense of belief in God works with other theistic traditions as well (like Islam and Judaism).

Harry J. Gensler, S.J., (1945–2022) retired from Loyola University Chicago in 2021, and earlier in his life had taught at Gonzaga University, the University of Scranton, John Carroll University, Marquette University, and the University of Wuhan in China. His main areas of study were logic, ethics, and religion. This is his 17th philosophy book, many of which have been translated into other languages. Some of his other books include: *Anthology of Catholic Philosophy* (2005); *Ethics and the Golden Rule* (2013); *Ethics and Religion* (2016); *Introduction to Logic*, 3rd ed. (2017); and *Ethics: A Contemporary Introduction*, 3rd ed. (2018).

Reasoning about God

An Introduction to Thinking Logically about Religion

Harry J. Gensler

NEW YORK AND LONDON

First published 2023
by Routledge
605 Third Avenue, New York, NY 10158

and by Routledge
4 Park Square, Milton Park, Abingdon, Oxon, OX14 4RN

Routledge is an imprint of the Taylor & Francis Group, an informa business

© 2023 Taylor & Francis

The right of Harry J. Gensler to be identified as author of this work has been asserted in accordance with sections 77 and 78 of the Copyright, Designs and Patents Act 1988.

All rights reserved. No part of this book may be reprinted or reproduced or utilised in any form or by any electronic, mechanical, or other means, now known or hereafter invented, including photocopying and recording, or in any information storage or retrieval system, without permission in writing from the publishers.

Trademark notice: Product or corporate names may be trademarks or registered trademarks, and are used only for identification and explanation without intent to infringe.

Library of Congress Cataloging-in-Publication Data
A catalog record for this title has been requested

ISBN: 978-1-032-34173-6 (hbk)
ISBN: 978-1-032-34172-9 (pbk)
ISBN: 978-1-003-32092-0 (ebk)

DOI: 10.4324/9781003320920

Typeset in Bembo
By Apex CoVantage, LLC

 Printed in the United Kingdom by Henry Ling Limited

7.6 *Analysis: Mysticism* 91
7.7 *Analysis: Why One God?* 92
7.8 *Analysis: A Pagan-Christian Debate* 93

8. Does Suffering Disprove God?   98

8.1 *Skepticus: The Problem of Evil* 98
8.2 *Skepticus: Did Adam's Sin Begin Disease and Death?* 100
8.3 *Skepticus: The Biblical Problem of Evil* 102
8.4 *Analysis: How Irenaeus Explains Evil* 103
8.5 *Analysis: What Kind of World Would God Create?* 106
8.6 *Analysis: Further Questions About Evil* 107
8.7 *Analysis: The Biblical Problem of Evil* 113

9. Why So Many Religions?   116

9.1 *Skepticus: Chaotic Religious Diversity* 116
9.2 *Analysis: Similarities and Differences* 117
9.3 *Analysis: Fellow GR Pilgrims, or Enemies?* 119
9.4 *Analysis: The Golden Rule* 121
9.5 *Analysis: Five GR Fallacies* 123
9.6 *Analysis: GR in Christianity* 128
9.7 *Analysis: GR in Other Faiths* 130
9.8 *Analysis: GR and Evolution* 134

10. Is Ethics Based on Religion?   136

10.1 *Skepticus: Divine Command Theory* 136
10.2 *Skepticus: Divine Command Objections* 138
10.3 *Skepticus: An Objection to Natural Law* 141
10.4 *Analysis: Natural Law and Racism* 141
10.5 *Analysis: Knowing God's Will* 145
10.6 *Analysis: Natural Law's Three Parts* 146
10.7 *Analysis: As Rational Beings* 147
10.8 *Analysis: As Biological Beings* 148
10.9 *Analysis: As Spiritual Beings* 150

11. The Meaning of Life   152

11.1 *Skepticus: Life Has No Meaning* 152
11.2 *Analysis: Life Has a Meaning* 153
11.3 *Analysis: Why Think That Life Has a Meaning?* 156

11.4 Analysis: Atheism's Dark Side 157
11.5 Analysis: Skepticus Errors 159
11.6 Analysis: Your Favorite Paths to God? 161

Bibliography   164
Index   170

Preface

Reasoning about God is a book for college students about philosophy of religion. Chapters begin with a passage from a fictional student, who raises intellectual problems against God; my analysis follows. This debate structure well presents the clash of ideas, gets students involved in the issues, and encourages critical thinking (since students are pushed to find flaws in the ideas). I followed this structure successfully in my ethics textbook (*Ethics: A Contemporary Introduction*), which is in three editions and has been translated five times into other languages. This structure works well in religion, even better than in ethics.

Here are some of the book's virtues:

- The writing is clear and concise and makes difficult issues easy to understand.
- The book makes a strong case for belief in God, based on various factors – including arguments about fine-tuning, Kalam, and near-death experiences – and approaches that are more instinctual or emotional. A major theme of the book is "There are many paths to God."
- While there is much on traditional topics of philosophy of religion (like the problem of evil), there is also much on other related topics of interest (like whether religion is harmful, life after death, the variety of world religions, and the meaning of life).
- There is much on science and how it connects to God's existence. I argue that recent science is friendlier toward religion than older science.
- While I'm Christian, my defense of belief in God works with other theistic traditions, too (like Islam and Judaism).

I hope you enjoy the book. I hope it helps you to think and reason more clearly about one of life's most important questions: "Is there a God?"

Harry J. Gensler, S.J.
I retired from Loyola University Chicago
http://www.harrycola.com
http://www.harryhiker.com

Publisher's note: Harry Gensler passed away during the production of this book. The publishers would like to express their sadness at Harry's passing, their thanks to him for being a pleasure to work with, and their gratitude for his many contributions to Routledge philosophy. Harry asked that the following words be added: "Gensler died of cancer, but he was happy that he finished this book while still alive."

Introduction

Reasoning about God is a book for college students about philosophy of religion. So what is *philosophy of religion*? But first, what is *philosophy*?

A. Philosophy

Philosophy is *reasoning about the big questions of life*. Here we focus on the biggest question: *Is there a God?* We also deal with related questions, like: Is there life after death? Is science the only path to knowledge? How ought we to live? What is the meaning of life? . . . Such questions are difficult and controversial; we'll *reason* about them.

Other disciplines study the big questions in their own way. We can study the *history* of belief in God, its *psychological* causes or stages, or its treatment in *literature* or *religious traditions*. While valuable, these studies don't replace *philosophy* – which rationally debates the big questions (like whether God exists).

B. Logical Reasoning

Reasoning in philosophy resembles other reasoning. We reason about who committed the murder, what car to buy, whether there's a greatest prime number, or how to cure cancer. As we approach these, we clarify the issue and gather background information. We review what others have said. We consider alternative views and objections to them. We make distinctions and weigh pros and cons. We may do experiments. The climax in philosophy comes when we take a stand and try to justify it. We explain that the answer must be such and such, and we point to other facts to justify our answer; this is *logical reasoning*, where we go from premises to a conclusion.

Logical reasoning concludes something from something else. We may conclude that the butler committed the murder from the beliefs that (1) either the butler or the maid did it, and (2) the maid didn't do it. If we put such reasoning into words, we get an *argument* – a set of statements consisting of premises and a conclusion (here "∴" is short for "therefore"):

1. Either the butler or the maid did it.
2. The maid didn't do it.
∴ The butler did it.

This argument is *valid*, which means that the conclusion follows logically from the premises: if the premises are true, then the conclusion must be true. When arguing for a conclusion, we try to give a *sound argument*, which is a *valid argument with true premises*.[1] If we satisfy both conditions (our premises are all true, and our conclusion follows logically from them), then our conclusion has to be true. When arguing, we try to find strong premises and may try to answer objections against them. When criticizing an argument, we need to dispute its logical validity (show that the conclusion doesn't follow from the premises) or attack premises (show that some are false or doubtful).

Doing philosophy involves much logical reasoning. We can often attack a view P by showing that it leads to an absurdity Q:

1. If P is true, then Q would be true.
2. Q is false.
∴ P is false.

It's important to examine a view's implications and look for flaws. We can show a view to be false by showing that it has false or even contradictory implications; we at least cast doubt on a view by showing that it has doubtful implications.

Here's a complicated argument important in philosophy of religion:

1. If God doesn't want to prevent evil, then he isn't all good.
2. If God isn't able to prevent evil, then he isn't all powerful.
3. Either God doesn't want to prevent evil, or he isn't able.
∴ Either God isn't all powerful, or he isn't all good.

This *problem of evil* argument, which has been discussed for thousands of years, is the most important objection to belief in God, or at least in a God who is all good and all powerful. Why doesn't evil in the world show that such a God can't exist? We'll later hear more about this argument and how to respond to it. For now, keep in mind the importance of logic and carefully worded arguments to philosophy of religion.[2]

---

1 We also need to avoid circularity and a few more things (Gensler 2017a: ch. 1 & §4.1).
2 If you've had a logic course, you'll find it useful. I suggest Gensler (2017a) if you want to learn logic on your own (it uses many philosophy-of-religion examples). The bibliography at the back of the book has further information about works that I refer to.

In developing our philosophical views, *reasoning* and *personal commitment* *(faith)* are both important. Reasoning alone won't resolve all the disputes. After considering arguments on both sides, we have to make up our minds. But if we pick a view with strong objections, we need to respond to these. Philosophy doesn't argue from religious revelation or tradition; arguing from these is *theology*, not *philosophy*.

I like the "stepping stone" analogy, where a stepping stone is a stone that helps you cross a stream without getting your feet wet; reason is like stones that we can use to get to faith on the other side.[3] Human reason can be a definite help to faith; faith isn't just a random eyes-closed leap in the dark but rather needs as much deep thinking as we can muster. But human reason is seldom 100% rock solid, and it often involves some risk. We need to find good ways to combine faith and reason.

One of my favorite slogans is *"There are many paths to God."* You can see many paths if you study a group of believers (like the twelve apostles, Christian philosophers, or Jesuits) and see what attracted them to God. The stepping-stone analogy can be extended. In hiking across a stream, we sometimes have to search out which stepping stones to use – and we may use different stones than others use. Sometimes a possible stepping stone won't work well, since it's poorly anchored in the creek or covered with slippery algae; we may have to look elsewhere to find a piece of human reason that will help us on our path to God. But there are *many rational stepping stones* that can help us on our path to God, and that's a theme of this book.

The 11 chapters to follow cover these topics:

1. Growing Up, Freud, Science
2. Is Religion Harmful?
3. Logical Positivism *(science is everything)*
4. Is There Life After Death?
5. Is There a First Cause?
6. Is the Universe Designed?
7. Three Paths *(ontological argument, reformed epistemology, mysticism)* + polytheism *(why ONE God and a pagan-Christian debate)*
8. Does Suffering Disprove God?
9. Why So Many Religions? *(plus much on the golden rule, which is their common teaching)*

---

3 I use a picture slide in class (see following link) of a stepping stone for crossing Hermit Creek in the Grand Canyon. I pretend to jump on the stone, and then across to the other side, without losing my balance and getting my feet wet.

https://harryhiker.com/gc19/html/11.htm or https://harrycola.com/gc19/html/11.htm. (I have two identical Web sites, harryhiker.com and harrycola.com, and if one doesn't work, then try the other; I pay for the first one, and it will likely not work after I die, while Routledge Press pays for the second one, which should continue to work.)

10. Is Ethics Based on Religion?
11. The Meaning of Life

Questions about God lead us into many interesting directions.[4]

C. Mere Monotheism

C.S. Lewis's (1952) *Mere Christianity* defended Christianity's broad features, common to different branches (like Catholicism, Protestantism, and Eastern Orthodoxy); it didn't argue for one branch against another. I might have called this present book *Mere Monotheism*, because I defend the broad features of monotheism (belief in one supreme God) but don't argue for one monotheist faith against another.

The three major monotheist religions – Judaism, Christianity, and Islam – are called "Abrahamic religions," because they all stem from Abraham of the Old Testament. They believe in one supreme God, and they've shared ideas over the ages.[5] While I myself am Christian (and Catholic and Jesuit), most of what I say will apply to Jews, Muslims, or those of other monotheist religions.

When I use the word "God" in this book, what do I mean? I intend it to be understood as in the great monotheist religions, roughly as Frederick Copleston (1948) and Bertrand Russell agreed to in their radio debate: "a supreme personal being – distinct from the world and creator of the world." I'll assume traditional definitions of "theist," "atheist," and "agnostic." A *theist* (*monotheist*) is one who believes that there's a God; this belief may be seen as certain or uncertain, as backed up by firm argument or not. An *atheist* believes there's no God (again seen as certain or not or as backed up by firm argument or not). An *agnostic* takes no stand on whether there's a God (and thus is undecided about God).[6]

So this book defends theism in general, instead of Christianity or Catholicism. Why this focus? For one thing, I have more interest and background

---

4 For more on a topic, try a Web search for a chapter or section title (like "Is there life after death?" or "What kind of world would God create?"). Many titles are helpfully descriptive.
5 Thinkers of monotheist faiths often learn from other such faiths. St. Thomas Aquinas's (1274) *Summa Theologica*, perhaps Christian thought's greatest work, often refers to Muslim thinkers, especially Ibn Sina (Avicenna, 46 references) and Ibn Rushd (Averroes, 12 references). The important Kalam argument (§5.5) for God's existence has a Muslim name and origin. And six books that I wrote were translated into Persian or Arabic or both.
   See http://harryhiker.com/books or http://harrycola.com/books.
6 Richard Swinburne (2016: 1) suggests this definition of "God," which would work just as well for my purposes: "a being with most of the following properties: being a person without a body (that is, a spirit), present everywhere (that is, omnipresent), the creator of the universe, perfectly free, able to do anything (that is, omnipotent), knowing all things (that is, omniscient), perfectly good, a source of moral obligation, eternal, a necessary being, holy, and worthy of worship."

in general questions about God. Also, I'm good at cooperating and learning from others – instead of arguing that my tradition is right while others are wrong. This *cooperative* (instead of *combative*) approach to other faiths nicely fits Jesus's example (Gensler 2013a: 42):

> Jesus lived in an interfaith environment and often praised those of other faiths. Those outside the Judeo-Christian tradition portrayed positively in the gospels include the Wise Men from the East (perhaps Hindus) who visited the infant Jesus (Mt 2:1–12), the Roman Centurion whose servant Jesus cured (Mt 8:5–13), the demented Gentile who lived among the pig-raisers (Mt 8:28–34 & Lk 8:26–39), the Ninevites who reformed their lives after Jonah confronted them (Mt 12:39–41), the queen of the South who visited Solomon (Mt 12:42), the Canaanite woman (Mt 15:22–8 & Lk 7:25), Pilate's wife (Mt 27:19), the Roman Centurion at Jesus's death (Mt 27:54 & Lk 7:2–9), the Gentile widow that Elias visited (Lk 4:26), Naaman the Syrian leper who was cured (Lk 4:27), the Good Samaritan who helps a stranger (Lk 10:24–37), and the cured Samaritan leper who gave thanks (Lk 17:12–9). All are praised or presented positively; they're not called "followers of Satan."

I see people of different faith traditions (and even atheists and agnostics) as fellow travelers on life's great pilgrimage back to God.[7]

D. Skepticus and Analysis

Chapters that follow have a debate structure. Each starts with a passage, by a fictional college student named *Skepticus*, with persuasive objections to God or religion. Take Skepticus's view seriously and understand it. Try to explain it accurately (as if to a third party) without slanted language; a good motto for doing philosophy is "Understand before you criticize." After you understand the view, reflect on how plausible you find it and how well it fits your own thinking. Then look for objections.

Read the fictional passage several times. First read for the general idea. Read it again for details; be sympathetic, as if you were listening to a friend explain her views. Read again critically, trying to uncover weak points and problems. Finally, after you've read the rest of the chapter and perhaps discussed the view in class, read it again to see where you stand.[8]

---

7 While I'm optimistic about interfaith relations, I admit that perverted religious factions that teach hatred (§2.5) require qualifying my optimism, even though I may not always make this explicit.
8 For some chapters, your teacher may assign a short paper. You may be told to read just *Skepticus* sections in a chapter (but not *Analysis* sections) and then turn in for the next class a one or two page REACTION PAPER. This paper, based only on the *Skepticus* sections (further outside reading is forbidden), gives your reaction to Skepticus's ideas, including criticisms and further

Each chapter, after *Skepticus* sections, has *Analysis* sections, where I respond to Skepticus. I may point out errors in his thinking or other ways to look at the issues. Skepticus is often too simple in how he approaches God; you should get better at recognizing problems in his thinking as you work through this book.

After you digest both passages – from Skepticus and from me – see if you can explain both sides clearly and without distortion. Being able to explain opposing views is important in philosophy and life; it helps you and your opponent cooperate better to find the truth. We get nowhere if we just distort each other's views. Look at those who disagree with you as collaborators in a common search for truth.

Where do I stand about religion? I believe in God and am a firm Christian. But my goal in writing this book isn't to get you to agree with me; my goal is to help you make choices about religion in a more reflective and rational way – however you decide. I'll argue that belief in God makes the stronger case; I believe God intends reason to support faith and that deeper reflection should lead to belief. You'll need to read this book to see if you agree with this.

---

reflections. When I assign reaction papers, I grade them as GOOD (most people get this), VERY GOOD (an unusually good paper, only a few get this), POOR (unusually bad paper, I give very few of these), or NOT DONE (zero, for no work). Student reaction papers improve as the course goes on; they give a good way to build critical thinking.

1

Growing Up, Freud, Science

We'll begin by listening to the fictional student Skepticus explain his objections to religion. He'll talk about his early years, when he was raised religious, and how in high school he gradually lost his faith. In college, he found science and how Freud explained why people find God so attractive. As you read Skepticus's passage, first try to understand it in a sympathetic way, and then try to find problems with it. We'll later consider objections.

1.1 Skepticus: Growing Up

Hello, my name is Skepticus. While my family was religious, I gradually gave up religion as I grew older and more mature in my thinking.

When I was young, my parents taught me to believe in the tooth fairy, Santa Claus, and God. They did this to make me feel better. At first, I found these ideas interesting and attractive; later, I asked questions. What does the tooth fairy look like? How does the tooth fairy put money under my pillow without waking me up? One night, I felt a tug on my pillow and saw Mom put a $5 bill where my baby tooth was. While I thought this was strange, it took me time to figure out that there really was no tooth fairy. Later still, I got angry at being duped. Why couldn't my parents just tell me the truth instead of telling me fairy tales that they think will make me feel good – but in the end just make me feel bad?

With Santa Claus, I knew what he looked like: plump, red outfit, big white hair. I sat on his lap and told him what gifts I'd like if I were a good little boy; I didn't think it strange that his busy schedule let him come to my department store. Here my intellectual problem was how Santa could bring gifts to every house on the planet on Christmas Eve. Let's say there are a billion houses to visit in 24 hours; this gives Santa 0.000086 seconds to bring gifts to each house – which is impossible! So Santa was a lie, too – and a lie that encouraged us to be good little boys and girls who would be so happy to get presents for good behavior.

God was harder to evaluate. In high school, my friends and I had intellectual doubts and felt awkward about having to go to church with our families. I was gradually drifting away from religion and God.

1.2 Skepticus: Freud and Science

In college, I became a chemistry major. I came to love science and scientific method, where you experiment to find out what's true or false; what makes you *feel good* is irrelevant. I found an objective way to discover truth about the world. I read thinkers who argued for a science-based approach to life instead of a religious one. I was impressed by Sigmund Freud (1856–1939).

Freud (1927: ch. 6) made three main claims about religion:

1. We have no right to believe when there isn't strong evidence.
2. Religion is an illusion and a neurosis.
3. Science is the only path to knowledge; we have no right to believe anything on the basis of our feelings.

(1) *Need strong evidence.* Chemistry gives strong evidence, while religion doesn't. I'd go further and say that *we shouldn't accept what isn't proved*. There's no proof or disproof for the existence of the tooth fairy, Santa Claus, or God; so we shouldn't believe that such things exist. Believing in such things is childish and irresponsible.

Beliefs based on strong evidence can become a common property among people; such beliefs hold for others as well as for us, and we can safely communicate them to others. We all grow stronger by such solid beliefs. But beliefs formed on flimsy evidence are evil; they harm our ability to know and communicate truth to others, which is what separates us from savages. Forming beliefs on flimsy evidence has long-term bad consequences.

(2) *Religion is an illusion and a neurosis.* Religion, as an *illusion*, is a *belief based on wishful thinking*; we believe what makes us feel good, because it fits what we'd like to be true – even though there's no evidence. Religious beliefs arose in ignorant, primitive times, before modern science. As Freud says:

> We shall tell ourselves that it would be very nice if there were a God who created the world and was a benevolent Providence, and if there were a moral order in the universe and an after-life; but it is a very striking fact that all this is exactly as we are bound to wish it to be. And it would be more remarkable still if our wretched, ignorant and downtrodden ancestors had succeeded in solving all these difficult riddles.

Freud's *projection of a father figure* leads us to God. A child's life can be difficult; children can fear harm, abandonment, and death. Our human fathers, while they sometimes protect us, are very limited. So we dream up a perfect, make-believe father in the sky – a God of supreme knowledge, love, and power – and this father will protect us perfectly. We believe in this God because he makes us feel good. Such a belief is childish and irresponsible.

Religion, as a *neurosis*, is a *harmful mental disorder*; it separates us from reality and makes us miserable. Religion is a mental disease and has us believe in a dream-world of wishful thinking. The cure for religion is Freud's theory of the mind (which replaces religious beliefs) and psychotherapy (which replaces religious practices).

(3) *Science, not feelings, is the only path to knowledge.* Forming our beliefs on the basis of our feelings is childish and irresponsible. Once humanity has achieved science and scientific method, these should be our guide to discover a reality outside of ourselves.

What I most like about Freud is how he nicely explains how religion arose (through childish wishful thinking) and points to science as an adult replacement. Freud was a key step in my growing up and rejecting religion in favor of science. I expect that more and more people will give up religion as they get educated and learn about science.

There's much more to say about all this, but we'll have to wait for later.

> Before going on, reflect on your reaction to Skepticus's passage. Do you see any problems with it?

1.3 Analysis: Good and Bad Skepticism

Rethinking what we were taught is an important part of growing up. Maybe we'll radically change what we were taught about religion – moving to more religion, less religion, or a different approach. Or maybe we'll accept what we were taught, but make it more authentically ours. My book is intended to help us to make such choices in a more reflective and rational way. I believe that reflection and rationality should help to lead us to belief. God intends reason to support faith.

My fictional student's name "Skepticus" isn't meant to be derogatory. There's *good skepticism* and *bad skepticism*. *Good skepticism* is *critical thinking*; we need it to do philosophy well. The core of good skepticism is being able to find problems in a flawed view that at first sounds very reasonable. This book should help you develop good skepticism. The student passages will often be flawed, and you'll be challenged to think deeply and look for problems. You should get better at *good skepticism* (critical thinking, finding problems with a view) as you work through this book.[1]

---

1 My ethics textbook (Gensler 2018) follows this same pattern – *fictional student passages* followed by a *deeper analysis* – but it's about ethics instead of religion. Since you're encouraged to find flaws in

Skepticus, although his passage may at first sound reasonable, makes some illogical moves. He needs to develop good skepticism toward his own core ideas. He needs to ask, "What exactly are my core ideas saying? How would they work in practice? Do they have crazy implications? Are they consistent?"

Here are three of Skepticus's flawed core ideas:

1. We shouldn't accept what isn't proved.
2. We shouldn't believe anything on the basis of our feelings.
3. Science is the only path to knowledge.

(1) *Need proof.* This view has problems. Consider "*We shouldn't accept what isn't proved.*" This statement itself isn't proved. So then, if it were true, we shouldn't accept it. So the statement is *self-refuting* – it's inconsistent with itself. Skepticus's first core idea violates what I see as reason's first principle: *Be consistent*.

There's also an infinite-regress problem. Suppose you prove conclusion A by premises B and C, which you also accept – then you need to prove B and C using further premises D and E, then you need to prove these, and then further premises, endlessly. So Skepticus's principle would be impossible to satisfy.

Need proof conflicts with responsible scientific practice. In medical trials that follow good scientific method, we often get *probable conclusions* but not clear-cut *proofs*. Consider medical trials about COVID vaccines; the idea that *we shouldn't accept what isn't proved* would have us reject most of these trials (which give only probable conclusions) and harm our effort to fight the virus. Skepticus needs to get clearer on how science actually works.

Need proof clashes with how we live. We all have controversial unproved beliefs (about politics, sports, weather, philosophy, and so on); there's nothing wrong with this. If I'm sick, believing that I have a good chance to recover (even without proof) may motivate me to recover, and so believing in a recovery may help it to come about. But, yes, there are areas in life where we need to be very careful; if I'm going to hike in a narrow slot canyon, where a sudden rainstorm could fill the canyon and drown me, I'll try to find a very good weather report.

Need proof is unbalanced and leads to *excessive skepticism*. William James (1842–1910) thought truth-seekers need two different norms (1896): "Believe truth" ("Believe as many truths as possible") and "Avoid error"

---

the student passages, I hope you'll use these to grow in your critical thinking (good skepticism). But don't expect poor Skepticus to similarly grow in his critical thinking as the book progresses; you'll need him to keep making mistakes that you can try to uncover.

("Believe as few falsehoods as possible"). We can maximize true beliefs by believing every idea and its negation; we can minimize false beliefs by believing nothing. Both norms are harmful and unbalanced; we need a balance between the two. Skepticus's "We shouldn't accept what isn't proved" is too skeptical; it prevents us from accepting important truths that have strong probability but not proof. James prefers a moderate-risk approach; this would gain many more truths at cost of only a few more errors.

William James applied this to believing in God. Suppose this is an important issue, but there's no proof either way (for or against God). What should we do? Skepticus says, "Don't believe, there's no proof." But James says, "We have a right to believe, at our own risk, even if there's no proof." Here, he thought, we must and rightfully may follow our *feelings*; and his *pragmatic method* favored views that help us to live better (which he, unlike Freud, saw as favoring belief).

(2) *We shouldn't believe anything on the basis of our feelings.* James saw a role for feelings; we need to combine thinking and feeling in forming our beliefs. Consider veteran scientists whose thoughts and feelings have been trained by years of scientific study and research; they'd likely use both together in appraising hypotheses.

James would say that Skepticus's *need proof* idea comes from his *fear of being wrong* (a feeling). James has this fear too, but he also has a *fear of losing truths* by accepting a *bad skepticism* that sets the standards for belief-acceptance unreasonably high.

Science rests in part on feelings (including hopes). From a theoretical side, we need a confident hope that our sensing and thinking can generally be trusted to bring knowledge (and aren't just a big hallucination or dream). From a practical side, our feelings (including reasonable hopes) drive much medical research, as we hope to learn more to help us fight cancer. Against Skepticus, we need thoughts, feelings, and actions to work together.

(3) *Science is the only path to knowledge.* Do we know this? Then it would have to be known by science – but how can this be? Please show me scientifically that *science is the only path to knowledge*. Since there's no way to do this, (3) is self-refuting. So Skepticus's core ideas (1) and (3) violate what I see as reason's first principle: *Be consistent.*

Science and religion are friends. Science arose in part from believing that a supreme God created the world to run by rational, knowable laws (so lightning is caused by divine laws, not by gods throwing lightning bolts). Most Nobel Prize winners are Christians (search the Web for "What percentage of Nobel Prize winners are Christians?"). Pope Francis was a college chemistry major and later used his science background to energize humanity against climate change. And science departments thrive at Christian schools.

"*Science is the only path to knowledge*" is an enemy of religion. But science itself isn't an enemy of religion.

1.4 Analysis: Freud Wasn't So Scientific

Freud used to be a huge force in psychology and against religion. Over the years, his influence decreased. Psychologists came to see much of his thinking as based on armchair speculation instead of data. Many of his views (like the Oedipus complex and highly sexual nature of young children) have little or no evidence.

Do religious beliefs arise by the projection of a father figure, as Freud claims? This wouldn't explain polytheism or animism or why religion works similarly whether or not children experience a father. Freud underemphasizes how well families deal with childhood distresses. And there are other explanations of how religious beliefs arose, like a built-in thirst for God (Augustine), mystery-awe-fascination (Otto), mystical experiences (James), and instinctive reactions triggered by experiencing nature (Calvin and Plantinga); these are often used to *defend* belief in God.

Many doubt the effectiveness of Freudian psychoanalysis. Seeing your analyst is expensive and time consuming and has few results.

Freud was wrong in thinking that religion is a *neurosis*, a *harmful mental disease*. Recent research shows that religion hugely promotes our health and happiness, which is the opposite of being harmful. We'll go further into this in the next chapter, which is about "Is religion harmful?"

Skepticus expects that more and more people will give up religion as they get educated and learn about science. But according to Gallup polls, the religious nature of America's population has changed little over many decades (Glynn 1997: ch. 2 and Iannaccone 1998). Roughly 94% of all Americans believe in God, 90% pray, and 71% believe in life after death (although the numbers depend somewhat on how we ask the questions); the numbers have remained relatively stable over the years.

American intellectuals (like scientists and college professors) tend to be more skeptical about religion than the general population. At one time, only 1% of the American Psychological Association believed in God; my psychology students told me that this had gone up to 30% and perhaps higher. Big factors here are Freud's declining influence and strong evidence for religion's positive life benefits.

Over the last 50 years, science has become friendlier toward religion and God. Often criticisms of religion are based on older science (like Freud), while newer science better supports religion; we'll see this again and again in further chapters.

1.5 Analysis: Augustine Versus Freud

Augustine (354–430) spent much of his life searching for God, showing both good and bad skepticism, until he became one of the greatest Christian thinkers. He summed up his faith journey: "You have made us for yourself, O Lord, and our hearts are restless until they rest in you."

Freud and Augustine both thought humans find God attractive. Freud thought there's no God, so this attraction is false and illusory. Augustine thought the opposite; there's a God, and God created us to find our completion in him. God made us to hope for a world of justice and love, a world of meaningfulness and purpose, a world of eternal life with God, a better world where God fulfills us completely. Alasdair MacIntyre (2009) put it eloquently:

> Finite beings who possess the power of understanding, if they know that God exists, know that he is the most adequate object of their love, and that the deepest desire of every such being, whether they acknowledge it or not, is to be at one with God.

While not everyone experiences this magnetic attraction to God as strongly as Augustine, some of this may well be part of us all (today, too; see Fulwiler's 2014 charming conversion story).

Freud's *father figure* explanation is separable from his atheism. Freud could have believed in a God who uses this *father figure* mechanism to get us to believe in him; indeed, Christians pray to God as "*Our Father* who art in heaven." Let me generalize this point. When atheists, to discredit religion, propose some mechanism (whether psychological, evolutionary, or whatever) that leads to belief in God, ask yourself, "Could this mechanism be part of God's plan to help people believe in him?" If so, then the proposed mechanism needn't discredit belief in God.

1.6 Analysis: Family Issues

I've been a university professor most of my life; this book focuses on struggles that college students have with faith and how philosophy can help. But this chapter also raises family issues, like these, where I'm less sure what to say:

- Should parents teach children to believe in the tooth fairy and Santa Claus?
- How should parents respond when their children have faith problems? Should they try to defend faith, or perhaps help their children understand both sides and make their own decision? Should they suggest that their children read this present book (or something else)?

Parents need to think about such questions. https://www.crediblecatholic.com (Robert Spitzer's site) has many helpful materials, like videos for students.

2
Is Religion Harmful?

We'll begin by listening to the fictional student Skepticus explain his admiration for Bertrand Russell and why they both think religion is very harmful. As you read Skepticus's passage, first try to understand it in a sympathetic way, and then try to find problems with it. We'll later consider objections.

2.1 Skepticus: Russell and Religion's Harmfulness

This is Skepticus again. Here I want to talk about Bertrand Russell (1872–1970) and why he and I both think religion is a very harmful force in the world.

Bertrand Russell, a top twentieth-century philosopher, was born into an aristocratic British family. After he lost his parents, his grandmother raised him Christian. As a teenager, he struggled with faith, but he still accepted God as first cause. On reading Mill's objection to the *first cause* argument, he rejected God, too; he remained a nonbeliever all his life, rejecting God on intellectual and moral grounds.

Like Freud, Russell thought religion is a make-believe story that clashes with science and is accepted because it comforts us in a fearful world; adult minds ought to accept beliefs on scientific evidence, instead of emotions and fantasy. Unlike Freud, Russell also attacked traditional arguments for God's existence.

Here I'll focus on Russell's (1930) moral objection, which claims that religion is a very harmful force in the world (which Freud would agree with):

- Religion, from a primitive barbaric age, promotes cruelties that modern consciences reject. So the Old Testament told the Jews to exterminate conquered peoples, including women, children, and animals.
- Religion pushes people to believe groundless dogmas, be closed minded, and persecute dissenters. It poisons the intellect, divides society, and opposes scientific progress.

- Religion teaches individualistic morality that neglects social consequences. It brings guilt about healthy sex. And an adulterer who finds a cure for a disease is seen as morally worse than a faithful husband who negligently lets his children die from preventable diseases.
- Religion, as it becomes stronger, increases in dogmatism and cruelty; recall witch burnings and Inquisition tortures. Religion today is more moderate, but only because of influence from free thinkers.

Russell saw religion as a disease born of fear and a source of misery. It benefited humanity in only two ways: in fixing the calendar and in studying eclipses; it had no other benefits. He also raised the problem of evil: the world has so much suffering that God, if he existed, would have to be a moral monster.

Russell admitted that Christ had some good ideas – like giving our goods to the poor, being non-violent, and not punishing adulterers, but the Church ignores these and promotes its own power. Christ wasn't as virtuous and wise as Socrates, since he preached damnation for his opponents, told disciples to hate their parents, cursed the unproductive fig tree, and believed that his second coming would happen soon.

Russell thought we were heading to a golden age of knowledge and universal concern. But first we need to slay the dragon that opposes this, which is religion.

After reading Russell, I wrote this paragraph about how religion harms believers:

> Believers are anti-science, authoritarian, blindly obedient, narrow minded, fundamentalist, intolerant, judgmental, anti-gay, racist, guilt-ridden, and hypocritical; they act morally only to avoid hell, hate those of other faiths, think they're better than others, and try to force their beliefs on others.

Gee, maybe I'm overstating things a little?

> Before going on, reflect on your reaction to Skepticus's passage. Do you see any problems with it?

2.2 Analysis: We Need to Appeal to Science

"Is religion harmful?" How can we answer this question? I propose that we use science. We need to look at scientific studies comparing believers and nonbelievers and see how the two groups differ (if they do). Using science, we'll see that religion, on the whole, benefits humanity greatly – psychologically, medically, and ethically. Much empirical data backs this up.

Skepticus, Russell, and Freud admire science, saying things like "Adult minds ought to accept beliefs on scientific evidence" (§2.1), but then they ignore scientific evidence when asking "Is religion harmful?" Instead, they argue from a few bad cases (faulty stereotypes) to negative generalizations about believers. Russell firmly believes on flimsy evidence the worst: *religion has been almost totally negative and has benefitted humanity in only two minor areas* (calendars and eclipses). This is really absurd; the slightest research would show this. Let me mention a few other ways that religion benefits humanity.

Religion contributes much to education. Cambridge University, where Russell studied and taught, had a religious origin, and many of its colleges have religious names (like Jesus, Corpus Christi, Trinity, and St. John's). Religion promotes charitable works (like hospitals, orphanages, soup kitchens, and shelters for battered women) and helps people with special needs (like alcoholics, the bereaved, and couples about to be married). Religion helps to create great art (including paintings, architecture, and music) and moral heroes (like Martin Luther King, Mahatma Gandhi, Nelson Mandela, and Mother Theresa). Religion gave birth to modern science and taught the world a universal *golden rule* ethics. And religion enhances the lives of countless people in joy, benevolence, and life's meaningfulness.

Russell couldn't find how religion benefits humanity (apart from calendars and eclipses)? Did he even look? Russell thought it wrong to believe without strong evidence, but he believed bad things about his opponents on flimsy evidence. Can anyone detect the inconsistency? Every racial, ethnic, and religious group has good and bad. It's bigotry to see only good on your side and bad on the other; by this measure, Russell was a religious bigot, not the voice of reason.

Opponents of religion divide usefully into two groups:[1]

- *Older (traditional) atheists.* These include David Hume (1711–76), Bertrand Russell (1872–1970), A.J. Ayer (1910–89), J.L. Mackie (1917–81), Antony Flew (1923–2010), and many others.
- *Four horsemen of the new atheism.* Richard Dawkins (1941–), Daniel Dennett (1942–), Christopher Hitchens (1949–2011), and Sam Harris (1967–).

The older group has better thinkers. They present, often in clear and well-argued ways, challenges which religious philosophers need to take seriously. Without such thinkers on the other side, religious philosophy would be

---

1 Some prefer to be called "agnostics" (taking no stand on whether there's a God) instead of "atheists" (taking a stand against God). Russell described himself both ways and thought it made little difference. Russell saw "There's a God" as having the same credibility as "A teapot orbits the sun"; while neither is completely disprovable, both for him have close to zero credibility.

superficial. Religious thinkers need to thank God every day for such critics of religion.

The new atheists are popularizers who often understand religion poorly. They delight in abusive language and distortions; they give insults instead of clear reasoning. Their theme is often religion's great harmfulness, which they handle in an unscientific way, like Russell but worse. While the new atheists have sold many books, they're often poor dialogue partners for religious philosophers.

2.3 Analysis: Belief's Psychological Benefits

Freud saw religion as a harmful neurosis; Russell and the new atheists agree. But their approach was unscientific; they generalized from their own faulty stereotypes instead of appealing to scientific studies comparing believers and nonbelievers. Science leads us to conclude that belief contributes strongly to happiness and mental health.

Glynn (1997: ch. 2) refers to studies about the happiness and mental health of believers versus nonbelievers:

- *Suicide.* Nonbelievers commit suicide much more than believers (and especially believers who live out their faith more deeply).
- *Alcohol and drugs.* Nonbelievers abuse alcohol and drugs much more than believers (and especially believers who live out their faith more deeply).
- *Depression and stress.* Here again, believers do much better.
- *Divorce.* Nonbelievers divorce much more, and believers more often say they'd marry the same spouse again (a measure of marital satisfaction).
- *Marital and sexual satisfaction.* These are much higher among believers, who often list religion as contributing to a happy marriage.
- *Overall reported happiness and well-being.* Again, believers are much higher.

Glynn bases most of these on groups of studies, some large studies, or both. Archer (2017) refers to further, more recent studies and draws similar conclusions.

Why do believers tend to have greater happiness and mental health? Does God reward believers? More likely, belief promotes factors – like optimism, self-esteem, and meaningfulness – that contribute to happiness and mental health. Religion teaches faith, hope, and love; these are keys to good living, here and in the hereafter.

This section is about whether believers *in general* are happier and better mentally adjusted, and the evidence is strong that they are. From this, we can't draw conclusions about individual cases: we can't conclude that *this believer* will be happier and better adjusted that *that nonbeliever*. The results here are general tendencies and reveal themselves in large numbers.

The happiness and psychic benefits of belief don't prove that there's a God. But, if we're pragmatists, they can incline us to belief. For pragmatists like William James, on important questions where we can prove neither side to be correct (like God and free will), we can and must allow our passionate nature to help us decide; if belief helps us to live better lives, that can be an important part of our decision.

2.4 Analysis: Belief's Medical Benefits

If you see medicine holistically, with factors like attitude and exercise contributing to our health, you'll suspect that belief's *psychological* benefits also lead to *medical* benefits. So yes, studies (Glynn 1997: ch. 3) show that believers tend to do better with medical problems (like arteriosclerosis, cirrhosis of the liver, pulmonary heart disease, and high blood pressure) and describe themselves as *healthier*; the effects are greater if the believers live more religiously. Again, religion is *beneficial*.

Studies also show that prayer promotes health and recovery. The type of prayer matters. *Ritual prayers* (standard formulas) and *petitional prayers* (praying for favors) have less effect, while *colloquial prayers* (talking to God in your own words) and *meditative prayer* s(feeling God's presence) have more effect. Also useful is *transcendental meditation*, where you repeat a mantra (often "Om," but some prefer "Jesus" or "The Lord is my shepherd") while blocking distractions.

Why should prayer promote health and recovery? Prayer likely doesn't convince God to help or reward us. Prayer changes us rather than changing God. So prayer during an illness can help us to appreciate suffering's role in God's plan for us and can emotionally deepen our love of God.

2.5 Analysis: Belief's Ethical Benefits

When I read militant atheists, I see many stereotypes about believers. Skepticus in §2.1 has a powerful paragraph using these:

> Believers are anti-science, authoritarian, blindly obedient, narrow minded, fundamentalist, intolerant, judgmental, anti-gay, racist, guilt-ridden, and hypocritical; they act morally only to avoid hell, hate those of other faiths, think they're better than others, and try to force their beliefs on others.[2]

---

[2] Atheists suffer from stereotypes, too. They're sometimes seen as amoral, relativistic, selfish, dogmatic, untrustworthy, evil, bitter, disrespectful, and angry; they worship science, criticize what they don't understand, have meaningless lives, and would love to persecute believers (as did many Marxist atheists). Both sides need to move away from stereotypes. I myself find most atheists to be honest people with high standards of evidence.

Most believers I know aren't like this; they're tolerant, non-fundamentalist, pro-science, and so on. But *some* believers have some of these bad features and even follow a perverted religion that promotes hatred.

Frederick Douglass (1855: 151), an ex-slave who experienced perverted religion, distinguished good from bad forms of Christianity:

> I love the religion of our blessed Savior. . . . I love that religion that is based upon the glorious principle, of love to God and love to man; which makes its followers do unto others as they themselves would be done by. If you demand liberty to yourself, it says, grant it to your neighbors. If you claim a right to think for yourself, allow your neighbors the same right. . . . It is because I love this religion that I hate the slaveholding, the woman-whipping, the mind-darkening, the soul-destroying religion that exists in the southern states of America.

Jesus also criticized a perverted religion of mechanical rules and hating enemies; he taught forgiveness, loving enemies, and following a loving God.[3]

When we read those who say religion in general is evil, we have a right to protest against false stereotypes. But we must admit that *perverted religion (religion that teaches hate instead of love)* is evil and ought to be resisted. Fortunately, perverted religion isn't dominant. On the whole, religion is a very powerful force that supports universal loving and moral living; much research data backs this up. The best presentation of the research data that I know is a book written by an atheist.

To understand religion's moral benefits, I recommend Bruce Sheiman's (2009) *An Atheist Defends Religion: Why Humanity Is Better Off With Religion Than Without It*. Its introduction claims: "By any empirical measure – defined in terms of theism's practical impact on individuals, society, and culture – religion is profoundly beneficial." Sheiman displays strong empirical evidence that religious people, while accepting similar norms as nonbelievers, tend to live out morality better and be healthier and happier. Believers come out better by practically any measure: charitable giving, volunteering, donating blood, depression rates, suicide attempts, drug addiction, divorces, exercise, heart attacks, criminality, longevity, marital satisfaction, self-acceptance, moral purpose, peacefulness, and personal happiness. Religion secures moral standards, teaches universal love and moral objectivity, and is a strong force for morality and personal happiness. Militant atheists who see religion as harmful ignore huge empirical data to the contrary. And yet, Sheiman is an atheist; while seeing religion's tremendous value, he can't accept it himself.

---

3 The *genuine/perverted religion* distinction cuts across faith boundaries. There are those who stress love (or hate) in Christianity, Islam, Judaism, Hinduism, and so on. I often feel a closer bond with those of other faiths who *love* than those of my own faith who *hate*.

2.6 Analysis: Russell's Daughter

Skepticus began this chapter by defending Russell about religion's harmfulness. We'll finish the chapter with Katharine Tait's (1975) book: *My Father, Bertrand Russell*.

Kate (Katharine) had a deep love for her famous father, whom she saw as the greatest and most charming human being she had ever met. Yet she came to see his imperfections. Kate was raised a strict atheist at her father's school, where students would supposedly study both sides of an issue fairly and be free to make up their own minds. But in fact, Kate complained, Christianity was always painted with negatives that her father experienced as a child. Kate's family life was unhappy, since her father had three divorces and often was bitter and unfaithful toward the current wife. As an atheist too, Kate was unhappy and felt empty.

Kate was transformed later in life when experiencing a more authentic Christianity. She found it easier to believe in a world created by an eternal God than one that just happened. And her belief in a loving and forgiving God felt like sunshine after many rainy days. God is always there for us, absolutely; we can't ever earn God's love, but we can't ever lose it. Kate's life was a search for God, and finally she found God.

Kate thought her father Bertrand had been searching for God too, but in a twisted way. She thanked God for giving her Bertrand as her father, and she'd have loved to have brought the two together. After her earthly father died, she imagined him with God, finally getting all his questions answered – and she thought that someday she'd be there with both of them.

3
Logical Positivism

We'll begin by listening to the fictional student Skepticus explain his admiration for logical positivism (a *science is everything* approach) and its view that statements about God and morality aren't true-or-false claims, even though they may express emotions. As you read Skepticus's passage, first try to understand it in a sympathetic way, and then try to find problems with it. We'll later consider objections.

3.1 Skepticus: Logical Positivism and God-Talk

This is Skepticus again. I'm now a double major, doing philosophy and chemistry, with interest in philosophy of science. I discovered a fascinating view called *logical positivism*, that fits me perfectly; the *logical positivist* A.J. Ayer is now my favorite thinker.

Like Ayer (1946), I respect scientific method, which I see as the only way to gain knowledge about the world. Science has us propose a view and then experiment to see if the view is correct. Ayer says that a view about the world (as opposed to one about math or logic) must be testable by sense experience – or else it makes no sense.

Here's a more precise definition. *Logical positivism* holds that *all genuine truth claims (claims that are true or false) are empirically testable or true by definition*. Only statements of these two groups make claims that are objectively true or false.

Empirically testable statements can in principle be shown by sense experience to be true, or at least highly probable. An example is "It's snowing outside"; we could go outside and look. Ayer saw "The other side of the moon has mountains" as empirically testable – even though, when he wrote, we weren't able to build rockets to let us see the moon's other side; it's enough that we could *describe* what an empirical test would be like. Another example is "This battery has 1.4 volts," which we can test using a voltmeter; logical positivism allows statements about unobservables if these have testable consequences.

True by definition (*analytic*) statements are true because of the meaning of words. An example is "All *bachelors* are single"; this really means "All *single men* are single" (and so we needn't observe bachelors to see that the statement is true). "2 + 2 = 4" is true by definition too; we can see this if we substitute "1 + 1" for "2" and "1 + 1 + 1 + 1" for "4." This gives us "1 + 1 + 1 + 1 = 1 + 1 + 1 + 1," which is true by definition (since our rules for " = " stipulate that statements of the form "x = x" are automatically true).

Science covers what's *empirically testable*, while math and logic cover what's *true by definition*. These two groups exhaust the set of objective true-or-false claims. If your statement isn't in either of these two, then it's factually meaningless and not a truth claim. Suppose you say "True reality is spiritual" – but your claim isn't empirically testable or true by definition. Then you say nothing that's true or false. You may express feelings, but you aren't making a truth claim if what you say isn't empirically testable or true by definition.[1]

"There's a God," while purporting to be a genuine statement, isn't empirically testable or true by definition, so it isn't a genuine true or false claim. While "There's a God" may express vague feelings, it's factually meaningless and so not true or false.

So am I an atheist? An *atheist* is one who believes that "There's a God" is *false*. I don't believe this; I think "There's a God" is neither true nor false, since it fails logical positivism's conditions needed to make a genuine truth claim. So, strictly speaking, I'm not an atheist (but I don't protest too much when people call me this).

Or am I a mystic? Some religious mystics say "We can't speak about God" or "Human speech about God is impossible." This doesn't literally make any sense, since both statements are grammatically *about God*. If I want to express my core religious beliefs clearly and without paradox, I talk about language, about the word "God" having no factual meaning, since it fails the *logical positivism* test.

3.2 Skepticus: Flew's Gardener

Antony Flew (1955)[2] told a story to explain logical positivism's objection to God-talk. Imagine two hikers who pick a nice wilderness camping spot. Believer says "This is someone's garden; see how the rocks are arranged, someone comes here to care for it." Skeptic disagrees, "No, instead chance arranges the rocks, no one comes here." The two set up devices to detect a gardener, but no gardener is detected. Believer persists,

---

1 David Hume (1748) had a similar idea: "If we take in our hand any volume; of divinity or school metaphysics, for instance; let us ask, Does it contain any abstract reasoning concerning quantity or number? No. Does it contain any experimental reasoning concerning matter of fact and existence? No. Commit it then to the flames: for it can contain nothing but sophistry and illusion."
2 Flew's example was in his brief "Theology and Falsification," first presented at a meeting chaired by C.S. Lewis. This became the most widely reprinted philosophy paper of the next 50 years.

"I still claim that there's a gardener, but one that's invisible and makes no sound and can't be detected in any way." Flew objects that these qualifications kill the statement about the gardener, nothing is left that could matter to our experience; there's no difference between "a gardener who's invisible and makes no sound and can't be detected in any way" and no gardener at all.

So too with God. What difference is there between a God who's invisible and makes no sound and can't be detected – and no God at all? There can't be a meaningful difference to us. So our talk about such a God can't make a genuine truth claim.

3.3 Skepticus: Godless Religion

Logical positivism holds that all genuine truth claims (claims that are true or false) are empirically testable or true by definition. Some logical positivists want to keep God-talk as meaningful in some way. I can think of three ways to do this.

(1) One might see "There's a God" as true by definition. The ontological argument, which goes back to St. Anselm (1033–1109) of the Middle Ages, holds this. It claims that if you deny that God (*the being than which no greater can be conceived*) exists, then you're trapped in a contradiction. But this argument doesn't work (§§7.1–7.2).
(2) One might see "There's a God" as an empirical assertion – perhaps like "The universe is subject to knowable laws (like the law of gravity)" or "Some people feel warm and fuzzy when they sing *Amazing Grace*." But this changes "There's a God" into something other than what most believers take it to mean.
(3) One might take "There's a God" as purely emotional – like "How amazing and deep is this world!" This is compatible with logical positivism but not with what most believers take "There's a God" to mean. A nontraditional religion based on this idea could see God-talk as emotional or poetic, not fact-stating.

Rabbi Sherman Wine (1928–2007) founded a Godless religion called Humanistic Judaism (1985). He rejected God on the basis of logical positivism. He called his view "ignosticism" (the concept of "God" is *factually meaningless*) instead of "atheism" ("There's a God" is *false*). He had a Jewish synagogue and congregation, like a regular rabbi, but he avoided "God" and words like "Yahweh" and "Lord," instead of using them to express emotions. His Humanistic Judaism celebrates Judaism while dropping God; it appealed to scientifically minded Jews who valued their Jewish identity and traditions but lost their faith in God.[3]

---

3 In the 1960s, some Christian thinkers – like Altizer (1966), Vahanian (1961), and Van Buren (1963) – promoted the death-of-God movement, but atheist Christianity didn't catch on like atheist

Godless religions are quasi-religious communities that drop supernatural beliefs. What are they like? Let's look at them from four angles: creed, code, cult, and community.

(1) While God is optional or rejected, atheist religion may have a minimal *creed* that affirms tolerance, honesty, justice, and community.
(2) Atheist religion can have a *code* based on "Love your neighbor" or "Treat others as you want to be treated" – and subsidiary principles about tolerance, justice, human rights, and helping others.
(3) Atheist religion can have a non-theist *cult* (worship) celebrating aspects of life, like birth (a naming ceremony instead of a baptism), coming of age (like bar/bat mitzvah or confirmation), marriage, death (celebrating a life but no afterlife), religious holidays, and weekly worship (celebrating living and virtuous living).

Non-theist prayer can have a role. We can appreciate life's good things (instead of thanking God), express hopes (instead of petitioning God), and feel peace in the world's presence (instead of God's presence). To grasp this better, I created non-theist forms of the Our Father and the Grace before Meals:

> Our Father is the earth that brought us forth; let us respect it with a deep sense of mystery and awe. As brothers and sisters of this planet, let us promote harmony among all people. May we have food to eat every day. May we forgive others as we ourselves want to be forgiven. And may we be freed from evil and temptation. Amen.
>
> We are appreciative for this food – to the earth and the farmers who grew it, and the cooks who prepared it. May it nourish our bodies and our togetherness, and may we share with those who have less. Amen.

Individual prayer is possible. We can set aside quiet time to review our day, enjoying good things and regretting failings, reflecting on our values and how to follow them, and appreciating being a child of the universe.

(4) Atheist religion can form *communities* that celebrate life, contribute to one's identity (perhaps as members of St. Darwin's Parish), and reach out to help others. And atheists can have their own religious charities (like soup kitchens, homeless shelters, and alcoholic treatment centers).

Judaism. Today, atheist religion is represented by Harvard's humanistic chaplain, Greg Epstein (2009) and by Unitarian Universalism (McGowan 2013: 139–42).

What do I, Skepticus, think of such Godless religion? Would I become part of it? I don't know what to think – the concept is too new and alien. But I appreciate that you could be part of such a religion without having to believe in God.

3.4 Skepticus: Emotivist Ethics

This is still Skepticus. Since many religious people connect God to ethics, we need to talk about ethical judgments – which, following A.J. Ayer and most logical positivists, I take to express feelings and not truth claims, so I deny moral truths, moral facts, and moral knowledge. This view is called *emotivism*.

Why should we reject moral truths? Logical positivism's argument here parallels its argument that "There's a God" doesn't make a truth claim:

1   All genuine truth claims are empirically testable or true by definition. (logical positivism)
2   No moral statements are empirically testable or true by definition.
∴   No moral statements are genuine truth claims. (And so moral statements can only express feelings.)

Consider "Racial hatred is bad." This isn't empirically testable or true by definition. By logical positivism, it isn't a genuine truth claim – it isn't objectively true or false. So it expresses only negative feelings. "Racial hatred is bad" is like "Boo on racial hatred!"

Some thinkers, denying premise 2, think moral ideas like "good," "bad," or "ought" can be analyzed into empirically testable ideas. For example, *cultural relativism* defines "good" as "socially approved" (this is relativized to a specific culture, usually that of the person making the statement). If this definition worked, "Racial hatred is good" would be empirical. We could test its truth by seeing if racial hatred *was* socially approved in the society in question; this would make ethics part of sociology. But the definition doesn't work; "good" in our language doesn't mean "socially approved," since it's consistent to claim that *some socially approved things aren't good*. If I lived in a society that approved of racial hatred, I could still say "Racial hatred is approved in my society, but it isn't good – boo on racial hatred!" My moral beliefs are about *my feelings* – my BOOs and HURRAHs – not those of my society.

I discovered a great book on ethics (Gensler 2018: chs. 1–3) that discusses and refutes empirical definitions of moral terms like these:

- *Cultural relativism.* "Good" means "socially approved."
- *Subjectivism.* "X is good" means "I like X."

- *Ideal-observer view.* "X is good" means "We'd desire X if we were fully informed and had impartial concern for everyone."
- *Supernaturalism* (also called "divine command theory"). "X is good" means "God (the creator of the universe) desires X."[4]

None fits how we use "good" in ordinary speech. It's consistent to say (against subjectivism) "I *like* to sleep in – but it isn't good – boo on this!" or (against ideal-observer) "Sharing wealth equally would be *what we'd desire X if we were fully informed and had impartial concern for everyone* – but I think that, as it would hurt me, it isn't good – boo on this!" Supernaturalism is religious, not empirical, but it's wrong for the same reason; it's consistent to say "If the creator of the universe desired that we all hate each other, then, even so, this wouldn't be good – boo on this!"

Ethical intuitionism, while agreeing that moral beliefs aren't empirical, claims that basic moral principles are known by "rational insight," like how we grasp the laws of arithmetic. But intuitionists are wrong about arithmetic. Since "2 + 2 = 4" is true by definition (a short way to say "1 + 1 + 1 + 1 = 1 + 1 + 1 + 1"), it's very different from moral statements like "Racial hatred is wrong," which aren't true by definition. Moral statements instead reflect how we *feel* about things, which usually follows what our culture taught us, although some follow their own feelings instead.

Let me repeat my argument. By logical positivism, moral beliefs could be truth claims only if they were either empirically testable or true by definition. But moral beliefs fit neither category. It follows that they aren't genuine truth claims. Moral beliefs, instead, are exclamations: "X is good" means "Hurrah for X!" – and "X is bad" means "Boo on X!" An exclamation doesn't state a fact and isn't true or false. Since moral judgments are exclamations, there can't be moral truths or moral knowledge.

Don't take "hurrah" and "boo" too literally. English has many words to express positive or negative feelings. Instead of "boo," we could say "hiss," "yeech," or "tsk tsk" – or shake our finger in disapproval. These fit different feelings and contexts. Perhaps no English exclamation is exactly equivalent to "bad." The main point is that "bad" expresses negative feelings, as does "boo," and functions like an exclamation.

Don't confuse our view with *subjectivism*. We hold that moral judgments express *feelings* but not *truths about feelings*:

- *Just express feelings (emotivism).* "Brrr!" "Ha, ha!" "Wow!" "Hurrah for X!"
- *Truths about feelings (subjectivism).* "I feel cold." "I find that funny." "I'm impressed." "I like X."

---

4 To avoid circularity, we can't here explain the meaning of "God" using "good" (§10.1).

As you shiver in the cold, your "Brrr!" isn't literally true or false; it would be wrong to respond "That's true." Suppose you say "I feel cold." Here you're saying something true – since you *do* feel cold. A moral judgment is like "Brrr!" (just expressing your feelings) and not "I feel cold" (a truth claim about your feelings).

This distinction avoids problems. Suppose that Hitler, who likes the killing of Jews, says "The killing of Jews is *good*." In subjectivism, his statement is *true* (it just means that he *likes* the killing of Jews). This is bizarre. We think his statement is an exclamation ("Hurrah for the killing of Jews!") and thus not true or false. We can't say that Hitler's moral judgment is false, but at least we don't have to say that it's true.

Besides expressing our feelings, moral judgments can also *influence others*; when I tell my baby sister "It's *good* to pick up toys," I'm trying to get her to feel positively about picking up toys and to act accordingly. We sometimes use moral judgments to *influence ourselves*. When the alarm went off this morning, I got up for chemistry lab, but I felt like staying in bed. I said to myself, "It's *good* to get up now!" This is like "Hurrah for getting up now!" Part of me is cheering on another part, as conflicting emotions in me fight for supremacy. And I may sometimes feel like being nasty, but part of me says "That's bad – boo!"

3.5 Skepticus: Simplicity Argument for Emotivism

I based emotivism on logical positivism, but I also have a *simplicity argument:*

1 Any view that's simpler and explains more is a better view.
2 Emotivism is a view that's simpler and explains more.
∴ Emotivism is a better view.

Premise 1 ("Occam's razor") is obviously true; in philosophy, as in science, a view is better if it's simpler and explains more. I'll make three points in favor of premise 2.

(1) Emotivism explains morality more simply: *evaluative judgments express positive or negative feelings*. What could be simpler? We don't bring in complications. Supernaturalists have to defend belief in God – which brings difficulties. Intuitionists have to defend objective, irreducible moral facts. Suppose you're a materialist, holding that all facts are expressible in the language of physics and chemistry. How do objective, irreducible moral facts fit into your world? Are moral facts composed of chemicals, or what weird things are they? How could we ever know such mysterious facts? Emotivism avoids these problems and explains morality more simply.

(2) Emotivism explains more about morality. Because morality is emotional, we can't define "good" in purely descriptive terms, we can't

resolve basic moral differences intellectually, and we differ much on moral beliefs. Emotivism makes morality more understandable.

(3) Emotivism fits how we speak. I was at a restaurant with my girlfriend, and we decided for fun to switch from "good" to "hurrah." It felt funny at first, but it made sense. We could express everything we wanted to say. We didn't feel that we changed what we were talking about (as we would if we switched from "good" to "socially approved" or "desired by God"). So emotivism is accurate linguistically. If you doubt this, try the same experiment yourself.

3.6 Skepticus: Moral Reasoning on Emotivism

This is still Skepticus. I need to explain how emotivism handles moral reasoning.

We can reason about moral issues if we assume a system of norms. We can then appeal to empirical facts to show that, given these norms and these empirical facts, such and such a moral conclusion follows. Suppose we all feel that lying is wrong; we can then appeal to empirical facts (that the president lied) to establish a moral conclusion (that the president acted wrongly). Such reasoning can be useful within a group that shares common norms.

We can't reason about basic moral principles; we can use emotion at this point – but not reason. If you argue with Nazis, you'll likely disagree on some basic moral principles. Maybe you think all races are to be treated with respect, while they think their race is to be treated better. We see this as conflicting feelings, while intuitionists see it as conflicting intuitions about an objective moral reality, but neither view can progress further by reasoning. Intuitionism has no practical advantage over emotivism. Instead, emotivism has the advantage, since it shows that we can go further by appealing to emotion. To convince Nazis, we have to make them *feel* differently and change their hatred and hostility into *feelings* of toleration or friendship.

Reason in ethics helps us to get our facts right; then our feelings take over. This is how we all make moral judgments, regardless of our theory. So influencing *basic* moral beliefs requires emotional means.

We argue about global warming much like intuitionists. The dispute may come to a clash of basic moral principles. Perhaps it's "We ought not to do what *may destroy the planet* for future generations" versus "We ought not to make major life changes based on *some global-warming theory with no certainty*." We see the clash as about feelings.

We approach moral education much like intuitionists, but it's about feelings instead of truths. Parents need to get clear on their feelings about how to live; then they can teach these to their children by personal example, verbal instruction, praise-blame, and reward-punishment. If their teaching succeeds, their children will share their feelings about how to live. But nothing prevents children from changing their feelings later on.

People sometimes claim that emotivism would destroy morality and the moral life. This is mistaken. We emotivists for the most part live out our values in the same way as intuitionists. But we don't think there's anything objective behind our values. Morality is about feelings, not about truths.

Emotivism would be difficult to combine with belief in God, as in Abrahamic religions like Judaism, Christianity, and Islam. Abrahamic believers, however they see morality philosophically, add a religious dimension: *morality is God's will for us*. We can be moral because God created us in his image and likeness, and so we can know right from wrong and choose between them. Morality is serious, objective, and part of our personal relationship to God. Right living has religious motives, both higher (unselfish love and gratitude) and lower (punishments and rewards), and pushes us toward our destiny of eternal happiness with God. This doesn't sound like emotivism, where there are no objective standards and moral judgments are just emotional grunts, expressing our individual BOOs and HURRAHs. Again I say, all the worse for religion.

> Before going on, reflect on your reaction to Skepticus's passage. Do you see any problems with it?

3.7 Analysis: Problems With Logical Positivism

Before I joined the Jesuits in 1967, I did a four-year undergraduate college degree at the Detroit diocesan seminary, majoring in philosophy. All the philosophy courses were in the last two years. I wanted to start early, so I read, on my own, St. Thomas Aquinas's (1225–74) *Summa Contra Gentiles* (1265), which defended God and Christianity. I decided to go into philosophy and pursue Aquinas's thought.

During my college years, the Vatican II Council (1962–65) moved the Church into the modern world (see Swindal and Gensler 2005: 285–92). The seminary philosophy program changed, too; while it used to teach Thomism (after St. Thomas) in Latin, it switched to history of philosophy and contemporary philosophy. The latter had two main approaches – *analytic philosophy* (more popular in the United States and other English-speaking countries) and *continental philosophy* (more popular on the continent of Europe). I preferred *analytic philosophy*, with its clarity and logical rigor.

The analytic philosophy I read during my undergraduate days had heavy logical positivist and anti-religious bias, which I hated. Much of it sounded like A.J. Ayer and his *Language, Truth and Logic* (1946), which I wanted to refute someday.

I didn't have to refute logical positivism. It died by itself, from intense criticism, and by now (as you read this) has been almost universally abandoned by philosophers. Even A.J. Ayer had problems with the view. In class, I play a video clip from Bryan Magee's BBC interview with Ayer on logical positivism (Ayer and Magee 1976). After discussing the history and doctrines of logical positivism, Magee asked whether it had any shortcomings. Ayer responded:

> I suppose the greatest defect . . . is that nearly all of it was false. (laughter) Perhaps that's being too harsh on it. I still want to say that it was true in spirit in a way, that the attitude was right. But if one goes for the details, first of all the verification principle never got itself properly formulated. I tried several times and it always let in either too little or too much, and to this day it hasn't received a properly logically precise formulation. Then, the reductionism just doesn't work. You can't reduce statements, even ordinary simple statements about cigarette cases and glasses and ashtrays, to statements about sense data. . . . If you go in detail very, very little survives. What survives is the general rightness of the approach.

Since philosophers abandoned logical positivism, why should we be concerned with it here? The answer, as my students emphasize, is that the same logical positivist ideas (like "Science is everything" and "What can't be scientifically tested is meaningless") remain strong, but often vaguely presented, OUTSIDE philosophy departments among attackers of religion. We need to bring such anti-religious ideas into the open, express them clearly, and show what's wrong with them. Logical positivism's beauty is that it's clear and attractive – but can be shown to be wrong so well that even its main defenders gave it up. So when we hear an attack on religion that depends on similar ideas, it's good to know how to criticize such ideas.[5]

What led to logical positivism's demise? Its first problem is that its central idea "*All genuine truth claims are empirically testable or true by definition*" is self-refuting.[6] Assume that the idea is true. On its own terms, this italicized idea isn't a genuine truth claim (since it's neither empirically testable or true by definition) and so can't be true. Logical positivism is self-refuting; if we assume it's true, we can show that it isn't true.

---

5 After logical positivism's decline, many who were poorly informed still thought analytic philosophers were mostly logical positivists. I suffered from this stereotype. How can Gensler (a Jesuit) even believe in God – since he's an analytic philosopher and so a logical positivist?

6 We could add an exception to logical positivism: *Except for this principle itself, all genuine truth claims are empirically testable or true by definition*. But then why not add further exceptions, perhaps for religious and ethical statements?

Philosophers who worship science often contradict themselves. They make claims, which can't be based on science, about science being the only path to truth. Such thinkers violate our first duty as rational beings, which isn't the impossible demand that we prove all our claims, but the humble demand that our claims be consistent with each other.

Ayer and other positivists were logical people; they gave up their view when they saw it was self-refuting. Another problem is that it proved impossible to clearly define "*empirically testable*" – and so, as Ayer notes, "The verification principle never got itself properly formulated." What's the problem? Consider these statements:

"All swans are white." (This is a *empirically testable*.)[7]
"Glurks glurkle." (This has meaningless terms that I just invented.)
"This is white." (This is an "observation statement" – a statement that in some sense can be *directly observed* to be true or false.)[8]

Which statements are *empirically testable*? Ayer at first suggested this definition:

> An *empirically testable statement* is one that, when conjoined with a bridge statement B, logically entails an observation statement O that isn't entailed by bridge statement B by itself.

It's easy to find a bridge statement to show that "All swans are white" fits this definition of *empirically testable*:

1 All swans are white.
2 If all swans are white, then this is white. (*bridge statement*)
∴ This is white. (This is the logically entailed *observation statement* – which the bridge statement doesn't directly entail by itself.)

It's also easy to find a bridge statement to show that "Glurks glurkle" fits Ayer's definition of *empirically testable*:

1 Glurks glurkle.
2 If glurks glurkle, then this is white. (*bridge statement*)
∴ This is white. (This is the logically entailed *observation statement* – which the bridge statement doesn't directly entail by itself.)

---

7 Ayer required that "empirically testable" statements be "*verifiable*" (*able to be shown by empirical evidence to be at least highly probable*, so here we'd check out random samples of swans and see if they're all white). Flew required only that "empirically testable" statements be "*falsifiable*" (*able to be shown by empirical evidence to be false* – actually, Australia has some black swans, so these refute "All swans are white"). I won't worry about the difference.
8 Maybe our example should be "This *appears* to be white" or "This *now appears to me* to be white." I won't worry about the difference.

By Ayer's definition, "Glurks glurkle" is *empirically testable*, as are "There's a God" and "Racial hatred is bad" and every other statement. Oops!

Ayer's second edition (1946) tried a new definition to avoid the problem, but it didn't work. Could a further revision cleanly distinguish statements that were *empirically testable*? While much work was done on this problem (Hempel 1950), no one could solve it. So logical positivists came to see "*empirically testable*" as imprecise and the distinction between science and non-science as somewhat vague.

Believers happily pointed out that belief in God can be "empirical" in broader but legitimate senses:

- *Afterlife verification.* Believers and nonbelievers are like hikers on life's trail who disagree about the trail's end. Believers think that at death they'll experience God's "eternal city," the heaven that religions teach about; nonbelievers disagree. So theism's experiential test involves dying and then seeing what happens. (§§4.4–4.7)
- *Argument from design (fine tuning).* Recent physics shows that the fundamental constants in the laws governing our universe need to have been in a very narrow range for the universe to evolve intelligent life. What best explains this is that the universe was created by an intelligent being (God) who intended to produce life. So belief in God can be defended on a broadly empirical basis. (§6.4)
- *Instinctual basis (works like sense experience).* Most humans over the ages have believed in God and other supernatural beings on an instinctual basis that resembles ordinary sense experience. (§§7.3–7.4)

Objecting to such examples requires a clear notion of "empirical" that fits science but not these examples.

In addition, some clearly genuine truth claims aren't empirically testable or true by definition. The Jesuit philosopher Frederick Copleston used this in a debate with A.J. Ayer (1949): "The human race will someday have destroyed itself forever"; this could be true even though we humans couldn't verify it (we'd no longer exist). Ayer didn't know how to respond. The section that follows has further examples.

3.8 Analysis: Problems With Emotivism

Reducing moral beliefs to exclamations doesn't work.

(1) Moral judgments aren't always emotional. Some moral beliefs are emotional for us (maybe about racism), while others are unemotional (maybe about tax exemptions). Since moral judgments can be unemotional, we can't take them all as exclamations – like "Boo!" and "Hurrah!" – whose purpose is to express emotion.

Suppose we experiment to see if all moral judgments are emotional. We interview people, hook up a gizmo to measure emotions, and test whether all moral judgments are emotional (as emotivism holds) or go from highly emotional to highly unemotional (as I hold). I have no doubt about how the experiment would turn out.

(2) Some moral judgments translate poorly into exclamations. Consider these:

1. Do what is good.
2. Hurrah for good people!
3. Either it's good to go or it's bad to go.
4. This is neutral (neither good nor bad).

Here's what we get if we replace "good" and "bad" with exclamations:

1. Do what is hurrah!
2. Hurrah for hurrah! people!
3. Either hurrah for going! or boo on going!
4. Neither hurrah for this! nor boo on this!

If we use exclamations in a normal way, these don't make sense. Many sentences using "good" or "bad" have no plausible "hurrah" or "boo" equivalents.

Subjectivists can plausibly translate my four sentences. They'd translate 1 into "Do what I like" or "Do what I'd say 'Hurrah!' to." But this makes "X is good" into a truth claim about feelings, which emotivists reject.

(3) Skepticus gave this *simplicity argument* for emotivism:

1 Any view that's simpler and explains more is a better view.
2 Emotivism is a view that's simpler and explains more.
∴ Emotivism is a better view.

He claimed that premise 1 ("Occam's razor") is *obviously true*; in philosophy, as in science, a view is better if it's simpler and explains more. But premise 1 is an evaluative judgment (since "better" means "more good") and so, in his emotivism, it's an exclamation and not a truth claim (and thus not "obviously true"). It's unclear how to express premise 1 as an exclamation, but here's an attempt:

1 Hurrah more for any view that's simpler and explains more!

In Skepticus's emotivism, his premise 1 is an exclamation, not a truth claim, and so his simplicity argument fails (because its first premise isn't true).

This leads to a bigger problem, namely that norms of scientific method (like premise 1, "Occam's razor") in general aren't true or false but rather are exclamations that express feelings. Here are two important norms of scientific method:

- We *ought* normally to believe our sense experience.
- In our scientific theories, we *ought* to be consistent.

As exclamations, these two can't be true or false, so they'd be no more true than these next two norms:

- A view is *better* if it fits my horoscope.
- We *ought* to decide between scientific views by flipping a coin.

So emotivism destroys the objectivity of *both morality and science*.

(4) Emotivism also explains morality poorly, since it *denies* moral knowledge; a better view would *explain* moral knowledge. Imagine that we explained science using only economic factors (scientists experiment because they get paid for this) while denying that science can arrive at knowledge. This *explains away* science; a better view would show how to arrive at scientific knowledge. So too, a better explanation of morality (see NL §§10.4–10.9) would show how to arrive at moral truth and knowledge.

3.9 Analysis: Further Remarks on Logical Positivism

(1) Skepticus mentioned that logical positivism led to Godless religions, like Rabbi Sherman Wine's (1985) Humanistic Judaism. How do I react to such religions?

I see humans as fellow travelers on a long life-trail from God to him (see Augustine, §1.4). Some travelers of different faiths already accept God and share many beliefs about him, but some travelers of the same faith have conflicting views about God (some Christians even see God as racist, §2.6). And some travelers are hostile or indifferent to God. We should think of the travelers not as good people versus bad people but as a diverse group that can help each other grow on their journey, often by providing explanations or challenges.

I'm Christian, but I think we can learn from Godless religions. For example:

- We can learn the purely humanistic (non-supernatural) value of religious communities. Many today believe in God but want to do it alone, not part of any organized religion. Are they missing something

important in non-supernatural terms? Maybe we can learn about this from studying religions like Humanistic Judaism.[9]
- We can use Godless religions to better appreciate our religion's purely humanistic value (like Paul Van Buren's 1963 description of Jesus).
- We can better appreciate what I see as the most important part of religion – *love of God*, which should be central to our lives and our life search – but which Godless religions unfortunately lack.

So maybe we can learn from such Godless religions.

(2) I mentioned that intellectuals are becoming less hostile to religion, due to things like Freud's decline and psychology's new appreciation of religion's benefits. We see the same trend in analytic philosophy, which used to be very anti-religious; that changed much with logical positivism's decline and the rise of groups like the Society of Christian philosophers and individuals like Alvin Plantinga, Richard Swinburne, and John Hick. We'll see the same trend later in science, with newer religion-friendly views about fine tuning and the world's beginning. But often today, anti-religious thinkers still appeal to views (like Freud and logical positivism) that are horribly out of date.

(3) We'll see later that two logical positivists did some rethinking about religion. Antony Flew and Habermas (2004; Flew 2007) came to believe in God on the basis of the *fine tuning* argument (§6.5). A.J. Ayer (1988a) had a near-death experience (§4.5); his initial description, which he later tried to repudiate, included: "I was confronted by a red light, exceedingly bright, and also very painful even when I turned away from it. I was aware that this light was responsible for the government of the universe." Our next chapter asks "Is there life after death?"

---

9 Americans (mostly believers) with no church membership have been big, covering 83% of the population during the American revolution and 66% in the mid-1800s but only 40% at the end of the 1900s (Iannaccone 1998: 1468). Today unchurched believers are again increasing.

4 Is There Life After Death?

We'll begin by listening to the fictional student Skepticus explain why, on the basis of science, he rejects life after death. As you read Skepticus's passage, first try to understand it in a sympathetic way, and then try to find problems with it. We'll later consider objections.

4.1 Skepticus: There's No Life After Death

This is Skepticus again, but this time asking "Is there life after death?" My answer is a clear no.

Yesterday, due to my messy roommates, I found a cockroach on our kitchen floor. I stepped on it, crushed it, and killed it. Then I threw outside the remains, which will turn to soil. So the cockroach, which had been a living organism, suffered death. And sorry, Mr. Cockroach, once you're dead, you stay dead; there's no afterlife.

All living organisms, like cockroaches, are complexes of chemicals. Being a *living organism*, as we learn in biology, requires being able to take in food, grow, move, respond to the world, and reproduce. A living organism requires intricate chemical complexes. Crushing the cockroach destroys these complexes, so it destroys the special abilities that life brings; the cockroach dies, never to return to life.

That's our scientific understanding of how living organisms die, and it applies to humans too. Humans follow the same biological laws as other organisms. Humans, like cockroaches, are chemical complexes with special living abilities, which cease when death destroys the complexes that makes these possible. When these chemical complexes are destroyed, with humans and cockroaches, death comes and is permanent – there's no return to life or conscious experience.

Humans have bigger brains than cockroaches, but death destroys both equally well. Our brain's size brings new factors: we can *care* about loved ones, *suffer* when they die, and *worry* about our future death. Since death brings us greater distress, we invent fantasies that deny death's cold, hard reality and say that we (or perhaps our "souls") somehow survive death. So maybe there's life after death, an afterlife? While this fiction goes against what science teaches about organisms, many accept it because it makes them feel good. (See §1.2 about Freud.)

Societies create afterlife myths to help us endure death's sorrows and anxieties, encourage social norms (this supposedly benefits us in the afterlife), and explain dreams about those who have died. Models of the afterlife differ; ancient Greeks believe in a permanent spiritual soul apart from a body, Hindus believe in a reincarnation whereby a soul can go into a different human or animal body (perhaps a cow), and Christians believe that the soul enters an enhanced human body. Many see an eternal heaven and hell at the end; some think those of their religion enjoy eternal happiness, while others suffer eternal torment. Still others see nirvana as the end of reincarnations, whereby we're freed from desires and suffering and no longer reborn. These afterlife myths have no scientific basis.

Apart from reincarnation views, there's usually life after death only for humans. Sorry, Mr. Cockroach. A few believe in an afterlife for their pet dogs or cats; I hope that mosquitoes don't get included! My view is simpler; death is terminal for all biological organisms – there's no return to life, no life after death, for any species.

After we've physically died, we may "live on" in memories of those who loved us and in how we affected the world. This a metaphorical sense of "living on." Bertrand Russell (1927: 54) eloquently expressed the literal truth: "I believe that when I die I shall rot, and nothing of my ego will survive."

"Cyber immortality" is possible. Suppose that, before you die, we download your brain (beliefs, desires, and habits) to a disk. Later we upload this data into another human, robot, or cyborg – which we'll call NEWYOU (now with all your beliefs, desires, and habits). We could continue to upload the data into further beings, forever. Could you achieve personal immortality this way, through endless time? I think not. Each NEWYOU is only a *copy* of you, a *clone*; a NEWYOU isn't you. So personal immortality is impossible (but endless cloning is possible).

Even with help from computers, you and I won't survive death. We both, with cockroaches and other organisms, are merely complexes of chemicals. We live because our chemical parts have a certain complex but delicate organization; when death destroys this, our life ceases, we die and rot, and nothing remains of our ego.

Before going on, reflect on your reaction to Skepticus's passage. Do you see any problems with it?

4.2 Analysis: Religion and the Afterlife

The afterlife's plausibility is heavily influenced by our religious views (this section) and our philosophical views on the body-soul problem (the next section).

When we study ancient cultures, we mostly find religious beliefs and funeral practices (like Egyptian pyramids) affirming the afterlife. Evidence for burials goes back 100,000 years and often included tools or food for the next life. Given a belief in supernatural beings, it's easy to believe that humans have a supernatural element and that death moves us to a higher life. A few ancients rejected the afterlife, like Epicurus of Greece and Sadducees of Jesus's time. While many religions imaginatively develop detailed descriptions of the afterlife, some follow the cautious Bahá'í approach that we shouldn't expect to understand the afterlife now better than an unborn fetus would understand life after birth.

Today, studies show, most people across the globe believe in life after death; for the US data, search for "How many Americans believe in life after death?" Most theist religions believe that God loves us and put into us a desire for eternal happiness with him; such religions would strongly believe in the afterlife. In Christianity, the afterlife has a special place, since the authenticity of Jesus's message is tied to his physically rising from the dead; for Christians, Jesus conquered death (his and ours) and shows how death is an entrance into a different and better life.[1]

Skepticus explains our attraction to religion and the afterlife emotionally; these beliefs make us feel good. As noted in §1.4, this emotional explanation, even if true, doesn't disprove the beliefs. Perhaps God, to lead us to believe in him and the afterlife, put into us a natural desire for eternal happiness with him, and we can see ripples of this desire in human history, from ancient times to the present.

Suppose that you (with Skepticus) believe both of these:

1. *Atheism.* There's no God.
2. *Materialism.* Everything in the universe is just a complex of chemicals.

If you believe both, you pretty much have to reject belief in the afterlife.

Atheists who reject materialism sometimes believe in an afterlife. They may accept Plato's view that a human is a combination of a material body with an eternal, immaterial soul; at death, the eternal, immaterial soul separates from the body but goes on existing. But most atheists tend to be materialists and reject an afterlife.

---

1 Several argue for the authenticity of Jesus's physical resurrection (and his message) on the basis of what they see as strong historical evidence. The evidence is the large number of people who attested to having experienced the resurrected Jesus (or who were reported to having experienced him but didn't repudiate this report, even though this would have been easy) – and who were committed to die for their belief if need be (many were killed by the Romans for their faith). See Craig (1981, 2010: ch. 9), Flew and Habermas (2004), Olson (2016), Pannenberg (1968), Swinburne (2003), and Wright (2003). I see this historical argument as plausible, although I haven't studied it deeply.

Christians and other theists are sometimes materialists but still believe in an afterlife. They may believe that at our death, God miraculously puts us into a better body that won't decay or die; this is a miracle (violating normal scientific laws) that God does for us, the gift of an afterlife that continues forever. God can perform such miracles.

Christians and other theists sometimes reject an afterlife, seeing their religion's talk about the afterlife as metaphorical. I'm not advocating this.

Christianity thinks how we die is very important – with love in our hearts toward God and our fellow human beings, asking forgiveness for failings on these, often in a life that's been purified by suffering, in preparation for the life to come.[2]

4.3 Analysis: Body-Soul and the Afterlife

I'm a human being, a human person. But what is that? Is a human being merely a complex of chemicals (materialism), a immaterial spirit (idealism), a combination of a material body and immaterial soul (dualism), or something else? The difficult body-soul problem connects closely to the afterlife. So we need to consider the *body-soul problem* (or *body-mind problem*; I'll use "soul" and "mind" interchangeably).

Monistic body-soul views say I'm just ONE ENTITY. Here are three options:

- *Materialism*. I'm only a body (a complex of chemicals). What I call *thoughts* and *feelings* are chemical brain processes or outer behavior.
- *Idealism*. I'm only a mind (an immaterial spirit). What I call *matter* is just mental images, and matter has no reality apart from these.
- *Double-aspect theory*. I'm one entity with material and mental properties:
    - "*I* weigh 84 kilos" ascribes a *material property* to me. To speak of "my body" is to speak of my *material properties*: "*My body* weighs 84 kilos."
    - "*I* feel joy" ascribes a *mental property* to me. To speak of "my mind" is to speak of my *mental properties*: "*My mind* feels joy."

Materialism, Skepticus's view, makes the afterlife impossible, unless we bring in a divine miracle at each death (see previous section).

When I feel pain, there's *chemistry* (chemical brain processes, including outer behavior) and *experience*. Materialists claim that the *experience* is

---

2 When I started struggling more with cancer, retired from teaching, and was told that I had not long to live, I wondered if I had time to write one more book, my seventeenth book, which would become *Reasoning about God*. If you're reading this book now, then yes, I was able to get this into publishable shape before dying. For me, writing this book was a wonderful way to prepare for death.

reducible to the *chemistry*; the materialist "identity theory" says both describe the *same identical event* – but maybe this isn't so clear. The two differ conceptually: we can imagine the *chemistry* happening without the *experience* or the *experience* without the *chemistry*. The two differ ethically too: we inherently care about what happens to a sentient being's *experience* (pain hurts!) but not what happens to its *chemistry*. I'll argue later (§4.7) that recent empirical data show that materialism is false.

Idealism is compatible with an afterlife, since then your death in the material world is just mental images that you, as an immaterial spirit, experience, as on a television screen. Idealism's problem is that it's difficult to believe that the material world has no independent existence but is just mental images.

Double-aspect theory is my favorite approach. It fits how we think and speak and avoids weird implications. It's compatible with life after death, where our mental properties continue, but our material properties change more. Its weakness is that it doesn't explain how a being with material properties can also have mental properties[3] ("The hard problem of consciousness") and how life after death is possible, but perhaps these are wonderful things that we'll never understand very well.

I like to combine the double-aspect theory with ideas from Pierre Teilhard de Chardin (1881–1955), a Jesuit scientist who wrote about how Christianity fits into an evolutionary world. Teilhard (1966, see Swindal 2005: 326–29), thought everything in the universe has both material ("the outside") and mental ("the inside") properties; at low complexity (like an ice cube), mental properties are negligible. His *law of complexity-consciousness* says that the evolutionary cosmic process tends toward beings appearing of increasing material complexity ("the outside") and consciousness ("the inside"). This has stages from atoms, to complex molecules, to one-cell organisms, to multi-cell organisms, to humans (with the ultra-complex brain going with a greatly enhanced mind), to increasingly complex forms of human society, to eventually the final goal and culmination of the process, which he calls the Ω *omega point* and identifies in faith with the Christian *Kingdom of God*. Life after death becomes possible at the human level, where the ultra-complex human brain makes possible a greatly more powerful mind.[4]

---

3 Interestingly enough, this puzzling fact can become a *first principle* about how to understand our universe; see the next paragraph about Teilhard.
4 Teilhard hoped to recast our understanding of the basic scientific laws governing the universe, to make proper room for consciousness ("the inside of things"). Those who argue for the authenticity of near-death experiences (see the next few sections) hope for a similar recasting of scientific laws. Skepticus may object that our current science (taken in a materialistic way) should last forever, and so we need to repel all who invade its sacred territory. But the history of science shows continual change; recall how Madame Marie Curie's study of radium disproved that atoms were indivisible. Healthy science is open to change when needed.

Dualistic body-soul views say I'm TWO ENTITIES – a material body and an immaterial mind (or soul). Again, there are three options; these differ on whether your two parts interact with each other:

- *Interactive dualism*. Body and mind causally interact with each other.
- *Epiphenomenalism*. Body influences mind, but mind doesn't influence body.
- *Occasionalism*. Body and mind don't interact causally; God influences mind and body so they seem to interact (so when the stone hits my head, God causes my mind to feel pain).

Interactive dualism is the most popular dualism (so when I speak of *"dualism"* without qualification, I mean *"interactive dualism"*). How I think, feel, and choose can influence my body (permitting a nondeterministic free will – I can freely decide to exercise more, and this can affect my body) – and my body can influence my mind (maybe I feel tired from exercise and can't think well). This view is compatible with life after death, where your soul leaves your body and exists in no body or another body. Dualism, while close to double-aspect theory in practice, sees me as TWO entities, instead of just ONE entity with two sets of properties.

Epiphenomenalism sees thoughts and feelings (as experienced and mental) as differing from chemical brain processes but totally depending on the latter. This denies nondeterministic free will; chemical processes cause both our experience of choosing and our choice. The view also makes it impossible for us (or our souls) to think or feel without a functioning brain. Since our thoughts and feelings totally depend on chemical brain processes, which death destroys, life after death is impossible (unless, as with materialism, God miraculously creates another brain to fuel the soul). I'll argue later (§4.7) that recent empirical data show that epiphenomenalism is false.

Occasionalism is weird and not popular today. It assumes that entities totally different in nature, like body and soul, can't causally interact, so God's causality fills the gap (sending pain to our soul when the rock hits our head). This view seems compatible with free will and life after death.

Not all neuroscientists are materialists. The eminent neuroscientist John Eccles (1989: 241), for example, is a dualist (or a more complicated trialist, 1984) and strongly opposed to materialistic reductionism:

> The human mystery is incredibly demeaned by scientific reductionism, with its claim in promissory materialism to account eventually for all of the spiritual world in terms of patterns of neuronal activity. This belief must be classed as a superstition. . . . We have to recognize that we are spiritual beings with souls existing in a spiritual world as well as material beings with bodies and brains existing in a material world.

In evaluating anti-religion criticisms supposedly based on science, make sure that the science is right and the critic isn't making further nonscientific assumptions. Skepticus assumes a materialist view; recall what he said in §4.1:

> Living organisms, like cockroaches, are complexes of chemicals. Being a *living organism* . . . requires intricate chemical complexes. Crushing the cockroach destroys these complexes, so it destroys the special abilities that life brings; the cockroach dies, never to return to life.
>
> That's our scientific understanding of how living organisms die, and it applies to humans too. . . . When these chemical complexes are destroyed, with humans as with cockroaches, death comes and is permanent – there's no return to life or conscious experience.

Dualists question lumping humans with cockroaches as being *just complexes of chemicals* (materialism) and not returning to conscious existence when death comes. Many dualists think organisms of high mental sophistication have *an immaterial soul* and aren't just complexes of chemicals; death separates the soul from the body but doesn't kill the soul or stop conscious experience. Skepticus *assumes that dualism is false and humans have no soul*. Since Skepticus supposedly bases his case on science, he needs to give us scientific grounds for rejecting dualism in favor of materialism, and he doesn't do this.

We can consistently imagine ourselves dying and then continuing our conscious experience on the other side; the idea is logically possible, and we can create consistent stories or movies where it happens. Are there experiential signs that this ever actually happens, that people experience life after death? Perhaps there are.

4.4 Analysis: Near-Death Experiences

A *near-death experience* (NDE) is *a lucid experience associated with perceived consciousness apart from the body occurring at the time of actual or threatened imminent death* (from the world's largest NDE Web site, https://www.nderf.org, which we'll discuss later).

I learned about NDEs while teaching at Loyola University Chicago. Our campus was used to film part of the *Flatliners* movie (1990), about medical students who experimented with NDEs. They'd stop a student's heart for a few minutes, the student had an NDE, and then they'd talk about it. (Don't try this at home!) While most of them thought the NDEs gave a genuine experience of life after death, the one atheist thought they were just hallucinations.

The "near-death experience" interest (and phrase) started earlier, with *Life After Life* by Raymond Moody (1975), a medical doctor with philosophy and psychology PhDs. Moody interviewed 150 patients who experienced death's beginning, due to causes like a heart attack. They told similar stories, and these themes often came up:

- sensing peace, love, well-being, coming home
- being out of your body but able to perceive the world better than before
- moving to a different place (maybe above the operating table to observe your operation or through a tunnel to a heavenly landscape)
- being reunited lovingly with dead family members
- encountering a loving divine being who shines with a brilliant light (Christians may see him as Jesus, while Hindus see him as Krishna)
- having your life reviewed non-judgmentally about loving your neighbor (you still need to grow in love)
- being returned to ordinary life (often reluctantly)
- finding the experience clear, coherent, real, and difficult to dismiss (unlike a dream or hallucination)
- having afterwards less fear of death, more motivation to love your neighbor, and less concern for honors and wealth.

Many hesitated to speak of their NDEs, fearing that people would think them crazy. How would you react to a patient who wakes up and says "I experienced God"?

If I view *often highlighted passages* for Moody's book on my Kindle, I get these:

> You experience a divine and totally loving personal being as a very bright light. It leads you to review your life, not to bring punishment or reward, but to help you live better in love and knowledge. You no longer fear death. So your spirit survives death and leads you to a more divine life.

Similar NDEs occur in all cultures and ages. NDEs are described in ancient Egyptian and Tibetan texts, for example, and at the end of Plato's *Republic*. NDEs are more common today, because of modern medical techniques like cardiopulmonary resuscitation; roughly 5% of Americans will experience an NDE. NDEs happen to those of all faiths and to those of no faith.

4.5 Analysis: Ayer's Near-Death Experience

A.J. Ayer, a prominent logical positivist who rejected God, was featured in Chapter 3. He had an NDE toward the end of his life (Ayer 1988a). While in the hospital for pneumonia, Ayer choked on smoked salmon, and his heart stopped for four minutes; his heart monitor flatlined, fitting a common definition of "death." Then he woke up and spoke lucidly. He said "You are all mad"; he later thought this meant they were wrong in rejecting the afterlife. He said to a friend: "Did you know that I was dead? The first time that I tried to cross the river I was frustrated, but my second attempt succeeded. It was most extraordinary. My thoughts became persons." Later he mentions the ancient Greek myth that souls of the dead cross the river Styx.

Ayer (1988a) later writes:

> The only memory that I have of an experience, closely encompassing my death, is very vivid. I was confronted by a red light, exceedingly bright, and also very painful even when I turned away from it. I was aware that this light was responsible for the government of the universe. Among its ministers were two creatures who had been put in charge of space.... The experience suddenly came to an end.

"The bright red light that governs the universe" suggests God, since many NDEs associate this with God. Did Ayer claim to have experienced God? Later Ayer tries to avoid this conclusion.

Ayer struggled with what to believe. Like most, he was strongly drawn to believe that his NDE was genuine and revealed a new reality, but his life and writings had attacked belief in God and the afterlife, and now he hesitated to change. What should he believe now? He says that, while his experience may have been delusive, a friend's similar experience suggests that it may have been veridical – which would give strong evidence that death doesn't end consciousness. He suggests that maybe the brain kept working with no blood flowing through it.

Dr. Sam Parnia et al. (2014, 2017, 2019) led the large AWARE medical trial on this last issue and would reject Russell's suggestion. The brain's cerebral cortex, responsible for thought and sensation, shows no activity (no brain waves) within 2 and 20 seconds of the heart stopping; brain death follows hours later. AWARE and other studies suggest that the mind or consciousness – the psyche, the "self," the thing that "makes me Sam" and who we are – may not originate in the brain and may be a separate, undiscovered scientific entity. Modern science lacks the tools to show it. Death needn't immediately annihilate consciousness or self.

Ayer says an afterlife wouldn't prove God's existence. He mentions philosophers who accept the afterlife but reject God. He concludes:

> My recent experiences have slightly weakened my conviction that my genuine death, which is due fairly soon, will be the end of me, though I continue to hope that it will be. They have not weakened my conviction that there is no god. I trust that my remaining an atheist will allay the anxieties of my fellow supporters.

Ayer's (1988b) doctor tested him, and there was no brain damage. Ayer reportedly told him: "I saw a Divine Being. I'm afraid I'm going to have to revise all my various books and opinions." Later Ayer changed his mind on this.

The NDE changed Ayer, who called himself "a born-again atheist." Ayer's wife said, "Freddie became so much nicer after he died. He was not nearly so boastful. He took an interest in other people." He appreciated more the beauty of nature. And he grew closer to his Jesuit friend and debate partner (§3.7), Frederick Copleston.

4.6 Analysis: Kübler-Ross, Evidence for Life After Death

Dr. Elisabeth Kübler-Ross is known for her work on death; her *On Death and Dying* (1969) explored the grief we go through when loved ones die. Her later book, *On Children and Death* (1985), discusses family issues, including coping with a child's death. Ross's last chapter focuses on how NDEs with children give evidence for an afterlife. She introduces this timidly, fearing that many would see this as pseudo-science and think she's crazy for mentioning the idea. But she can't deny what she has heard over and over again in her work with children, and that, yes, this does give objective evidence for life after death.

Families sometimes have car accidents where family members die. The seriously injured may go to multiple hospitals. Sometimes a child, call him "Jimmy," has an NDE and reports visiting family who died. When Jimmy wakes up, *he knows exactly which family members died* (let's say Marcia and Daddy).[5] Often, by normal means, he shouldn't know this; he didn't see them die, and no one told him about their deaths. Is this a coincidence? Does he just guess right about who died? Ross thinks this very unlikely, since the same thing happens again and again, in different places and cultures, and the child always gets it right about who died. Other researchers also get correct reports from NDE children. What explains this? *How does the child know which family members died?* The best explanation is that the child's NDE is genuine and the child met with dead family members.[6]

---

5 Sometimes the child wakes up, says "Marcia and Daddy are waiting for me," smiles, and dies. In another case, the child talked about meeting his twin brother whom he didn't know about, since he had never been told that he had a twin brother who died at birth.

6 "In all the years that I have quietly collected data from California to Sydney, Australia; from white and black children, aboriginals, Eskimos, South Americans, and Libyan youngsters, every single child who mentioned that someone was waiting for them mentioned a person who had actually preceded them in death, even if by only a few moments. And yet none of these children had been informed of the recent death of the relatives by us at any time. Coincidence? By now there is no scientist or statistician who could convince me that this occurs, as some colleagues claim, as 'a result of oxygen deprivation' or for other 'rational and scientific' reasons." Ross (1985: 210–11)

Ross (1985: 202) has optimism about others coming to accept life after death:

> Since the consciousness of the people on this planet earth is unfolding at an accelerated rate, it is only a matter of a couple of decades until all people of all creeds, of all cultures, of all places will *know* that this life on earth is just a small, yet the most difficult, part of our long journey from the source we call God, back to our final home of peace, back to God.

If the evidence is strong, will people come to accept this?

4.7 Analysis: Long, Evidence for Life After Death

Dr. Jeffrey Long has worked to give the strongest possible NDE argument for the afterlife. This requires getting clear on two questions:

- What do NDE reports say?
- Why does the best explanation for these reports require an afterlife?

To get a good NDE database, Long in 1998 set up the Near-Death Experience Research Foundation and https://www.nderf.org Web site. He gathered as many NDE reports from as many cultures as possible, checking them for authenticity and consistency. The site now has an impressive 5000 NDE reports; previous studies used far fewer reports and were more localized. Long's work is very thorough.[7]

Long's book, *Evidence of the Afterlife: The Science of Near-Death Experiences* (2009), deals with the second question: "Why does the best explanation for these reports require an afterlife?" He gives nine points; I'll comment more on earlier ones.

1. *Lucid death.* This point is strengthened by Dr. Sam Parnia's (2014) large AWARE medical trial about what goes on medically after our heart stops. Within 2 to 20 seconds, the brain's cerebral cortex, responsible for thought and sensation, shows no activity (no brain waves). We can have lucid thinking for several minutes after this, with no brain activity; this disproves materialism and epiphenomenalism (§4.3). Parnia says there should, by conventional thinking, be no consciousness. "Yet, paradoxically, what we started to see is that millions of people

---

[7] Maybe everyone who gave one of the 5000 reports was lying? This is very unlikely, especially since NDE reports from other sources are similar.

have now been resuscitated, and many of them have reported these very lucid, well-structured thought processes. They're able to form memories, describe conversations and what people were wearing. Except that their brain has shut down and they've gone through death. Which is completely a paradox, it should not happen. If your mind is simply a product of your brain, if your brain has shut down, there should be no consciousness" (Parnia 2019).

2. *Out of body.* Often an NDE patient is being operated on, with eyes closed, and positioned poorly to see the operation. Afterward, the patient says he floated to the ceiling to get a better look – and he can describe accurately the details of the operation. In other cases, the patient may go into the waiting room, outside, or through a tunnel toward the light.
3. *Blind sight.* Those blind from birth can see well, and all can use telepathy.
4. *Impossibly conscious.* People are conscious even when under total amnesia, which shouldn't happen.
5. *Perfect playback.* The non-judgmental life review has your life flash on a screen and is evaluated in terms of loving your neighbor. It's accurate and often includes almost forgotten items.
6. *Family reunion.* People reunite with family, as in the Kübler-Ross section.
7. *From the mouths of babes.* Children under five report the same experiences; they can't be repeating what they were taught about NDEs, since they were too young to have learned about these.
8. *Worldwide consistency.* People from all cultures report similar experiences; this is based on analyzing reports in the NDERF database, which come from all over the world.
9. *Changed lives.* People afterwards believe more in life after death, fear dying less, become more loving and spiritual, appreciate life and nature more, have more confidence, are happier, and care less about money and honors. Their NDE is their life's most transforming experience.

Skeptics try to explain NDEs as hallucinations, but the two differ in many ways. NDEs are seen as real and fully believable – "as real as you and me sitting here talking"; hallucinators tend to be aware that it isn't real. Those who have had both experiences say they're very different. NDEs are highly coherent and consistent across cultures; hallucinations tend to be incoherent and idiosyncratic. NDEs bring peace and other good life consequences, while hallucinations bring anxiety and disturbance. Or maybe those who have NDEs suffer from oxygen deprivation? Again, the features are different, and people having an NDE tend to have normal oxygen levels. NDEs seem impossible to explain away by normal medical means.

I think Elisabeth Kübler-Ross and Jeffrey Long make a strong case for life after death, but you have to judge this yourself. For more, read Long (2016), *God and the Afterlife: The Groundbreaking New Evidence for God and*

Near-Death Experience, and Miller (2012), *Near-Death Experiences as Evidence for the Existence of God and Heaven*, and view Robert Spitzer (2020).[8]

Skepticus in §4.1 mentioned three views of the afterlife:

> Ancient Greeks believe in a permanent spiritual soul apart from a body, Hindus believe in a reincarnation whereby a soul can go into a different human or animal body (perhaps a cow), and Christians believe that the soul enters an enhanced human body. . . . These afterlife myths have no scientific basis.

In NDE reports, the dead and near-dead have *enhanced human bodies* (with illnesses cured and some superpowers added, like telepathy). So visited dead relatives aren't *disembodied spirits* or *reincarnated* into other human or animal bodies. I see NDE research as giving scientific support for the *enhanced human bodies* view.[9]

Here's how NDE data support a theological view. Compare these two views:

(1) God is deeply loving and desires that his creatures love each other.
(2) While God created the world and us, he's utterly indifferent to us and our lives. (This is an extreme *deism*[10] and held by some who believe in God but see no reason God would care about us.)

NDE data strongly favor (1) over (2). This supports the core belief of most believers that God is a *loving being* and that *we were created to love one another*.

I expect that when I die, which may be soon, my first experience will be a loving hug from God, with "Welcome home, son." I'll have many questions. How can I be experiencing this? And how can an embodied being on earth have experiences – how can this be? I'll have much to learn about who and what I am.

---

8 Would eternal life eventually bring boredom? I'm sure that God could solve this problem. I can watch the same movie every few years – and it's like seeing it afresh, because I forget the details. So something simple like forgetting could be part of the solution.

9 St. Paul (1 Cor 15:42–45), who may have had an NDE, puts it this way: "So is it with the resurrection of the dead. What is sown is perishable, what is raised is imperishable. It is sown in dishonor, it is raised in glory. It is sown in weakness, it is raised in power. It is sown a physical body, it is raised a spiritual body. If there is a physical body, there is also a spiritual body."

A short time before he died, St. Thomas Aquinas had an intense experience of God, which may have been an NDE, compared to which he saw all his theorizing as bring "like straw" in value.

10 A *deist* is one who, while believing that there's a God (often on the basis of reason), rejects divine revelation and minimizes God's concern for and involvement in the world. Thomas Jefferson and other deists were prominent in early American history.

5
Is There a First Cause?

We'll begin by listening to the fictional student Skepticus explain why he rejects the *first cause* argument (and related arguments) for God's existence. As you read Skepticus's passage, first try to understand it in a sympathetic way, and then try to find problems with it. We'll later consider objections.

5.1 Skepticus: There's No First Cause

This is Skepticus again, and I'm getting interested in arguments for God's existence. One of my favorite philosophers, Bertrand Russell (1927), talks about these:

> Perhaps the simplest and easiest to understand is the argument of the First Cause. It is maintained that everything we see in this world has a cause, and as you go back in the chain of causes further and further you must come to a First Cause, and to that First Cause you give the name of God.

The young Russell accepted God on the basis of this argument. John Stuart Mill's criticism changed his mind (my italics):

> I for a long time accepted the argument of the First Cause, until one day, at the age of eighteen, I read John Stuart Mill's Autobiography, and I there found this sentence: "My father taught me that the question, 'Who made me?' cannot be answered, since it immediately suggests the further question, 'Who made God?'"
>
> That very simple sentence showed me, as I still think, the fallacy in the argument of the First Cause. *If everything must have a cause, then God must have a cause. If there can be anything without a cause, it may just as well be the world as God,* so that there cannot be any validity in that argument. . . . There is no reason why the world could not have come into being without a cause; nor, on the other hand, is there any reason why it should not have always existed. *There is no reason to suppose that the world had a beginning at all.*

DOI: 10.4324/9781003320920-6

Since I've been learning symbolic logic (using Gensler 2017a), I put the *first cause* argument, as Russell understands it, into a strict premise-conclusion form:

1 Everything has a cause.
2 If the world has a cause, then there's a God.
∴ There's a God.

This is valid – the conclusion follows logically from the premises – as we can see intuitively or prove using quantificational logic.[1] One problem is that premise 1 ("Everything has a cause") can equally well show that there's no God (since if *everything* has a cause, then *God* has to have a cause too):

1 Everything has a cause.
2 If there's a God, then something doesn't have a cause (namely God).
∴ There's no God.

Premise 2 is true because God, of necessity, has no cause; if God had a cause, he'd be a creature, not God. We can't hold "Everything has a cause" – since, with other true premises, it leads to contradictions ("There's a God" and "There's no God").

Russell and I saw that this *first cause* argument is really stupid – since premise 1 leads quickly to contradictions. Could believers really be that stupid? I asked Faith, a philosophy-major friend who believes in God. Faith said Russell distorts the *first cause* argument, whose classic sources *don't say* "Everything has a cause." She said this premise is really stupid and is used mainly by college freshmen who don't know any better or atheist thinkers who want to make believers look dumb. St. Thomas Aquinas (1225–74), Faith emphasized, doesn't include this stupid premise as part of his argument:[2]

> The second way [to show God's existence] is from the nature of cause. In the world of sense we find there is an order of causes. There is no case known (neither is it, indeed, possible) in which a thing is found to be the cause of itself; for so it would be prior to itself, which is impossible. Now in causes it is not possible to go on to infinity, because in all causes following in order, the first is the cause of the intermediate cause, and the intermediate is the cause of the ultimate cause, whether the intermediate cause be several, or only one. Now to take away the cause

---

1 Some arguments in this present book are also in my logic textbook as homework problems to work out (three in this section are in Gensler 2017a: 200, 201, and 129).
2 I use "cause" for Aquinas's "efficient cause"; these mean the same in English. This text is from Aquinas (1274: first part, question 3, article 3, body), also in Swindal (2005: 170).

is to take away the effect. Therefore, if there be no first cause among causes, there will be no ultimate, nor any intermediate cause. But if in causes it is possible to go on to infinity, there will be no first cause, neither will there be an ultimate effect, nor any intermediate causes; all of which is plainly false. Therefore it is necessary to admit a first cause, to which everyone gives the name of God.

A *first cause* (*uncaused cause*) is something that brings other things into existence while nothing brought it into existence. This reasoning is valid in propositional logic.

1 Some things are caused (brought into existence).
2 Anything caused is caused by another.
3 If some things are caused and anything caused is caused by another, then either there's a first cause or there's an infinite series of past causes.
4 There's no infinite series of past causes.
∴ There's a first cause.

Premise 1 says that some things are caused (brought into existence). Suppose you make some spaghetti (you bring it into existence). What is the cause of the spaghetti? We could give a long answer – the cause is YOU + the spaghetti maker + preexisting materials, but the argument works equally well if we just pick a prominent cause. So let's say that your SPAGHETTI MAKER (which turns dough into pasta noodles) caused the SPAGHETTI. Then we can ask, did anything cause (bring into existence) your SPAGHETTI MAKER? Here we could give one of three answers:

1. No, your SPAGHETTI MAKER has no cause. Then it's a first cause: "Something that brings other things into existence while nothing brought it into existence." Sorry, this won't work; only God can be a first cause. So no, your SPAGHETTI MAKER doesn't exist without a cause.
2. Yes, your SPAGHETTI MAKER has a cause, since it brought itself into existence. Sorry, this won't work either, since it violates premise 2 and common sense (since nothing can bring itself into existence). So no, your SPAGHETTI MAKER didn't bring itself into existence.
3. Yes, your SPAGHETTI MAKER has a cause. To keep it simple, let's say that the cause was the PASTAIO FACTORY.

In case 3, we can ask the same question again: Did anything cause the PASTAIO FACTORY? Let's keep asking this question for whatever answer we get. What will eventually happen? We'll either keep on going forever and get an *infinite series of past causes* – which premise 4 claims is impossible – or we'll get a *first cause* – something that causes other things to exist while nothing caused it to exist – which is God. So we eventually get to a *first cause*, and hence God.

I can see two problems with the argument. First, maybe premise 4 is wrong; maybe there's an infinite series of past causes. While some may see this as absurd or self-contradictory, Aristotle and many scientists over the years have accepted it; they think the universe goes back infinitely in time, with no beginning. Why could this not be? Russell says *"There is no reason to suppose that the world had a beginning at all."*

Another problem is, if there's a first cause, it might be a purely physical event like the Big Bang and not a personal creator like God.

So I think the *first cause* argument doesn't work – either in Russell's simple version or in Aquinas's more complex version.

5.2 Skepticus: Aquinas's Five Ways

Aquinas's "five ways" argue for God's existence. Some came from Plato, Aristotle, or Moses Maimonides; Aquinas put them together and many later discussions use them. I'll sketch these five ways, intended to prove God's existence, as:

1. first mover,
2. first cause (we just discussed this one),
3. necessary being,
4. greatest being, and
5. world's designer.

None of them work, and pointing out their flaws can get complicated. If you get a headache, just skip to the end of the section.[3]

(1) The *first mover* argument uses "move" for any kind of change; "*x moves y*" means "x changes y in some way." So a *first mover* (*unmoved mover*) is what changes other things, while nothing changes it. Here's how Aquinas presents the *first mover* argument (which sounds much like *first cause*):[4]

> I answer that the existence of God can be proved in five ways. The first and more manifest way is the argument from motion. It is certain, and evident to our senses, that in the world some things are in motion. Now whatever is in motion is put in motion by another, for nothing can be in

---

[3] Gensler comment: These arguments are classics, but their reasoning is poor, their flaws are complicated, and you'd lose little by just skipping to the end of the section.

[4] Aquinas (1274: first part, question 3, article 3, body) has this, also in Swindal (2005: 169–71). My logic textbook (Gensler 2017a: 227–28, prob. 22 and 23) gives the *necessary being* argument as a homework problem. This has cartoon versions of the five ways:

https://web.archive.org/web/20000531123855/http://members.xoom.com/cartoontruth/p2.htm

motion except it is in potentiality to that towards which it is in motion; whereas a thing moves inasmuch as it is in act. For motion is nothing else than the reduction of something from potentiality to actuality. But nothing can be reduced from potentiality to actuality, except by something in a state of actuality. Thus that which is actually hot, as fire, makes wood, which is potentially hot, to be actually hot, and thereby moves and changes it. Now it is not possible that the same thing should be at once in actuality and potentiality in the same respect, but only in different respects. For what is actually hot cannot simultaneously be potentially hot; but it is simultaneously potentially cold. It is therefore impossible that in the same respect and in the same way a thing should be both mover and moved, i.e., that it should move itself. Therefore, whatever is in motion must be put in motion by another. If that by which it is put in motion be itself put in motion, then this also must needs be put in motion by another, and that by another again. But this cannot go on to infinity, because then there would be no first mover, and, consequently, no other mover; seeing that subsequent movers move only inasmuch as they are put in motion by the first mover; as the staff moves only because it is put in motion by the hand. Therefore it is necessary to arrive at a first mover, put in motion by no other; and this everyone understands to be God.

This version of the *first mover* argument is valid in propositional logic.

1   Some things are in motion (changing in some respect).
2   Whatever is in motion is moved by something else.
3   If some things are in motion and whatever is in motion is moved by something else, then either there's a first mover or there's an infinite series of past movers.
4   There's no infinite series of past movers.
∴   There's a first mover.

This *first mover* argument has the same two problems we saw with *first cause*. (1) Maybe premise 4 is wrong; maybe the universe existed for an infinitely long time (an infinite number of moments) and its state at any moment was brought about by a previous state. (2) A first mover might be a physical event like the Big Bang and not a personal creator like God – and it might not still exist.[5]

The *first mover* argument has three further problems. (3) Against premise 3, ants and automobiles presumably move themselves; the *first cause* version avoids this problem (since neither brings itself into existence). (4) If God is

---

5   Or we could deny premise 1 about motion's reality (as did ancient thinkers Zeno and Parmenides). Or we could question premise 3, mentioning possible endless-but-finite loops: A was caused by B, B was caused by C, C was caused by D, . . . , and Z (the last one) was caused by A; then world history, like a rubber band, has a finite number of elements but no beginning.

a first mover, then he can't change in any way (a first mover, by definition, can't change), but do we really want to view God as absolutely changeless? Is a changeless God compatible with the Bible? Again, the *first cause* argument avoids this problem (since it just claims that nothing brought God into existence – he JUST IS, without beginning, eternally). (5) God in the *first mover* argument might *change* preexisting matter instead of *creating it out of nothing*. The *first cause* version gives a stronger conclusion about God being *Creator* (*he brings the world into existence*).[6]

(2) The *first cause* argument was already discussed in the previous section.

(3) The *necessary being* argument is the most difficult to understand and the most flawed logically. I'll introduce two technical terms:

- A *contingent being* is one that exists but *could have failed to exist* (since it doesn't exist of necessity). You're a *contingent being*, one that exists but could have failed to exist.
- A *necessary being* is one that exists and *couldn't have failed to exist* (it exists of necessity; it couldn't have not-existed). Many think that God is a necessary being and perhaps the only necessary being.

Aquinas argues that there has to be a necessary being (God). His argument has two parts, which we can express as follows:

1   If every being is contingent, then nothing exists now.
2   Something exists now.
∴   Not every being is contingent. (intermediate conclusion)
3   If not every being is contingent, then some being is necessary.
∴   Some being is necessary.

What I call the FIRST PART of Aquinas's argument is the first three lines, with further premises added, which are supposed to establish the intermediate conclusion "Not every being is contingent." Aquinas tries to establish this by assuming "Every being is contingent" and then showing that this leads to an impossibility. This is what Aquinas says about the FIRST PART of his argument:

> [FIRST PART] The third way is taken from possibility and necessity, and runs thus. We find in nature things that are possible to be and not to be, since they are found to be generated, and to corrupt, and

---

6 Arguments for God's existence were controversial in the Middle Ages. William of Ockham (c. 1285–1349, see Swindal 2005: 220–22), emphasized faith over reason. While criticizing the *first mover* argument as a strict proof, he accepted it on probable grounds (perhaps as a "weak conjecture") as more simply explaining the world since it avoids an infinite series. He saw "There's a God" as a universal presupposition instead of something that could be demonstrated.

consequently, they are possible to be and not to be. But it is impossible for these always to exist, for that which is possible not to be at some time is not. Therefore, if everything is possible not to be, then at one time there could have been nothing in existence. Now if this were true, even now there would be nothing in existence, because that which does not exist only begins to exist by something already existing. Therefore, if at one time nothing was in existence, it would have been impossible for anything to have begun to exist; and thus even now nothing would be in existence – which is absurd. Therefore, not all beings are merely possible, but there must exist something the existence of which is necessary.

This is how I'd express Aquinas's fuller reasoning for the FIRST PART:

1 Assume that every being is contingent.
2 Each contingent being at some time fails to exist.
∴ There's some time at which every being fails to exist.
3 If there's some time at which every being fails to exist, then nothing exists now.
∴ Nothing exists now.
4 Something exists now.
∴ Not every being is contingent.

Premise 1 assumes that every being is contingent; it assumes this to show that it's impossible, since it leads to lines that contradict each other ("Nothing exists now" and "Something exists now"). Thus we can conclude the last line ("Not every being is contingent"), the opposite of the assumption (line 1).

Premise 2 ("Each contingent being at some time fails to exist") could be false, since some contingent beings might be eternal (always exist). God could have created an eternal sun which always exists and yet is contingent (it might not have existed, since God could have decided not to create it). That's the first flaw in the argument.

The inference from premise 2 to the first intermediate conclusion is invalid, which is a second flaw:[7]

1 Each contingent being at some time fails to exist.
∴ There's some time at which every being fails to exist.

---

[7] This error in relational logic derives from "(x)(∃y) ... " the corresponding "(∃y)(x) ... " formula. This is the quantifier-shift fallacy (Gensler 2017a: 222). A simple form of this would be "Everyone loves someone ∴ There's someone that everyone loves" ("(x)(∃y)Lxy ∴ (∃y)(x)Lxy"), which is invalid because we might all love different people; maybe we all love our mothers (and thus all love at least one person), but yet there's not any one single person that absolutely everyone loves.

Imagine a world that contains only two beings, both contingent, Adam and Eve:

- Adam exists on every day of the week except Monday.
- Eve exists on every day of the week except Tuesday.

In this world, premise 1 is true ("Each contingent being at some time fails to exist"), while the conclusion is false ("There's some time at which every being fails to exist"). Some think our world works this way; while individual beings aren't eternal, these beings get transformed into other beings when they're destroyed – so there's always something. Recall the spaghetti, which changes from dough to spaghetti to tummy-contents to . . . things that are "destroyed" transform into other things.

If you're still confused on this, here's a pair of examples:

1   Every student is at some time away from campus.
∴   There's some time at which every student is away from campus.

1   Every being at some time fails to exist.
∴   There's some time at which every being fails to exist.

Both are invalid, since we can consistently imagine a situation where the premise is true but the conclusion false.

Premise 3 ("If there's some time at which every being fails to exist, then nothing exists now") could be false if there's a future time (but no past time) where everything goes out of existence at once. Premise 4 ("Something exists now") is surely true. But the argument has three major flaws, and so doesn't work.

Aquinas says this about the SECOND PART of his *necessary being* argument:

> [SECOND PART] Therefore, not all beings are merely possible, but there must exist something the existence of which is necessary. But every necessary thing either has its necessity caused by another, or not.[8] Now it is impossible to go on to infinity in necessary things which have their

---

The quantifier-shift fallacy is like arguing "Everyone lives in some house, so there must be some (one) house that everyone lives in." Maybe we mostly live in different houses. Some great minds have committed this fallacy. Aristotle argued, "Every agent acts for an end, so there must be some (one) end for which every agent acts." Aquinas argued, "If everything at some time fails to exist, then there must be some (one) time at which everything fails to exist." John Locke argued, "Everything is caused by something, so there must be some (one) thing that caused everything."

8 I'm unclear what this means. Just ignore this complication, as I do.

necessity caused by another, as has been already proved in regard to efficient causes. Therefore we cannot but postulate the existence of some being having of itself its own necessity, and not receiving it from another, but rather causing in others their necessity. This all men speak of as God.

I'd express his reasoning as before:

1 If every being is contingent, then nothing exists now.
2 Something exists now.
∴ Not every being is contingent. (intermediate conclusion)
3 If not every being is contingent, then some being is necessary.
∴ Some being is necessary.

The first three lines are from the flawed FIRST PART. The rest of the argument works, but earlier errors ruin the reasoning. And why is this necessary being a *personal God who created the world*? Couldn't a prime number be a necessary being? We need further reasoning to go from "necessary being" to "God." For many reasons, the *necessary being* argument fails.

(4) The *greatest being* argument is very implausible (unless you accept a weird metaphysics) and is seldom defended today. Here's what Aquinas says:

> The fourth way is taken from the gradation to be found in things. Among beings there are some more and some less good, true, noble and the like. But "more" and "less" are predicated of different things, according as they resemble in their different ways something which is the maximum, as a thing is said to be hotter according as it more nearly resembles that which is hottest; so that there is something which is truest, something best, something noblest and, consequently, something which is uttermost being; for those things that are greatest in truth are greatest in being, as it is written in [Aristotle's] *Metaphysics*, book 2. Now the maximum in any genus is the cause of all in that genus; as fire, which is the maximum heat, is the cause of all hot things. Therefore there must also be something which is to all beings the cause of their being, goodness, and every other perfection; and this we call God.

I'd express his reasoning this way:

1 Everything that has a quality (like being hot or good) must have this by virtue of something that has it in the highest degree.
2 Some things have the quality of *greatness* (which includes existence, goodness, and other qualities).
∴ Everything that has the quality of *greatness* has this by virtue of a being (God) that has *greatness* to the highest degree.

Premise 1, in our present view of the world, is crazy. Premise 1 implies that whatever (like your spaghetti) has a degree of heat has it by virtue of something that has heat to the highest degree – which the medievals thought was fire (but we now know of hotter things). Even worse, premise 1 implies that whatever has a degree of ugliness has this by virtue of something that has ugliness in the highest degree (what would this be?). And premise 1 implies that if this argument is really silly, then it has this by virtue of something that has the property of *being really silly* in the highest degree. So premise 1, to put it mildly, lacks the clear ring of truth.

(5) The *world's designer* argument is more plausible and important, but it's better to take it later, when we discuss evolution and whether the world has a purposeful plan (§§6.1–6.2). So we'll see this one later, including problems with it.

My conclusion, on these and other arguments for God's existence, is that none of them work. Believers will never succeed in proving God's existence; remarkably, many theist philosophers agree with this. Sorry for them all; atheism rules!

> Before going on, reflect on your reaction to Skepticus's passage. Do you see any problems with it?

5.3 Analysis: Arguments for God's Existence

Religious philosophers defend religious beliefs from two main angles:

1. *A general approach for forming rational beliefs about religion.* For example: in forming religious beliefs rationally, we need to be *consistent* and *factually informed* (especially about recent science and philosophy) and try to *promote progress on our life journey.*[9]
2. *Direct arguments for God's existence*: [premise], [premise] ∴ There's a God.

(1) Previous chapters used the first. So we:

- criticized attacks on religion based on *inconsistent ideas* (like logical positivism and the idea that we shouldn't accept what isn't proved),
- criticized attacks on religion based on *outdated and discredited scientific or philosophical ideas* (like Freudian psychology, faulty views about religion's harmful effects, logical positivism, and materialist ideas about NDEs not based on a serious study of cases),

---

9 We need a few more items, like *avoid views with crushing objections, provide paths for your main conclusions* (perhaps arguments, instincts, or pragmatic considerations), and *if possible provide multiple paths that strengthen each other.* I'm not trying to give a complete list of such items here.

- pointed out how to promote progress on our life journey (how elements of reason can be stepping stones on our path to God; Augustine's view of how God made us to search after him; how religion has psychological, medical, and ethical benefits; and how near-death experiences can change our lives in positive ways).

(2) This current chapter moves to *direct arguments for God's existence* ("[premise], [premise] ∴ There's a God"). We started by considering the *first cause* argument, which met seemingly strong objections from Russell and Skepticus; we'll see that their objections are based on outdated and discredited scientific views.

Many direct arguments for God's existence fit into four main categories.[10] There must be a God, these claim, because:

- *Cosmological argument*. The *world's existence* requires an explanation. ("Cosmos" is from the Greek for "world.") (Chapter 5)
- *Teleological argument*. The *world's order* requires a designer. ("Telos" is from the Greek for "purpose.") (Chapter 6)
- *Ontological argument*. The *idea of a supremely perfect being* requires existence. ("Ontos" is from the Greek for "being.") (§§7.1–7.2)
- *Moral argument*. Our *moral duties* require a source. (This could be "deontological," from the Greek for "duty.") (Chapter 10)

Despite the singular word "argument," each of these is a *family of arguments*. Distinct forms of the cosmological argument include the first four of Aquinas's five ways (first mover, first cause, necessary being, and greatest being); we'll later consider two stronger cosmological arguments: Kalam and sufficient reason. Aquinas's fifth way (the world's designer) is a teleological argument – as is the newer and stronger *fine-tuning* argument; we'll see these in the next chapter.

Religious philosophers vary in how they regard these direct arguments for God's existence. *Rationalists* see such arguments as essential and sometimes conclusive, while *fideists* think we should largely ignore reason (especially direct arguments) and believe just on faith.[11] My view is in the middle;

---

10 Many direct arguments for God's existence don't fit neatly into these four categories. A *near-death experience* argument could go this way: "[premises about why NDEs are genuine and how this entails God's existence] ∴ There's a God." *Pascal's wager* argument – after Blaise Pascal (1623–62), see Swindal (2005: 257–60), goes like this: "Our probable expected gain in believing in God is greater than our probable expected gain in not believing in God. If so, then we ought to believe in God. ∴ We ought to believe in God." Plantinga (2006b) has many other examples.
11 The fideist Tertullian (c. 160–220, Swindal 2005: 61f) asked "What has Athens to do with Jerusalem?" ("What has reason to do with faith?"). His answer was NOTHING, so Christians should avoid reason and be simple believers. In contrast, the most influential Catholic thinker, St. Thomas Aquinas (1224–74, Swindal 2005: 165–203), taught the harmony between reason and faith.

we need faith and reason to work together, and the reason part can include direct arguments. We'll see reasons for this dispute in the next section.

5.4 Analysis: How Much Evidence Would God Give Us?

I have my students imagine themselves being God and deciding how much evidence they'd give for their existence. If you were God, would you give:

1. conclusive evidence,
2. strong evidence,
3. weak evidence, or
4. no evidence

for your existence? I have students think about the choices and vote for one. I say that, since they're just expressing their mind, there's no right or wrong answer beyond that. I add that I'd be disappointed if some options got no votes.

(1) *Conclusive evidence* gets about 13% of the vote. So why would you, as God, give humans *conclusive evidence* for your existence? Students say "It's important for humans to know clearly that I exist, in order to live their lives, so I'd give indisputable evidence and proof about this." How would you make your existence so clear? Students respond like "I'd give a loud voice from the sky, and I'd say and do extraordinary things." Those who pick this option are often skeptical about God's existence. Some atheists have argued:

1 If there's a God, then we'd have conclusive evidence for God's existence.
2 We don't have conclusive evidence for God's existence.
∴ There's no God.

Most of my students think God *wouldn't* give us conclusive evidence and that God wants to remain at least somewhat elusive (Moser 2008).

Skepticus in §5.3 says (my italics) "Believers will never succeed in *proving God's existence*." Now "proof" is a very strong word, and few things can be *proved* conclusively. It's more useful to ask whether a specific argument gives *strong evidence* or *weak evidence* for God's existence (as I think some do), rather than whether it's a *conclusive proof*.

(2) *Strong evidence* gets a big 45% of the vote. Supporters say "While it's important for us to have some strong indication that there's a God, it's also important that we struggle with this issue – so our belief is to some extent our personal choice. So if I were God, I wouldn't provide an indisputable proof of my existence." I see myself and most of the Catholic intellectual tradition in this category.

(3) *Weak evidence* gets about 32% of the vote. Supporters say "While it's important for us to have *some* sign that there's a God, this needs to be weak and

ambiguous, so our belief is largely from personal struggle and choice." Since the two middle groups (strong and weak evidence) predominate, most students look for a balance between having some (incomplete) evidence and having some personal struggle and choice, and I think this is what God gave us.

(4) *No evidence* gets only 10% of the vote. Supporters say "We need to struggle and form our own belief about God; it's less important to get the right answer."

In the 1970s, I studied then-current arguments for God's existence (like Aquinas's five ways) and saw them as giving at best only *weak evidence* for God's existence. Now I think there's *strong evidence* – based on NDEs, Kalam, and fine-tuning. These have become popular since the 1970s and have increased belief in God among intellectuals. Arriving at strong arguments for God's existence requires better understanding of science and better intellectual opponents; Aquinas's time lacked these.

My multiple-choice format constrains student choices to four options that I give. Two other options might be popular if I offered them:

5. As God, I'd give humans strong evidence for my existence – but I'd make humans work hard to be open to it and get this evidence.
6. As God, I'd give stronger evidence for my existence to some individuals or eras than to others – so they could follow different paths to me.

These options make sense too. Option 5 sounds like what Augustine would say; he struggled much but then arrived at what he saw as strong evidence. Option 6 points out that reasoning may be more important for some, while feelings and instincts may matter more for others. Remember my slogan: "There are many paths to God." Some intellectual types may need a path that uses careful reasoning; others may follow a more emotional or instinctive path. In my mind, both may be fine.

5.5 Analysis: The Kalam Argument

The Bible (Genesis 1:1) starts boldly: "In the beginning, God created the heavens and the earth." This makes two statements: (G) "*There's a God* (a Creator-God)" and (B) "*There's a beginning* (when the world started)." Four combinations are possible:

- *Classical theism* (G and B). There's a God and a beginning.
- *Eternal-world theism* (G and not-B). There's a God but no beginning.
- *Classical atheism* (not-G and not-B). There's no God and no beginning.
- *Big Bang atheism* (not-G and B). There's no God but there's a beginning.

We'll consider first the two theist forms, then the two atheist forms.

Theist philosophers are mostly happy with *classical theism*: there's a *God* and a *beginning*. Medievals asked, "Can the world's beginning be *proved*?"

Bonaventure and many Muslims said yes; Aquinas said no. But Christians firmly accepted, either from reason or revelation, the world's beginning.

Since modern science at first seemed to accept the world's eternity, some Christians moved to *eternal-world theism*: there's a God but no beginning. *Creation*, then, isn't God causing the world to begin (since it didn't begin) but rather the world's eternal dependence on him for its existence, as an eternal light might depend on an eternal flame. An eternal world clashes with Genesis 1:1, but the Genesis details conflict and can't all be taken literally (§6.3). Eternal-world theism has less attraction now that science has moved away from the world being eternal.

Until recently, the standard atheist alternative to Genesis 1:1 was *classical atheism*: there's no God and no beginning (the world always was and always will be). While many believers think the world needs a cause, atheists (like Bertrand Russell and Skepticus) thought a world with no beginning or cause was just as plausible as a God with no beginning or cause. Many atheists saw their view as *simpler*: they accepted one principle (an eternal, uncaused world), while believers accepted two (an eternal, uncaused God + a caused world with a beginning).

There seemed to be an irresolvable dispute between two views:

- *Classical theism (religious view)*. There's a God and a beginning.
- *Classical atheism (materialist view)*. There's no God and no beginning.

The terms "religious view" and "materialist view" are from C.S. Lewis (1952: 21–22), who nicely describes the dispute:

> Ever since men were able to think they have been wondering what this universe really is and how it came to be there. And, very roughly, two views have been held. First, there is what is called the materialist view. People who take that view think that matter and space just happen to exist, and always have existed, nobody knows why; and that the matter, behaving in certain fixed ways, has just happened, by a sort of fluke, to produce creatures like ourselves who are able to think. By one chance in a thousand something hit our sun and made it produce the planets; and by another thousandth chance the chemicals necessary for life, and the right temperature, occurred on one of these planets, and so some of the matter on this earth came alive; and then, by a very long series of chances, the living creatures developed into things like us.
>
> The other view is the religious view. According to it, what is behind the universe is more like a mind than it is like anything else we know. That is to say, it is conscious, and has purposes, and prefers one thing to another. And on this view it made the universe, partly for purposes we do not know, but partly, at any rate, in order to produce creatures like itself – I mean, like itself to the extent of having minds.

Please do not think that one of these views was held a long time ago and that the other has gradually taken its place. Wherever there have been thinking men both views turn up. And note this too. You cannot find out which view is the right one by science in the ordinary sense.[12]

After Lewis, science began to question two parts of the materialist view: the world's eternity (here) and how easily a random world can produce life (next chapter).

First, science seemed to show that the world wasn't eternal but instead began to exist in a Big Bang explosion 14 billion years ago.[13] Part of the evidence for this is the *redshift* combined with the *Doppler effect*. The *Doppler effect* is the change in sound or light waves from an object coming toward you or going away from you. Imagine that a race car is coming toward you, passes you, and then goes away from you; the sound from the car goes from a higher pitch to a lower pitch as the car passes you:

Coming toward you, car sounds have a higher pitch (more beats per second).

))))))))

Going away from you, car sounds have a lower pitch (fewer beats per second).

))))))))

Source: Illustration of car from gnurf / Shutterstock

To dramatize this, hum a high-pitched car sound as the car comes toward you, and then lower the pitch as it goes away from you. Motion toward you compresses sound waves (more beats per second, higher pitch), while motion away expands them (fewer beats per second, lower pitch). *Colors* work the same way. A yellow car would look slightly green coming toward you and slightly orange going away, but this color shift would be too small to observe unless the car went extremely fast.

The *redshift* is the observed fact that light from distant stars gets shifted toward the red end of the color spectrum. So a heated element that's known

---

12 While C.S. Lewis tried to resolve the dispute using a moral argument for the religious view (which I don't think works; see §§10.1–10.2), appealing to recent science here is better.
13 Georges Lemaître, a Catholic priest, first proposed this idea in the 1930s. He spoke of "the Cosmic Egg exploding at the moment of creation."

to give off yellow light is more orangish. Scientists explain this redshift by the Doppler effect and the idea that distant stars are speeding away from us. So they think the world is expanding. If we wind back the process, we can figure out when the world exploded from an initial point, in the Big Bang. Scientists are getting better at dating this event; do a Web search for "age of the universe" to get our best current estimate of how many years ago the universe began (today they say it's about 13.77 billion years ago).

A longer story would discuss background radiation (which strengthens the argument), entropy (the world would have reached almost complete entropy had it existed forever), and much math. I won't go into details. A multiple-Big-Bang theory, that the world goes through an infinite cycle of expansions and contractions, used to be popular; but fewer hold this today, since gravity is what would contract the world, and calculations show that matter's density isn't enough to make it contract.[14] So our best science says that the world is a one-shot process and had a beginning in time.

If the world began to exist long ago, wouldn't this require a cause – and what could this be but a great mind? The *Kalam argument* (so called because it resembles a medieval Muslim argument) argues this way to God's existence:

1 Whatever began to exist had a cause.
2 The world began to exist.
∴ The world had a cause. (intermediate conclusion from 1 and 2)
3 If the world had a cause, then either a personal being caused the world or a material being caused the world.
4 A material being didn't cause the world.
∴ A personal being (God) caused the world. (from intermediate conclusion, 3, and 4)

Premise 1 is based on commonsense metaphysics; applying to *whatever began to exist*, it doesn't say whether an *eternal God or world* needs a cause. Premise 2 is based on current physics (and sometimes arguments about a physical infinite's conceptual impossibility). Premise 3 is based on commonsense metaphysics, that causes are either personal (free will) or material (antecedent conditions and causal laws). Premise 4 excludes a material cause, since matter can't without circularity cause the beginning of the totality of matter. The conclusion follows from the premises. So Genesis 1:1 ("In the beginning, God created the heavens and the earth") can be based on *faith and reason*.

How does J.L. Mackie, my favorite atheist philosopher, respond? Mackie is sure from the problem of evil that there's no God. So he concludes that

---

14 See Stephen Hawking (1998: 45–49). Hawking also argues that an eternal, static (not expanding or contracting) world wouldn't be stable, since gravity over an infinite period of time would eventually pull it together and make it collapse.

one of the premises here is wrong; he raises doubts about 1 and 2. Against premise 1, perhaps the world just popped into existence without a cause. (I see this as weird and implausible, but not entirely refutable, like the student excuse "An uncaused elephant popped into existence and ate my homework.") Or against premise 2, maybe current science is wrong and the world is eternal. (This is possible, but evidence for the world's beginning is stronger than before, and this option makes atheism look bad, since it rejects our best current science.) Mackie doesn't dispute premises 3 and 4.[15]

I take the Kalam argument to be *very strong but not absolutely conclusive*. Staunch atheists like Mackie (who's sure that there's no God) could say Kalam is based on our current science and so may change. Even so, we generally need to go with our current science, especially if it's solidly based, and this would apply to Kalam.

Some atheists, accepting that the world is about 14 billion years old, moved from *classical atheism* to what I call *Big Bang atheism*:

- *Classical atheism.* There's no God and no beginning.
- *Big Bang atheism.* There's no God but there's a beginning.

Big Bang atheism is less plausible. Before the Big Bang theory, few if any atheists thought the world had a beginning. I pity Big Bang atheist parents who now have to explain to their children: "We atheists believe the world just popped into existence, without any cause, about 14 billion years ago." This may cause children brought up atheist to question their atheist faith!

I see Kalam as an updated *first cause* argument. Often the older philosophy of religion (like Aquinas's five ways) just needs to be rethought.

5.6 Analysis: The *Sufficient Reason* Argument

I'll briefly discuss the *sufficient reason* argument for God's existence (an update of Aquinas's *necessary being*, §5.2). Frederick Copleston (1948) used it in his radio debate with Bertrand Russell; Richard Taylor (1991) and others also support it. The argument is based on the *principle of sufficient reason* – which goes back at least to Gottfried Leibniz (1646–1716), a philosopher who co-invented calculus. It says, roughly, that there must be a reason or cause for any *contingent fact* being so. Somewhat like before (§5.2), a *contingent fact* is one that could have been otherwise (like "You exist" and perhaps "The world exists"), while a *necessary fact* is one that has to be that couldn't have been otherwise (like "$2+2=4$" and perhaps "God exists").

---

15 See Mackie (1982: 24–49). For longer Kalam defenses, see William Craig (1979, 1994) and Robert Spitzer (2010).

In class, I like to use an example (http://harryhiker.com/utah/html/39.htm or http://harrycola.com/utah/html/39.htm) of an unusual round rock ball that I found while hiking on a Utah plateau. The rock's existence is a *contingent fact*, and we can ask "Why does this unusual rock exist?" By the *principle of sufficient reason*, there must be an answer, even though we may not know it. It isn't enough to say "It's eternal and so has always been there," for we can ask "Why is this eternal rock there, instead of something else or nothing at all?" And it isn't enough to say "It's part of an eternal sequence of similar rocks," for we can ask "Why is there an eternal sequence of rocks there, instead of something else or nothing at all?"

We can ask similar questions about the universe's existence, which is a contingent fact (since we can conceive of there being no universe): "Why does the universe exist at all?" Again, it isn't enough to say "The universe is eternal and so has always been there," for we can ask "Why is the universe eternal and has always been there, instead of something else or nothing at all?" And it isn't enough to say "The present state of the universe is part of an eternal sequence of similar states of the universe," for we can ask "Why is there an eternal sequence of similar states of the universe, instead of something else or nothing at all?"

We can express the *sufficient reason* argument as follows:

1 Every positive contingent fact has an explanation (in terms of necessary laws or a free choice).
2 The world's existence is a positive contingent fact.
∴ The world's existence has an explanation (in terms of necessary laws or a free choice). (intermediate conclusion from 1 and 2)
3 The world's existence doesn't have an explanation in terms of necessary laws.
∴ The world's existence has an explanation in terms of a free choice (and so a personal being, God, caused the world). (from intermediate conclusion and 3)

Premise 1 is a version of the *principle of sufficient reason*. Premise 2 applies this to the world's existence, which seems to be a positive contingent fact. Premise 3 is true because the world's existence is contingent, and thus isn't explainable as following from necessary laws. The conclusion about God follows – and is independent of what science may say about the world's eternity; even if the world is an eternal sequence of states of the universe, it still exists contingently and depends on the eternal free choice of God, who is the necessary being who created the universe.

Bertrand Russell (1948) and J.L. Mackie (1982) raise similar objections:

• Against premise 1, the world's existence and some other positive contingent facts may have no explanation. The world's existence may be a

brute fact, it just is, it needs no explanation. The principle of sufficient reason may apply to explaining parts of the world (like why the round rock exists), but not to the world's existence as a whole.
- "Necessary" here is ambiguous. Suppose we mean *conceptually necessary* (can't be consistently conceived not to exist); neither God nor the world seems *conceptually necessary* (since either could be conceived not to exist). Or suppose we mean *metaphysically necessary* (eternal, nondependent, indestructible); either God or the world could be plausibly seen as metaphysically necessary (eternal, nondependent, and indestructible).

These are strong objections. So I see this argument as weaker than Kalam, as giving a weak conjecture instead of a strong argument.

6
Is the Universe Designed?

We'll begin by listening to the fictional student Skepticus explain why he rejects the *teleological argument* (*argument from design*) for God's existence and how he thinks evolution fits in. As you read Skepticus's passage, first try to understand it in a sympathetic way, and then try to find problems with it. We'll later consider objections.

6.1 Skepticus: Initial Problems With the Design Argument

This is Skepticus again. I want to show what's wrong with the design argument for God's existence; this was the last of St. Thomas Aquinas's "five ways" (§§5.2–5.3). Let's start with what Aquinas says (Swindal 2005: 169–71, my italics):

> The fifth way [to show God's existence] is taken from the governance of the world. We see that things which lack intelligence, such as *natural bodies*, act for an end, and this is evident from their acting always, or nearly always, in the same way, so as to obtain the best result. Hence it is plain that, not fortuitously, but designedly, do they achieve their end. Now whatever lacks intelligence cannot move towards an end, unless it be directed by some being endowed with knowledge and intelligence; as the arrow is shot to its mark by the archer. Therefore some intelligent being exists by whom all natural things are directed to their end; and this being we call God.

This is sketchy. I wish Aquinas had given an example of "*natural bodies*," which "act for an end . . . to obtain the best result . . . not fortuitously, but designedly." Do these include *planets* or *biological organisms*? These suggest different arguments:

- *Orderly-things argument*. An orderly watch requires a watchmaker. And the world, with its orderly planetary motion, resembles a big orderly watch.

- *Plants-and-animals argument.* Complex purposeful organisms couldn't have come about by chance, so they require an intelligent designer.

We'll discuss the *plants and animals* argument in the next section.

Here's the orderly-things argument (Gensler 2017a: 90 and 153 prob. 4):

1. The world is orderly (like a watch that follows complex laws).
2. Most orderly things we've examined have intelligent designers.
3. We've examined a large and varied group of orderly things.
4. If most orderly things we've examined have intelligent designers and we've examined a large and varied group of orderly things, then probably most orderly things have intelligent designers.
5. If the world is orderly and probably most orderly things have intelligent designers, then probably the world has an intelligent designer.

∴ Probably the world has an intelligent designer (God).

Premise 1 is true because the world runs by orderly laws; we need these for our watches, cars, and computers to work. Premise 2 is based on our experience of orderly things – like watches, cars, and computers – having intelligent designers. Premises 3 to 5 are conceptual bridges, which our argument needs since it generalizes from a sample and uses inductive reasoning (Gensler 2017a: 75–77). The conclusion follows using standard propositional logic.

Premise 2 is weak. Yes, some orderly things clearly have intelligent designers. But this isn't clear for many other orderly things, like blades of grass, trees, animals, spider webs, sedimentary rock, crystals, and planets. So "*Most orderly things we've examined have intelligent designers*" isn't clearly true. The argument fails because premise 2 is weak; what hurts it isn't Darwin but orderly things that perhaps aren't designed.

6.2 Skepticus: Darwin Destroys the Design Argument

This is Skepticus again. Before Darwin and evolution, atheists struggled to explain how plants and animals came to be without an intelligent designer (God).

Pretend you're an atheist and know nothing about evolution. How do you explain how plants and animals came into existence? Biological organisms have a complex system of purposes. Consider the eye of a cat; the eye has a complex structure and seems finely engineered *in order to* (*purpose*) help the cat see the world, move, escape danger, and find food. Could this complex visual system have just happened, by chance? Can we shake elements in a jar randomly until the parts happen to come together to form a cat? Could there be a worse explanation than this? Isn't an intelligent designer (God) needed to create a complex purposeful organism like a cat?

St. Augustine struggled about God but then came to see that *there must be a God*. In an entertaining homily (Swindal 2005: 107–11), he marvels at the human organism's construction, with complex parts fitting together in a beautiful and purposeful way. What could bring about such a human organism but God?

> This setting up of a rational animal, this arrangement of soul ruling and flesh serving, of mind and spirit, of head and body and unseen natural parts, of knowledge and action; intelligence, sense, and movement, the reservoir of memory, the lessons of knowledge, the decisions of the will, the use and adornment of the body's limbs and organs, . . . – whom could it have as its author but God?

The *plants and animals* argument as an *inference to the best explanation* (Gensler 2017a: 105–6) looks like this:

1 We ought to accept the best explanation for empirical facts.
2 The existence of plants and animals (whose structure seems to exhibit complex purposefulness) is an empirical fact.
3 The best explanation for the existence of plants and animals is that they were caused by an intelligent being (the alternative is that they came to be by chance).
∴ We ought to accept that plants and animals were caused by an intelligent being (God).[1]

Before evolution, atheists found it difficult to counter this argument.

Then Charles Darwin (1809–82) and evolution appeared, and atheists can again hold their heads high. Thomas Huxley (1866: 297) wrote:

> [Darwin's work] did the immense service of freeing us [agnostics and atheists] forever from the dilemma – Refuse to accept the creation hypothesis, and what have you to propose that can be accepted by any cautious reasoner? In 1857 I had no answer ready, and I do not think that anyone else had. A year later we reproached ourselves with dullness for being perplexed with such an inquiry. My reflection [after studying Darwin] . . . was, "How extremely stupid not to have thought of that!"

What explains the existence of plants and animals? Pre-Darwin options were *chance* (randomly mixing material elements) or *design* (an intelligent being). *Chance* is implausible; you can't get a tree, cat, or human by randomly

---

1 The conclusion doesn't say that God caused *the world*, but only that he caused *plants and animals* (perhaps as part of a young god's science project?). This is weaker.

shaking material elements in a jar. *Design* by an intelligent being seems far better (as premise 3 claims).

Darwin killed premise 3: "*The best explanation for the existence of plants and animals is that they were caused by an intelligent being.*" We no longer need designers or purposes but only chance and mechanical laws. By evolution, plants and animals came to be through *random mutation (of inherited characteristics) and selection (survival of the fittest).*[2]

Over the years, evolution has become increasingly important in biology; big steps forward were the genetic code,[3] how radiation causes random genetic changes, and how these lead to random variations in inheritable features. Today, evolution is solidly based on how it explains a wide range of biological facts; evolution's central defense is an *inference to the best explanation* (Gensler 2017a: 105):

1 We ought to accept the best explanation for empirical facts about biological organisms (comparative structure, embryology, geographical distribution, fossil records, etc.).
2 The best explanation for empirical facts about biological organisms is evolution.
∴ We ought to accept evolution.

A fuller formulation would say what these empirical facts are, various ways to explain them, and why evolution explains them better than its rivals.

The atheist Richard Dawkins (1995: 132–33) well said that the universe in the evolutionary model shows no signs of design or purpose: "The universe we observe has precisely the properties we should expect if there is, at bottom, no design, no purpose, no evil and no good, nothing but blind pitiless indifference." Science rejects "design" and "purpose" in explaining the world, because it doesn't need them.

Aquinas imagined two objections to God's existence. The second is his *unnecessary hypothesis* objection (Swindal 2005: 169–71):

> Further, it is superfluous to suppose that what can be accounted for by a few principles has been produced by many. But it seems that everything we see in the world can be accounted for by other principles, supposing

---

2 What explains the appearance of the genetic code (DNA, inheritable characteristics) in the first place? Why would the primordial soup of the early oceans produce DNA? We as yet have no good explanation of this, and this is a big gap. But my further criticisms of the atheism model (§6.5) won't be based on this problem.
3 Skepticus won't tell you this, but Gregor Mendel (1822–84), a religious Augustinian friar, was the father of genetics. And the scientist Francis Collins (1950–), whose study of fine-tuning led to his conversion and a 2006 book about God, directed the mapping of the human genome (our complete genetic DNA structure). Believers do well at genetics.

God did not exist. For all natural things can be reduced to one principle which is nature; and all voluntary things can be reduced to one principle which is human reason, or will. Therefore there is no need to suppose God's existence.

Here's another form of the argument:

1 We ought to posit God's existence if and only if God is part of our best explanation of the empirical world.
2 God isn't part of our best explanation of the empirical world. (Our best explanation is science, which doesn't need God.)
∴ We ought not to posit God's existence.

Here we nonbelievers fully agree. Aquinas would respond that his proofs (his five ways) establish God's existence, but we nonbelievers don't think so.[4]

To explain the origin of plants and animals, science goes with *evolution*, but religion goes with *design*. The Bible's first book, Genesis, talks of God creating the world in a week, making plants and animals, and forming humans out of clay. The biological world is from God, as designer. This clashes hugely with modern science. Some liberal believers reject Genesis or don't take it literally. I see this as dishonest. For many centuries, believers took the Bible all literally, including Genesis; now they say no, Genesis is just a story, not to be taken literally, and we can be believers and still accept evolution. Consistent believers reject this and see that they need to choose between science and religion. While backward fundamentalist believers reject science, smarter believers eventually reject religion and its pre-scientific biblical fairy tales.

> Before going on, reflect on your reaction to Skepticus's passage. Do you see any problems with it?

6.3 Analysis: Biblical Interpretation

Much of the supposed conflict between science and religion comes from taking the Bible too literally. Skepticus repeats a common misconception, that *believers took the whole Bible literally* through most of history and only moved to nonliteral interpretations later, to avoid a conflict with science.

---

4 The *fine-tuning* argument (§6.4) criticizes premise 2 very effectively. I'd also dispute premise 1, since some good paths to God aren't based on science.

Skepticus thinks this change was dishonest, and true Christians need to take the Bible literally. Skepticus is historically wrong.

From early centuries, the most important Christian thinkers gave strong reasons for *not* taking the Bible all literally. Origen (c. 185–254) pointed out that Genesis creation accounts have inconsistencies and thus can't all be literally true (Swindal 2005: 71–76). He suggests that we focus on deeper meanings and not on colorful details.

Genesis has two creation stories (Genesis 1:1–2:3 and 2:4–25). These conflict about many details (for example, on whether animals were created *before* or *after* the first humans). Both have the same religious message, that humans and the world are from God. The first story just by itself even has problems, as Origen points out:

> For who that has understanding will suppose that the first, and second, and third day, and the evening and the morning, existed without a sun, and moon, and stars? And that the first day was, as it were, also without a sky?

Origen gives other biblical passages that shouldn't be taken literally, like:

- God walks in the Garden of Eden at night and Adam tries to hide himself under a tree. (Genesis 3:8)
- I am a God that makes peace, and creates evil. (Isaiah 45:7)
- Salute no man by the way. (Luke 10:4)

We need to look for the deeper meaning behind such passages instead of taking everything literally.

Often what we say *today* shouldn't be taken literally. I love the parody of the Ohio State fight song that starts "Annihilate Ohio State" (I went to the rival University of Michigan). But do I really want to *literally annihilate them (totally obliterate them, perhaps with a nuclear bomb)*? Surely not; I just want to beat them in football (as we did last week). To express our ideas, we sometimes overstate or say what can't be taken literally. While this is true today, it's even more important when we interpret passages written thousands of years ago, in another culture and language. A good Bible course will teach this, or else students will take the Bible to say really silly things. Most educated believers don't think God dictated the Bible word for word; instead, God moved humans to express his message in their own human way. Difficult passages need to be interpreted charitably in the Bible's wider context. Nonbelievers are often very crude in how they take biblical passages.[5]

---

5 I've had Catholic college students ask me whether Catholics can believe in evolution. I say, "Of course!" Pre-college Catholic religious education sometimes needs to be better.

Augustine (354–430) said we need sensitivity to language to interpret the Bible, and it's an error to take it all literally. He (Swindal 2005: 97–101) proposed this norm: "Don't take a verse literally if doing so clashes with *purity of life* (including love of God and neighbor) or *soundness of doctrine* (so we need to ignore minor factual errors). God, while inspiring the Bible's religious meaning, uses human beings to convey this meaning, and this can introduce confusions and errors."

Galileo Galilei (1564–1642), the father of modern science and a good Catholic, defended Copernicus's view that the earth revolved around the sun. Literally minded church officials objected that this contradicted the Bible, which spoke of "the sun rising." Galileo contended (Swindal 2005: 241–44) that this biblical literalism leads to absurdities and goes against major Christian thinkers. While the Bible's genuine religious message is true, passages can be difficult to interpret and sometimes can't be taken literally. We can know God through *creation and revelation*, which are consistent with each other if properly understood. The Bible is about religion, not physics; it shows the way to go to heaven, not how the heavens go. To learn physics, we have to apply our God-given minds to study the world; it's crazy to think the God who gave us sense and intellect doesn't want us to use them in learning about the world.

Galileo here raises a problem with *biblical literalism*. Why did God give us minds for doing science and clear signs of evolution's truth – when he didn't want us to use them? Did God want to mislead us? Fundamentalists say: "God wants us to choose between following *his word* (the Bible) and *flawed human thinking* (science)." But *maybe biblical literalism is flawed human thinking* which distorts God's word. Important Christian thinkers (like Origen, Augustine, and Galileo) argued that biblical literalism can distort God's word and make it crazy. God gave us minds to figure out the Bible's meaning in a consistent way, and this leads us not to take Genesis literally. If consistency is a key rational value given to us by God, then we should use it to interpret the Bible, as we use it to interpret ordinary human speech.

6.4 Analysis: Evolution and Purpose

Skepticus says (§6.2) "To explain the origin of plants and animals, science goes with *evolution* but religion goes with *design*." He speaks as if the two approaches are exclusive, but they can be combined.

Here's a principle I gave earlier: In evaluating anti-religion criticisms supposedly based on science, make sure that the science is right and that the critic isn't making further nonscientific assumptions (§4.3). Evolution, as a scientific view, explains biological processes using *random variation* and *survival of the fittest*, and these ignore purposes. But we can raise a further question: "Was our evolving universe created by a God with his own purposes?" Evolutionary scientists can answer this yes or no; evolution as a science is compatible with either. The NO-GOD answer is a nonscientific assumption, not a scientific claim.

Here's a parallel. We can explain how cars work internally by mechanical laws; based on such laws, turning the steering wheel will have such and such an effect. Such explanations needn't mention purposes. The same goes for explaining biological facts by evolution. Why do squirrels on the Grand Canyon's north side tend to have whiter tails than those on the south side? The answer is that, since the north has more snow, having whiter tails helps protect squirrels from predators. Such explanations use *mutation* and *selection*, not purposes. So we explain the inner working of cars and biology by mechanical laws, not purposes.

But we also can talk about the *human purposes* of cars, why we build them, and how it would be difficult to imagine cars existing without such purposes. Maybe we also can talk about the *divine purposes* of the biological world, why God created it, and how it would be difficult to imagine it existing without such purposes. Are there divine purposes behind our biological world? Using the next section's *fine-tuning* argument, I'd say *clearly yes*. Here I just want to say that evolution can be interpreted either way. Yes, explaining the inner working of cars and the biological world can keep to mechanical laws (and ignore purposes), but in a wider context, cars and the biological world may involve purposes in a big way. Many of us think that God created us using a long evolutionary process.

But why would God create life and thinking life by such a long evolutionary process, which brings suffering and is very inefficient (wasting much space and time)?

While I'm not sure of the answer, I can make a few points. First, suffering and the struggle against it are important aspects of creation (following the Irenaean account of evil §§8.4–8.6 that we consider later). Second, space and time are not, for God, scarce resources that need to be conserved; God has available an unlimited supply of whatever space and time he wants to use.

Perhaps God is attracted to fit cosmic creation into Teilhard's complexity-consciousness scheme (§§4.3 & 11.3), which is so simple in its idea but so complex in its execution. Or perhaps God is attracted to the beauty of this grand creative process and the good of its wide range of creatures (Swinburne 2004).

Or perhaps God creates thinking life using a huge universe to promote the WOW FACTOR. Believers praise God for the greatness and grandeur of the mountains and oceans. But the universe is so, so much bigger than that. Think of walking a mile, which takes maybe 20 minutes. And think of walking the earth's circumference, about 25,000 miles; this would take a year to walk nonstop, if we could do it.

Scientists say the observable universe is 93 billion light years in size. If you plug in the numbers, that's 500,000,000,000,000,000,000,000 miles (5×10^{23} miles, or "silly big" for short). So praise God, who in creating a world for us created a mind-numbing silly-big universe! And God himself, being infinite, is even greater than that. But can the WOW FACTOR get any greater?

Here's how. God in his creation is at the same time so NUMBINGLY HUGE (*silly big*) and yet so INTIMATELY CLOSE (knowing and loving us in the intimate details of our lives as no one else ever could, *silly close*). Wow! Silly, silly wow! Praise God, the infinitely awesome yet intimately loving Father of us all!

6.5 Analysis: The *Fine-Tuning* Argument

Here's a sketch of how atheists explain how intelligent life began (§5.5 or Lewis 1952: 21–22). The universe has 70,000,000,000,000,000,000,000 (7 × 10^{22}) stars. Suppose that a thousandth of these stars produce *planets with liquid water*,[6] a thousandth of these watery planets *evolve life*, and a thousandth of these planets with life *evolve intelligent life*. Then 70,000,000,000,000 (7 × 10^{13}) planets would *evolve intelligent life*. Even if these numbers are far off, still a huge random universe can easily evolve intelligent life.

Or maybe not. A paper by Brandon Carter (1974) claimed that, for life to evolve, physics laws and constants have to be within a very narrow range.[7] Stephen Hawking (1998: 125–31), Carter's Cambridge colleague, gave this example: "If the rate of expansion one second after the Big Bang had been smaller by even one part in a hundred thousand million million, the world would have recollapsed before it ever reached its present size." This would have stopped life's evolution. So expansion has to be correct to the 17th decimal place for life to evolve. Hawking goes on (my italics):

> The laws of science, as we know them at present, contain many fundamental numbers, like the size of the electric charge of the electron and the ratio of the masses of the proton and the electron.... The remarkable fact is that the values of these numbers seem to have been very finely adjusted to make possible the development of life. For example, if the electric charge of the electron had been only slightly different, stars either would have been unable to burn hydrogen and helium, or else they would not have exploded. Of course, there might be other forms of intelligent life, not dreamed of even by writers of science fiction, that did not require the light of a star like the sun or the heavier chemical elements that are made in stars and are flung back into space when the stars explode. Nevertheless, it seems clear that there are relatively few ranges of values for the numbers that would allow the development of any form of intelligent life. Most sets of values would give rise to universes that, although they might be very beautiful, would contain no one able to wonder at that beauty. *One can take this either as evidence of a*

---

6 Such planets with liquid water are said to be in the *Goldilocks zone*, after the fable character who liked her porridge not too hot and not too cold.
7 He proposed the anthropic principle ("What we can expect to observe must be restricted by the conditions necessary for our presence as observers") and the strong anthropic principle ("The Universe, and hence the fundamental parameters on which it depends, must be such as to admit the creation of observers within it at some stage").

Is the Universe Designed? 77

divine purpose in Creation and the choice of the laws of science or as support for the strong anthropic principle.

[Hawking criticizes the latter, which I call *parallel worlds*.]

Could the world *by pure chance* be so finely tuned to produce life? This seems very improbable. The world was more likely created by an intelligent being (God) who designed it very carefully to bring forth life.[8]

I created a Windows computer game to demonstrate this *fine tuning* argument. Go to http://harryhiker.com or http://harrycola.com/index.htm, click *Software* at the top, and then click on *Genesis*. When you start the program, a message comes up:

> The object of this game is to set up the basic laws of your universe in such a way that life will eventually evolve. If your universe brings forth life, you win; otherwise, you lose.

Then the program appears:

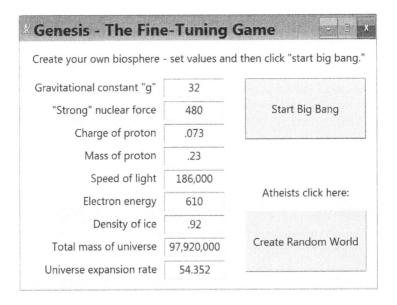

You set values for the constants and click "Start Big Bang." You'll get a noise and message that says:

---

8 For more on the *fine-tuning* argument, see F. Collins (2006: 63–84), R. Collins (1999), Flew (2007: 85–158), Glynn (1997: 21–55), Manson (2003), Plantinga (2011: 193–224), Spitzer (2010: 13–103), and Swinburne (2004: 172–88).

> Sorry, your world self-destructed and didn't produce life. Please try again.

Or you can look under the words "Atheists click here" and click "Create Random World." This puts random numbers into the constants and then attempts to create a world. You'll again get a noise and message that says:

> Sorry, your world self-destructed and didn't produce life. The RANDOM button gives you a chance to produce life of one in 100 trillion.

Students enjoy this program (which I use in class and students can use at home), and it quickly teaches what fine-tuning is about.

My program, however, has limitations:

- It needs more decimal places. As Hawking noted, the universe expansion rate has to be correct to the 17th decimal place for life to evolve.
- It lacks units. Should you give speed of light in *miles per hour* or *kilometers per second*?
- It needs more physical constants (I give only nine).[9]
- The chance of producing life by random numbers is much less than one in 100 trillion. I don't know what the number is.
- There's no parallel-worlds option. A checkbox could open multiple program copies with randomly different values for the constants.
- You can't beat the program and produce life. Since I don't know the correct values, I don't have my program accept them.
- A fancier program (which would require huge expertise to create) would give words and images for the world that fits your values: your world may lack stars, collapse quickly, or contain only hydrogen.

Despite these limitations, my program helps students understand fine tuning.

Let's say that a world is *fine-tuned* if the physics laws and constants governing it (like the gravitational constant "g," the proton's charge and mass, and water's density) are in the narrow range of what's required for life to be possible. The *fine-tuning* argument is an *inference to the best explanation*:

1. We ought to accept the best explanation for the world's *fine tuning*.
2. The best explanation for the world's *fine tuning* is that the world was created by an intelligent being intending to create life (this is better than the *chance* and *parallel worlds* explanations).
∴ We ought to accept that the world was created by an intelligent being (God) intending to create life.

---

9 http://www.godandscience.org/apologetics/designun.html gives 34 constants and says what happens to your universe if these constants are too high or too low.

Premise 1 assumes that the world is *fine-tuned*, which seems very solid, even though there are controversies about details. The big dispute is how *fine tuning* is to be explained and whether it needs an explanation.

The *chance explanation* says that it just happened (although very improbable) that the world was finely tuned for life. Long shots sometimes pay off – people do win the lottery. This gives another atheist alternative to Genesis 1:1:

> *Big-gamble Big Bang atheism.* There's no God, the world about 14 billion years ago just popped into existence without a cause, and the physics laws and constants just happened (in a zillion-to-one coincidence) to be in the narrow range that makes life possible.

This seems extraordinarily implausible.

Another explanation uses "parallel worlds," which are complete and real universes separate from each other (so there can't be causal interaction or travel between them). This view posits an infinity of parallel worlds, each governed by a different physics, and some of these would very likely produce life. Parallel worlds lack evidence but do permit an atheist worldview that makes intelligent life probable. This gives us another atheist alternative to Genesis 1:1:

> *Parallel-worlds Big Bang atheism.* There's no God. But there are an infinity of parallel worlds. Each popped into existence without a cause, and each is governed by a different set of physics laws and constants. Our world happens to be one of the very few that produced life.

This too seems extraordinarily implausible; one of my students called it an "Occam's razor nightmare." Genesis 1:1 ("In the beginning, God created the heavens and the earth") is simpler and more intuitive.

I have my students vote on which explanation they'd prefer if they were atheists: *big gamble* or *parallel worlds*. While they have a hard time taking either seriously, science-fiction fans often pick parallel worlds. The vote usually goes about 50-50.

I take fine tuning to be a very strong argument. The simplest and best explanation for fine tuning involves God: the world was caused by a great mind who "fine-tuned" its physics laws and constants to permit the emergence of life. This argument resembles Augustine's (about needing God to explain the existence of humans), but it avoids the evolution objection by talking about conditions needed for evolution to work; evolution can't explain why the physics is just right.

Antony Flew (1923–2010, §3.2), an atheist philosopher who spent much of his life attacking belief in God, was impressed by *fine tuning* and came to believe in God; he wrote a book called *There Is ~~No~~ A God.* (2007). He thought other critics of religion, like Bertrand Russell, might also have been impressed had the argument appeared earlier; he imagines how the Russell-Copleston (1948) debate might then have gone:

> Consistent with Russell's comments [that God hasn't produced sufficient evidence of his existence], Russell would have regarded these developments as evidence. I think we can be sure that Russell would have been impressed too. . . . This would have produced an interesting second dialogue between him and that distinguished Catholic philosopher, Frederick Copleston.
>
> (Flew and Habermas 2004: 211)

Fine tuning has led many scientists to believe in God.[10]

Dr. Francis Collins (1950–) is a prominent scientist with a PhD in genetics plus a medical degree. He directed the mapping of the human genome (our complete genetic DNA structure), which is a huge achievement; he's in the news a lot about COVID, as the National Institutes of Health (NIH) director. After he lost his faith in graduate school, the *fine-tuning* argument led him back to God, and he too wrote a book on this (2006). He became a strong Christian and often writes on science and religion; accepting God changed his life. In this, he differed from Anthony Flew, who came to believe in a remote deist God, not one who reveals himself or cares much about humans; believing in God had less effect on Flew's life, but it did shake up his philosophy.

Does the *fine-tuning* argument lead to believing in a remote deist God? It can do this, and it did this for Antony Flew (but not for Francis Collins). Following my "There are many paths to God" slogan, *fine-tuning* believers may need to add additional paths (maybe revelation or near-death experiences) that emphasize God's love for us.[11]

What does J.L. Mackie, my favorite atheist philosopher, say about the *fine-tuning* argument? Unfortunately, Mackie died in 1981, before fine tuning became popular. But he did make two brief comments (1982: 141):

- Mackie says we have no idea what worlds would result from alternative physical constants, and so we can't say they couldn't have produced life. *But we do know much about this.* Hawking and others mention that specific changes bring lifeless worlds that collapse immediately, lack stars, or have only light elements like hydrogen.
- Some debunk fine tuning by saying, "Of course the physics laws and constants are just right to allow us to have evolved! We shouldn't find

---

10 http://www.godandscience.org/apologetics/quotes.html
11 An argument (like Kalam or fine tuning) for the existence of the person who is God may not give us a wide understanding of God, but it can open the door to wider understandings.

this so surprising, since otherwise we wouldn't exist." Mackie thinks this is a poor objection, since we can consider possibilities which do not include our being there to experience them.

Elliot Sober (2009: 77) uses this second objection. He argues (against premise 1) that fine tuning, even if a fact, needs no explanation:
The standard criticism of this (*fine-tuning*) argument invokes some version of the *anthropic principle*. The rough idea is that, since we are alive, we are bound to observe that the constants are right, regardless of whether the values of those constants were caused by Intelligent Design (ID)[12] or by chance. We are the victims of an *observational selection effect*.

So *of course* observers can conclude, since they are alive, that physics is consistent with their being alive. Thus fine tuning (that the laws of physics happen to be consistent with human life) can be expected, is unremarkable, and requires no explanation.

This objection is based on a confusion. If observers are bound to observe some fact, that doesn't show that this fact requires no explanation. Here are examples:

- You're reading this sentence. This shows *that* you know English. But it doesn't explain *why* you know English. The explanation might be that you learned English as you grew up in an English-speaking country.
- You hurt your neck in a car accident. This shows *that* there was a car accident. But it doesn't explain *why* it happened. The explanation might be that another driver sent a text, lost control, and went into your lane.
- The concert pianist brags about how good your piano sounds. This shows *that* it's finely tuned. But it doesn't explain *why* it's finely tuned. The explanation might be that you recently had a piano tuner tune the piano.
- You exist. This shows *that* the laws of physics happen to be consistent with human life coming to be. But it doesn't explain *why* the laws of physics happen to be consistent with human life coming to be. The explanation might be chance, parallel worlds, or design.

Sober's approach suggests yet another atheist alternative to Genesis 1:1:

Observation-selection Big Bang atheism. There's no God; the world about 14 billion years ago just popped into existence without a cause, and the physics laws and constants just happened (in a zillion-to-one coincidence) to be in the narrow range that would make life possible. But,

---

12 "I" here is misleading; the *fine-tuning* argument (which accepts evolution) differs from *intelligent design (creationism)*, endorsed by biblical fundamentalists, which rejects evolution.

since the fact *that* we exist shows that the laws of physics happen to be consistent with the existence of human life, we needn't worry about *why* the laws of physics happen to be consistent with the existence of human life.

This is as crazy as the *big gamble* and *parallel worlds* options. The more we pursue alternatives to Genesis 1:1, the crazier these get – and the better classical theism and Genesis 1:1 appear.

One of my students had another objection. He conceded that fine tuning was a fact and that nontheist explanations for it were poor. But he thought the Great Mind idea was poor, too, since it clashes with how we think about the world; so it has a very small antecedent probability. Thus we have no idea how to explain fine tuning.

My response had three parts. (1) The Great Mind idea does explain the constants in a familiar and straightforward way; we've all experienced minds working out complex details to get a given result (e.g., working out a house plan in order to have a fine, livable home). (2) The Great Mind idea fits how most people explain the origin of the universe, as resulting from a divine plan; here too, it beats the alternatives. (3) The Great Mind idea may seem less likely to someone who thinks, for example, that only matter exists. But why think this? And isn't such thinking flawed if it makes us conclude that there's no good explanation of the emergence of life?

The Kalam and *fine-tuning* arguments for God's existence seem very strong. But there are reasons for not seeing them as absolutely conclusive:

- While these are based on our best current science, science could change.
- While alternatives to these arguments (like parallel worlds or worlds popping into existence without a cause) seem flimsy, we can't show that they're impossible.
- Many intelligent people reject these arguments. While their objections seem weak, maybe we're missing something – or maybe stronger objections will appear later.
  The *fine-tuning* argument uses an inductive inference to the best explanation, which isn't as clear-cut as deduction.[13]
- For the *fine tuning* argument (or any argument for God's existence) to penetrate, we need some openness to God. This may be lacking.

So the Kalam and *fine-tuning* arguments, while strong, don't *force* belief on us. There's still an element of struggle and personal choice.

---

13 Gensler (2017a: 75–111). We can raise questions like these: On what grounds should we evaluate one explanation as better than another? Should we accept the best possible explanation (even though no one may have thought of it) or the best currently available explanation (even though no current explanation may be very good)? And why is the best explanation most likely to be true?

Let me end by giving another answer to the question I asked before (§5.4): "If I were God, what evidence would I give humans for my existence?" If I were God, I'd make people as distinct individuals; some would be more like Augustine (who struggles about faith) and some more like his mother Monica (who believes more easily). I'd give people different paths to follow toward me – like feelings, religious instincts, and reasoning; which of these are most important would depend on the person. For those who pursue reasoning, I'd make it possible (but not easy) to find me this way too. For a scientific age, where many people (like Antony Flew, Francis Collins, and many scientists and intellectuals) are inclined to reject me on the basis of science, I'd give scientific signs of my existence – like Kalam and fine tuning.

7
Three Paths + Polytheism

This chapter has some miscellaneous items that don't go well elsewhere. The first few sections briefly discuss three further paths to God: St. Anselm's ontological argument, Plantinga's reformed epistemology, and mysticism. As usual, we'll begin by listening to the fictional student Skepticus explain why he rejects these. As you read Skepticus's passages, first try to understand them in a sympathetic way, and then try to find problems with them. We'll also consider objections.

The end of the chapter has two further sections, on "Why ONE God?" and "A Pagan-Christian Debate."

7.1 Skepticus: The Ontological Argument

This is Skepticus, and I'll discuss St. Anselm's (1033–1109) ontological argument, which argues from the *concept* of God to his *existence*. It's a verbal trick, but it's difficult to show what's wrong with it. Some believers take it seriously.[1]

We create our concept of God from projecting a father figure (§1.2, Freud). To shield us from life's difficulties, we dream up a perfect, make-believe father in the sky. This God isn't just the greatest being (who might be just a little greater than others); he's supremely great in every way (including knowledge, power, and goodness). He's even greater than we can imagine.

Anselm defines "God" as "a being than which no greater can be conceived." As such, God must of necessity exist; if he didn't exist, then we could imagine a similar being that does exist and would thus be greater than God (greater than a being than which no greater can be conceived), which

---

[1] See Anselm (1100), also in Swindal (2005: 133–37). My logic textbook gives various forms of this and related arguments (from René Descartes, Charles Hartshorne, and Alvin Plantinga) as homework problems: Gensler (2017a: 129 prob. 3 and 4, 240 prob. 12, 246 prob. 9, 248 prob. 26, 253–54 prob. 1–4, and 261 prob. 14 and 15).

DOI: 10.4324/9781003320920-8

is impossible. So, given Anselm's concept of God, such a God has to exist of logical necessity.

Here's a premise-conclusion version that's valid in propositional logic:

1   If God exists in the understanding and not in reality, then there can be conceived a being greater than God (namely, a similar being that also exists in reality).
2   "There can be conceived a being greater than God" is false (since *God* is "a being than which no greater can be conceived").
3   God exists in the understanding.
∴   God exists in reality.

Premise 1 points out what follows if God exists in the understanding but not in reality. Premise 2 says that what follows is false, given Anselm's definition of "God." Premise 3 says that God exists in the understanding. The conclusion follows using standard propositional logic.

Anselm's fellow monk Gaunilo, who believes in God but doubts Anselm's reasoning, raises two objections. First, Gaunilo says that God, who goes beyond our understanding, doesn't "exist in the understanding." Anselm responds that, while we don't fully understand God, he *does* exist in the understanding in that we grasp the consistent idea of "a being than which nothing greater can be conceived."

Second, Gaunilo objects that Anselm's reasoning could similarly prove the existence of unreal objects, like a perfect island greater than all other islands (but which wouldn't be so great if it didn't exist). But this isn't parallel to Anselm's argument; to be parallel, it would have to speak of *an island than which no greater can be conceived*. Anselm could claim that this idea is self-contradictory, since, for any finite island (and islands have to be finite), we could conceive a greater finite island. The case is different with God, whose infinite knowledge, power, and goodness can't be surpassed.

Alvin Plantinga (1974a, 1974b) contends that an ambiguity with "greater than" ruins the argument. Consider *Supergirl* (a fictional character with great superpowers) and my sister *Carol* (a real person with ordinary powers). Which is *greater*? We could take "greater" in either of two senses (these differ on whether we just compare real-or-imagined properties or whether existence automatically beats nonexistence):

- *Properties sense*. Supergirl is greater than Carol because Supergirl's imagined properties are greater. Here we compare real-or-imagined properties and ignore existence. Premise 2 (the definition of "God") assumes this sense.
- *Existence sense*. Carol is greater than Supergirl because Carol exists. Here existence automatically beats nonexistence. Premise 1 assumes this sense.

So Anselm's argument, to have its premises all be true, must shift the meaning of "greater" between premises. So his argument fails.

Again, we find another failed attempt to prove God's existence.

> Before going on, reflect on your reaction to Skepticus's passage. Do you see any problems with it?

7.2 Analysis: The Ontological Argument

St. Anselm (1033–1109), a Benedictine monk and Archbishop of Canterbury, was a founder of scholastic philosophy and theology; his example contributed much to the growth of these in the emerging medieval universities. Anselm is famous for his "ontological argument," which led to much reflection and debate by subsequent thinkers. Many think the argument is flawed, but they disagree about what the flaw is. Others defend their own version of the argument. Still others think Anselm wasn't giving an argument for God's existence but instead praying to God.

Skepticus mentions Alvin Plantinga's objection to the argument, which I agree with. Plantinga, however, gave his own improved ontological argument:

1   "Someone is *unsurpassably great*" is logically possible.
2   "Everyone who is *unsurpassably great* is, in every possible world, omnipotent, omniscient, and morally perfect" is necessarily true.
∴   Someone is omnipotent, omniscient, and morally perfect.[2]

In premise 1, "*unsurpassably great*" is understood as in premise 2, which stipulates what the term means (so premise 2 is true by definition). Plantinga sees premise 1 as reasonable but controversial. There seems to be no contradiction in there being someone who's the absolutely greatest being not only in the actual world but in every possible world, so it's reasonable to think it logically possible that someone is *unsurpassably great*.

The conclusion follows, given certain things about advanced modal logic (including system S5). To understand this argument, sorry, you have to understand an advanced area of logic; if you're interested, study my logic book, Gensler (2017a: 249–61).

Plantinga gives this argument not as a conclusive proof but as an argument with reasonable premises that concludes with God's existence. So he gives it as a weak but not insignificant argument; I agree with this.

---

2 Gensler (2017a: 261 prob. 15) is a version of Plantinga's (1974a, 1974b) ontological argument.

While Plantinga (2006a) accepts two dozen or so fairly good arguments for God's existence, he contends that such arguments aren't needed and aren't enough to sustain a strong personal faith. So he prefers his "reformed epistemology" approach.

I'll end this section by mentioning the attraction of the notion of God, as an *absolutely perfect being*, that the ontological argument uses. If Augustine is right, God built this attraction into us. René Descartes (1596–1650), after giving his own (not very good) version of the argument, says this prayer (Swindal 2005: 253):

> I think it proper to remain here for some time in the contemplation of God himself – that I may ponder at leisure his marvelous attributes – and behold, admire, and adore the beauty of this light so unspeakably great, as far, at least, as the strength of my mind, which is to some degree dazzled by the sight, will permit. For just as we learn by faith that the supreme felicity of another life consists in the contemplation of the Divine majesty alone, so even now we learn from experience that a like meditation, though incomparably less perfect, is the source of the highest satisfaction of which we are susceptible in this life.

7.3 Skepticus: Reformed Epistemology

This is Skepticus again, and I want to discuss Alvin Plantinga's (1932–) view that humans naturally and instinctively come to know God from life experiences.

"Reformed epistemology" is about *how we know things* ("epistemology") and has ideas from the *reformation* leader John Calvin (1509–64).[3] How do we come to know that we have two chairs in our bedroom (external objects), that we ate scrambled eggs this morning (memory), that our friend Dolores is in pain (other minds), and that there's a God (religion)? This is a traditional answer:

> *Classical foundationalism.* We start with two kinds of *basic beliefs*: truths about immediate sense experience ("I seem to see a blue image") and self-evident truths ("x = x"). Then we know some further fact just if it can be justified by a deductive or inductive argument from our basic beliefs.

This may sound good, but it doesn't work:

- *Classical foundation* is self-refuting, since it can't justify itself.
- It does a poor job of justifying further knowledge (about things like external objects, memory, other minds, and religion) – which need to be held more firmly than classical foundationalism permits.

---

3 See Plantinga (1983, 1993a, 1993b, 2000, 2006a, 2011, & 2015); the first of these is also in Swindal (2005: 478–87).

Plantinga contends that reformed epistemology gives better answers.

Consider how we come to know that our friend Dolores is in pain. Perhaps Dolores talks about her pain and shows pain behavior (like the behavior we have when we're in pain). Instinctively, after talking with her and seeing her behavior, but without going through a conscious reasoning process, we come to *believe* that she's in pain. Under proper circumstances, we *know* that she's in pain, and our *knowledge* is "properly basic," in that it's genuine but not based on any argument.

This process of gaining knowledge about other minds, while generally reliable, can go wrong. Maybe Dolores is lying about her pain. Maybe we're hallucinating. Or maybe Dolores is from another planet, where her behavior indicates pleasure.

For my *belief* that Dolores is in pain to be *knowledge* requires two additional things: (1) it must be *true* that Dolores is in pain and (2) I must have for this what Plantinga (2015: 156) calls "*warrant*" and defines as follows:

> A belief has *warrant* for a person S only if that belief is produced in S by cognitive faculties functioning properly (subject to no dysfunction) in a cognitive environment appropriate for S's kind of cognitive faculties, according to a design plan that is successfully aimed at truth.

In my example, my cognitive facilities (about knowing other minds) function properly, in an appropriate cognitive environment, according to a design plan successfully aimed at truth (ultimately God's design plan, and it works reliably).

Plantinga (2011: 307–50) argues that, if God guides evolution, then we'd have evolved thinking mechanisms designed to promote truth. From an atheist perspective, however, our thinking mechanisms would have evolved to promote not *truth* but *survival* (including the four Fs: "feeding, fleeing, fighting, and reproducing"). But then atheists have less reason to accept their beliefs as true, including beliefs about evolution. So the atheism + evolution combo toys with intellectual suicide.

We have a similar "sense of divinity" to arrive at beliefs and knowledge about God. Again, our God-given cognitive facilities use experiences – like of the beauties of nature, a newborn baby, God's love or forgiveness, a Gothic cathedral, the hymn *Amazing Grace*, or our need for God – that lead us to have beliefs about God. Under proper circumstances (adding truth and warrant), our beliefs about God can be *knowledge*, and our knowledge (perhaps that God loves me or that there's a God) is then "properly basic," in that it's genuine but not based on any argument.

Plantinga isn't here giving an *argument* for God ("[premise], [premise] ∴ There's a God"). Applying his structure presupposes that you believe in God, but it enables you *to explain your belief in God and why you think it's genuine knowledge* (when truth and warrant are added). So Plantinga explains religious knowledge for those who already believe in God, but he's not trying to convince nonbelievers to believe in God.

While I, Skepticus, am suitably impressed by Plantinga's approach, I'm *not convinced* to believe in God. Let me point out three problems. First, his approach gives no reason (no argument) for me to believe in God. Second, on Freudian grounds, I see this supposed "sense of divinity" as aimed not at truth but at making us feel good by believing in this make-believe father, so the last "warrant" condition fails. Third, as we'll see, there are strong *problem of evil* objections to God's existence; he sees these as possible "defeaters," but he doesn't take them seriously enough.

Rejecting instinctive ways to form beliefs about external objects, memory, or other minds may be intellectual suicide. But it's not intellectual suicide to reject, as I do, this supposed "sense of divinity." So again, we have yet another failed attempt to defend belief in God.

> Before going on, reflect on your reaction to Skepticus's passage. Do you see any problems with it?

7.4 Analysis: Reformed Epistemology

Alvin Plantinga (1932–) is the most influential philosopher of religion of the last few decades and the biggest force in restoring the respectability of religion in analytic philosophy. He's Calvinist and taught for many years at Calvin College in Michigan. In 1983, he accepted a major chair at Notre Dame; this points to how ecumenical philosophy has become at Catholic universities. His writing is a model of clarity and logical rigor. His work covers a wide range of topics, including criticisms of logical positivism, the problem of evil, arguments for God's existence, science and religion, God's nature, and reformed epistemology.

"There are many paths to God" is one of my favorite slogans. I see Plantinga's instinctual "sense of divinity" as a possible path to God. On the plus side, it seems to capture the experiential side of forming beliefs about God that's built into many of us; Augustine would be happy. On the negative side, as Skepticus brings out, it has little argumentative force against nonbelief; if you want to make nonbelievers squirm, tell them not about the sense of divinity but about fine tuning.

7.5 Skepticus: Mysticism

This is Skepticus again, and I want to discuss *mysticism* as a way to know God. Roughly speaking, a "mystical experience" is an alleged experience of

God that's much more direct and powerful than ordinary experience. If you feel awe at God's creation or joy over being forgiven by God, your experience needn't be mystical. But St. Paul's experience here (2 Corinthians 12:2–4) is definitely mystical:

> I know a person in Christ who fourteen years ago was caught up to the third heaven – whether in the body or out of the body I do not know; God knows. And I know that such a person – whether in the body or out of the body I do not know; God knows – was caught up into Paradise and heard things that are not to be told, that no mortal is permitted to repeat.

Sometimes what is experienced isn't God but rather reality's UNITY (that we're all ONE). If you study mysticism, which is present in every religion, you may find it confusing. People debate whether mysticism and mystical beliefs are somewhat similar in all religions and cultures – or whether these vary greatly by culture. And they debate whether mystical experiences give us genuine knowledge about a deeper reality (including about God).

Frederick Copleston (1948) used an argument (but not a strict proof) from mysticism in his radio debate with Bertrand Russell. He says:

> By religious [mystical] experience . . . I mean a loving, but unclear, awareness of some object which irresistibly seems to the experiencer as something transcending the self, something transcending all the normal objects of experience, something which cannot be pictured or conceptualized, but of the reality of which doubt is impossible – at least during the experience. I should claim that cannot be explained adequately and without residue, simply subjectively. The actual basic experience at any rate is most easily explained on the hypotheses that there is actually some objective cause of that experience.

He thinks people definitely have such mystical experiences, and the best explanation for them is that people genuinely experience God. He adds that such experiences often transform one's life for the better.

Bertrand Russell raises objections, and I'd agree with them. (1) Mystical experiences are very private (their content varies hugely between people, with little agreement); some say they experience the devil – how believable is this? (2) There's no way to check the accuracy of what's supposedly revealed; this is unlike seeing that the clock says 3 pm, which others can check. (3) While it's fine that mystical experiences transform some people for the better, this gives no evidence that such experiences teach us truth. (4) Mystical experiences are better explained as hallucinations than as a deeper perception of reality.

So again, we have yet another failed attempt to defend belief in God.

> Before going on, reflect on your reaction to Skepticus's passage. Do you see any problems with it?

7.6 Analysis: Mysticism

I don't have a mystical bone in my body, and I understand mysticism poorly. But I do respect people with such experiences, I see how it helps them to better love God and neighbor, and I regard mysticism as a genuine path to God for them. William James (1902), in his classic *Varieties of Religious Experience*, says mystical experiences are authoritative for those who have such experiences, but not for others; I'd agree.[4]

Mystical experiences can be special gifts from God. Ignatius of Loyola (1491–1556), the founder of the Jesuits, had several of these, including at the Cardoner River in Spain (where he was dramatically enlightened about many things, including his life's mission) and at the La Sorta chapel in Rome (where he had a vision of God the Father and of Christ with his cross, with words of encouragement). Mystical gifts can increase our energy and commitment.

Mysticism and NDEs (near-death experiences, §§4.4–4.7) both seem to reveal a higher reality. But NDEs seem to make a stronger case for God and the afterlife:

- NDEs (but not mystical experiences) often let us check the content's accuracy (for example, about which people died in the family car accident).
- NDE content is much more similar across individuals and cultures than is mystical content.
- NDEs are lucid and happen when the brain's cerebral cortex, responsible for thought and sensation, shows no activity (no brain waves) – conditions that make hallucinations impossible. It's more difficult to refute hallucination explanations of mystical experiences.
- NDEs have a much greater sample size (about 5% of Americans will eventually have an NDE, and their reports are somewhat similar).

Because of these differences, I contend that NDEs can provide a strong argument for God and the afterlife for others, too, and not just for those who have had NDEs.

---

4 The *Anthology of Catholic Philosophy* that I coedited (Swindal 2005) has several readings from authors who are mystics or have mystical tendencies. These include Plato, St. Paul, Philo of Alexandria, Plotinus, Pseudo-Dionysius, Meister Eckhart, Margaret Porette, Ignatius of Loyola, Pierre Teilhard de Chardin, and Herbert McCabe.

We need to explore how mysticism and NDEs connect. Both go beyond ordinary experience and give us an amazing look into our spiritual side. What more can we say?

7.7 Analysis: Why One God?

It hit me one day that my book neglected a key part of monotheism, the belief in ONE God. While I defended the existence of *a God* (where this could mean "one or more Gods"), couldn't *a committee of Gods* have created the world 14 billion years ago, fine-tuned it to bring forth life, and appear to us in near-death experiences? Why believe in *ONE God* instead of a *committee of Gods*? This is a difficult question. I put the issue in this miscellaneous chapter since I couldn't find a better place.

I use "God" here with a capital letter for "a supreme personal being – distinct from the world and creator of the world" and I normally take "supreme" to include "all-knowing, all-good, and all-powerful" – see §C of our introductory chapter). And I use "god" with a small letter for "one of several limited personal deities." While monotheism believes in one God, polytheism believes in many gods.

Polytheism was the dominant form of religion across the ancient world (including the Americas, Africa, Egypt, the Near East, India, China, and Europe).[5] Individual gods and goddesses were much like immortal humans with superpowers. So ancient Greece had a king-god Zeus and a love-goddess Aphrodite – and many more, with stories about each. Greek gods were often identified with Roman gods with similar superpowers, so the Roman Jupiter = the Greek Zeus, and the Roman Venus = the Greek Aphrodite. The gods of conquered peoples were added to the Roman gods, so all worshiped the same gods; thus religion helped unify the Roman Empire. While most polytheists were happy about this, Christians and Jews refused to worship pagan gods; the Roman Empire was unhappy about this.

Many biblical scholars think the ancient Jews started as polytheists but moved to a purer monotheism. Yahweh at first was thought of as one of many gods. Over time, Yahweh grew closer to the Jewish people, was seen as Creator of the heavens and the earth, and was recognized to be greater and greater. Eventually a more purely monotheistic belief in Yahweh as the ONE true God emerged.

"Henotheism" believes in many gods but that one of these is by far the greatest; this is between polytheism and monotheism. Hinduism can be seen as polytheistic (many gods), henotheistic (many gods, but Krishna is the

---

[5] Polytheism may have evolved from an earlier animism, which sees spirits everywhere.

greatest), or monotheistic (Krishna is the ONE true God; other gods are just ways to speak about Krishna).

Could there be more than one God (capital letter, supreme being)? There's a conceptual problem with having two all-powerful Gods. Suppose God-A makes it rain; then God-B is unable to make it not-rain and so isn't all-powerful. We could get around this by specifying that multiple Gods must be "of one mind" (same knowledge, goodness, actions, etc.).

Christianity believes that God is a Trinity, and there are three persons in ONE God. So Christianity insists on some plurality in God, although it also insists that there is just ONE true God. How this can be is a mystery.

In light of Christianity's doctrine of the Trinity, I'll ignore the problem (as too difficult for me) in this section's first paragraph. So, when reflecting on fine-tuning, I'll just say "God (the ONE true God) fine-tuned the universe." Is God here the Trinity? Yes, but I'm not smart enough to explain this further, sorry.

7.8 Analysis: A Pagan-Christian Debate

I just mentioned polytheism, and we'll now look at a charming Roman Empire debate between a polytheist ("Pagan") and a Christian ("Christian"). Minucius Felix (c. 200) wrote this in the second or third century; he was likely a Roman official or lawyer before converting to Christianity. He knew much philosophy and other areas; we know little else about him. This debate, perhaps not totally fictional, brings to mind controversies about God that have been important across the ages.

Pagan criticizes Christianity for its beliefs and practices. He makes four points against *Christian beliefs*:

1. We can explain the world without God.
2. Evils in the world disprove the existence of a perfect God.
3. Like Socrates, we need to be more doubtful about things, especially about our ability to answer life's big questions.
4. We should follow the religion of our ancestors, not this new thing.

(1) Pagan says we can explain the world without God, since the world is just a *mix of elements*:

> Man, and every animal which is born, inspired with life, and nourished, is a mix of elements. . . . So all things flow back again into their source, and are turned again into themselves, without any artificer, judge, or creator.

Christian contends that the world and its elements are set up in an ordered and purposeful way – with seasons that make possible our growing of food and intricate human bodies that make possible our lives – and this requires a designer (God):

> What can possibly be . . . so evident, when you lift your eyes up to heaven, and look into the things which are below and around, than that there is some Deity of most excellent intelligence, by whom all nature is inspired, moved, nourished, governed? . . . When the order of seasons and harvests is distinguished by steadfast variety, does it not attest its Author and Parent? As well the spring with flowers, and the summer with harvests, and the grateful maturity of autumn, and the wintry olive-gathering. . . . The very beauty of our own figure especially confesses God to be its artificer: our upright stature, our up looking countenance, our eyes placed at the top, as it were, for outlook; and all the rest of our senses.
>
> If, on entering any house, you should behold everything refined, well arranged, and adorned, assuredly you would believe that a master presided over it, and that he himself was much better than all those excellent things. So in this house of the world, when you look upon the heaven and earth, its providence, its ordering, its law, believe that there is a Lord and Parent of the universe far more glorious than the stars themselves, and the parts of the whole world.

Over the years (see Chapter 6), the design argument has gotten more complicated – first weakened by Darwin and later strengthened by fine tuning. But the basic idea is the same as many centuries ago.

(2) Pagan argues that *evils in the world disprove the existence of a perfect God*. If a perfect God controlled the world, justice would rule (and Socrates wouldn't have been killed unjustly) and Christians would be happy (instead of being so poor, cold, overworked, and hungry). To suffering Christians, Pagan asks: "Where is that God who is able to help you when you come to life again, since he cannot help you while you are in this life? . . . He either is not willing or not able to assist His people."

Christian says that God sends us suffering to build us up; it isn't "punishment" but rather "warfare." He continues:

> Fortitude is strengthened by infirmities, and calamity is often the discipline of virtue; in addition, strength both of mind and of body grows apathetic without the exercise of labor. Therefore all your mighty men whom you announce as an example have flourished illustriously by their afflictions.
>
> How beautiful is the spectacle to God when a Christian does battle with pain; when he is drawn up against threats, and punishments, and tortures; when, mocking the noise of death, he treads underfoot the

horror of the executioner; when he raises up his liberty against kings and princes, and yields to God alone.

When you get to the next chapter on "Does Suffering Disprove God?", you'll see that Felix agrees with Irenaeus (c. 120–200) about the value of struggling against suffering and doesn't see suffering as punishment from Adam's sin.

(3) Pagan argues that, like Socrates, we *need to be more doubtful* about things, especially about life's big questions. It's better to follow accepted beliefs instead of trying to figure things out ourselves. Since Christians tend to be uneducated and stupid, they do poorly in exploring big questions, like the existence of a supreme God.

Christian says that it's important to get clear about the big questions of life; Pagan needs to respond more directly to the arguments. Pagan's talk about the great value of DOUBT is evasive and inconsistent; Socrates didn't doubt God's existence, Pagan doesn't doubt his "mix of elements" explanation of the world, and Pagan doesn't doubt the evils he attributes to Christians on very flimsy evidence (see later).

(4) Pagan argues that we should follow the *religion of our ancestors, not this new thing*. Christian responds that traditional polytheism is beginning to fall apart in the Roman Empire, which is moving toward belief in one supreme God. He talks about what Plato and other philosophers say about God, Jupiter's rise to something close to God (henotheism), and the craziness of the polytheistic gods.

> Let us review, if it is agreeable, the teaching of philosophers. . . . Thales the Milesian said . . . that God was that mind which from water formed all things. . . . Although the first discoverer of atoms, does not [Democritus] especially speak of nature, which is the basis of forms, and intelligence, as God? . . . Aristotle . . . sets God above the world. . . . Plato has a clearer discourse about God, both in the matters themselves and in the names by which he expresses them. . . . God is by His very name the parent of the world, the artificer of the soul, the fabricator of heavenly and earthly things. . . . The same almost are the opinions also which are ours.
>
> I hear the common people, when they lift their hands to heaven, say nothing else but "Oh God," and "God is great," and "God is true," and "if God shall permit." Is this the natural discourse of the common people, or is it the prayer of a confessing Christian? And they who speak of Jupiter as the chief, are mistaken in the name indeed, but they are in agreement about the unity of the power.
>
> Jupiter's nurse is a she-goat, and as an infant he is taken away from his greedy father, lest he should be devoured. . . . The detected adultery

of Mars and Venus, and the violence of Jupiter against Ganymede . . . Cybele . . . who could not entice her adulterous lover . . . mutilated him, doubtless that she might make a god of the eunuch. . . . The Galli also worship her by the punishment of their emasculated body. Now certainly these things are not sacred rites, but tortures. . . . Do they not argue the contemptible and disgraceful characters of your gods?

The last point calls the gods "contemptible and disgraceful." Such gods aren't worthy of worship (or even moral admiration or imitation), don't help us to explain the world, don't contribute to the meaning of our lives, and aren't ideally loving "father figures" (but more like flawed older brothers and sisters). The ONE, true, perfectly loving God made us for himself; since he is much more religiously attractive to us, monotheism tends over time to trounce polytheism.

Pagan criticizes *Christian practices* in four ways:

1. Christians are irreligious, despising temples and religious practices that made the Roman Empire great.
2. Christians are ignorant, credulous, poor, and lower class.
3. Christians worship a convicted criminal.
4. Christians are notorious for their evil actions.

(1) Pagan says Christians are irreligious, despising temples and religious practices that made the Roman Empire great; recall that the gods of conquered peoples were added to the group of Roman gods worshipped by everyone (except Christians and Jews, who refused to participate). Christian responds that the Roman Empire's success had little to do with its religion and much to do with its army's power and cruelty.

(2) Pagan says that Christians are ignorant, credulous (especially the women), poor, and lower class. Because Christians often came from lower classes, they were seen as uneducated and ignorant, so defenders of Christianity needed to be educated and smart. Christian does a great job in the debate, in terms of the power and clarity of his arguments, his background knowledge, and his rhetorical skills.

Christian also talks about the value of poverty:

> That many of us are called poor, this is not our disgrace, but our glory; for as our mind is relaxed by luxury, so it is strengthened by frugality. And yet who can be poor if he does not want, if he does not crave for the possessions of others, if he is rich towards God? He rather is poor, who, although he has much, desires more. . . . Therefore, as he who treads a road is the happier the lighter he walks, so happier is he in this journey of life who lifts himself along in poverty, and does not breathe heavily under the burden of riches.

Early Christian communities shared their wealth.

(3) Pagan criticizes Christians for worshipping a convicted criminal (Jesus), which leads them to commit evil actions themselves. Did Pagan forget his praise of Socrates, also a convicted criminal? Both Socrates and Jesus were moral heroes, unjustly accused of wrongdoing.

(4) Pagan criticizes Christians for many evil actions; I'll just mention two. First, Christians love each other at once, without discrimination, and this leads to shameful and lustful sexual orgies. Second, Christians in their secret worship kill a young infant; they cover it with grain, stab it with swords, drink its blood, and eat it.[6]

Christian says these are lies and violate our duty to get our facts right when criticizing others.[7] Christians took marital fidelity seriously and rejected lustful sexual orgies common among the Romans. Christians took the right to life seriously too and rejected Roman practices like infanticide, abortion, and killing at gladiator games.

At the end, Christian wins the debate and Pagan converts immediately to believing in God and Christianity. This strikes me as implausible; conversions tend to work slowly. Our religious beliefs run deep and connect with our lives in many ways, and these have to be considered. With Augustine, the conversion process went very slowly – but then the final result likely came quickly: "I believe." With the Pagan, at least in Minucius Felix's account, the conversion happened very quickly.

---

6 I had fun with this one when teaching at Loyola. I told the students that we still kill infants at the popular 10:30 am Sunday mass in the Madonna Della Strada chapel, and that it's much fun – but the sacristans complain about having to clean up all the blood afterwards. (Just kidding!)
7 Like Bertrand Russell and others (§§2.1–2.2), Pagan criticizes believers for accepting God on flimsy evidence and then believes the worst about believers on flimsy evidence.

8
Does Suffering Disprove God?

We'll begin by listening to the fictional student Skepticus explain why he thinks suffering and other evils disprove God's existence. We'll also hear objections to *traditional theodicy*, which tries to defend God. As you read Skepticus's passage, first try to understand it in a sympathetic way, and then try to find problems with it. We'll later consider objections.

8.1 Skepticus: The Problem of Evil

This is Skepticus again. I want to defend the *problem of evil* argument. From premises about suffering and other evils, this concludes that there can't be a God (or at least an all-good, all-powerful God).

St. Thomas Aquinas (1274: I, q. 1, a. 3) gave this as the first of two popular objections to belief in God:

> Does God exist? It seems that God does not exist; because if . . . God existed, there would be no evil discoverable; but there is evil in the world. Therefore God does not exist.

Bertrand Russell (1927) said:

> It is a most astonishing thing that people can believe that this world, with all the things that are in it, with all its defects, should be the best that omnipotence and omniscience has been able to produce in millions of years. I really cannot believe it. Do you think that, if you were granted omnipotence and omniscience and millions of years in which to perfect your world, you could produce nothing better than the Ku-Klux-Klan?

I live in a city where many evils happen every year: deaths, diseases, poverty, robberies, tornadoes, and so on – bringing physical pain and mental suffering. Similar evils take place all over the world. Imagine that there's a being X, who either caused these evils or could easily have prevented them. X had the power to bring only joy to people, if he had so chosen, but instead brought about (or at least permitted) massive evils. If X exists, then X is a moral monster. But if God exists, then God is X. So if God exists, then God is a moral monster.

For thousands of years, the *problem of evil* argument has been the most important objection to belief in God. Here's the traditional formulation, which goes back to the ancient Greek Empiricus:

1 If God doesn't want to prevent evil, then he isn't all good.
2 If God isn't able to prevent evil, then he isn't all powerful.
3 Either God doesn't want to prevent evil, or he isn't able.
∴ Either God isn't all powerful, or he isn't all good.

Premise 1 is based on God being *all good*: an all-good being would *want* to prevent evil. Premise 2 is based on God being *all powerful*: an all-powerful being would be *able* to prevent evil. Premise 3 is based on arguing that if God wanted to prevent evil and was able to do so, then he'd do it and there'd be no evil – which goes against the clear fact that there's evil. The conclusion, which follows using standard propositional logic (Gensler 2017a: 153 prob. 5), requires rejecting God, his power, or his goodness.

Evils in the world roughly divide into main groups:[1]

- *Natural evils* (don't directly come from free choices). Diseases (like cancer and heart disease), natural disasters (like hurricanes, tornadoes, and floods), and death of natural causes.
- *Moral evils* (directly come from free choices). Hatred, injustice, revenge, war, murder, stealing, lying, and so on.

Do we think a perfect God would create a world with so much natural and moral evil? Surely not! Why shouldn't we conclude that the world *wasn't* created by a perfect God?

1 If a perfect God created the world, then the world wouldn't have much natural and moral evil.
2 The world has much natural and moral evil.
∴ A perfect God didn't create the world.

Here's a related argument:

1 If God loves us, then God would make us happy.
2 God doesn't make us happy (since many or most are miserable).
∴ God doesn't love us.

---

1 This distinction is useful but rough. In part, cancer may be caused by *bad eating habits* and hurricanes by *bad environmental habits*. Global warming is mostly moral evil, our fault.

How can believers respond to such arguments?

(1) Some *deny evil's existence*. Some say evil is an illusion, but since illusions are evil, this won't avoid the problem. Others see diseases as privations or lacks with no positive being; but this won't make it less bad to inflict diseases on others. Denying evil is difficult, since evils are big in our lives, and fighting them is big in every religion.

(2) Some think *it's all a mystery*, so we needn't worry about it. We should turn off our ears when we hear nonbelievers argue against God on the basis of evils. Trust that God has a reason to permit evil, even though our little minds can't grasp it. This answer is evasive and will bring scorn from those who use evil to attack belief in God. Those who struggle with faith also need a better answer. Believers need to give some answer about why God might permit evil, even if it's incomplete, as all human answers are. Believers need to raise doubts about the *problem of evil* argument, even if we'll never completely understand evil or God's purposes.

(3) Some construct a *theodicy (why a perfect God permits evil)*.[2] We'll see an example in the next section. Theodicies dispute premise 1 (*"If God doesn't want to prevent evil, then he isn't all good"*); they propose God's reason for sometimes permitting and not preventing evil.

I have a Catholic philosophy-major friend named Faith, and I asked whether her religion taught a theodicy. Faith said yes, and she told me about an Adam-and-Eve theodicy she learned in Catholic grade school. Since Faith started having doubts about this theodicy, she welcomed the chance to explain it to me.

8.2 Skepticus: Did Adam's Sin Begin Disease and Death?

This is Skepticus again. When I met with Faith, she explained the *traditional theodicy*[3] she learned in Catholic grade school. Then she raised objections.

Faith first summed up what she learned in grade school:

> God created the first humans, Adam and Eve, in a perfect world without suffering, disease, or death – in the Garden of Eden. God intended

---

2 Weaker than a *theodicy* is a *defense*, which gives a *possible explanation* (but not one you assert) for why a perfect God permits evil. Later I (Gensler) give something between a theodicy and a defense: an explanation of why a perfect God permits evil that I assert in a qualified way, as being roughly true but likely incomplete on details.

3 John Hick (1978) distinguishes two approaches to theodicy, the *Augustinian* and the *Irenaean*; we both much prefer the Irenaean view. I use "traditional theodicy" for what Hick calls "Augustinian theodicy," because Augustine seems to me to be more complicated than the first (traditional) approach. I and many of my students learned traditional theodicy in grade school; since this has so many problems, the Irenaean view is felt as a liberation.

that they and their descendants live there forever, in a world with no evils, either natural or moral. But God valued free will, so he made their continuing paradise existence depend on their choices. God commanded them not to eat fruit from a certain tree (anything else was OK); they'd suffer if they ate the "forbidden fruit." Unfortunately, after being tempted by the devil, Adam and Eve ate the fruit. So God punished them and their descendants by sending them natural evils (like suffering, disease, and death) and permitting (not stopping) moral evils (as when their farmer son Cain murdered their shepherd son Abel).

So why does our world, created by a perfect God, have evil? The evil came from the sin of Adam and Eve. All evil comes from the abuse of creaturely free will, as either a *just punishment* or a *natural consequence*. God *permits* evil because he could prevent it only by taking away our free will, and thus our capacity for moral goodness; taking away our free will would result in a less good world. "*Permits*" is important here. God doesn't *want* Cain to murder Abel (God forbids it), but he *permits* (doesn't stop) the action because he respects our free will – and he *justly punishes* the action.

I thanked Faith for describing *traditional theodicy* so well. I asked whether she had problems with the view. She said yes, and mentioned strong objections. She surprised me that she accepted evolution and didn't take the Bible all literally.

First, Faith said traditional theodicy clashes with evolution, which she accepts. Evolution shows that Earth, for billions of years before the first humans, had disease, death, and hurricanes. So these evils didn't start with the first humans but existed far earlier. And, from the evolutionary view, the first humans would have been immature, just higher than apes, and not perfect.

Second, Faith said, Genesis inconsistencies (e.g., whether animals came before humans) push us *not* to take the creation accounts literally. Early Christian thinkers, like Origen (c. 185–254) and Augustine (354–430), gave consistency arguments against biblical literalism [§6.3]. Why, then, should we take Adam and Eve so literally, especially since there are problems in doing this? And doesn't God's giving the very odd "Don't eat this fruit" as his sole moral norm for humanity instead of "Love your neighbor" suggest that this is a *story* and shouldn't be taken literally?

Third, Faith pointed out, a perfect Adam and Eve likely wouldn't have sinned. Did they poorly understand the consequences of eating the fruit – or were they tempted too strongly? If so, then wasn't that God's fault? Humans with normal self-control who understood the punishment would obey the simple "Don't eat this fruit."

Fourth, Faith asks, Would it be right for *humans* to punish innocent children because of sins by distant ancestors? Surely not. Then how is it right for *God* to inflict painful diseases on innocent children because of sins by Adam and Eve?

Fifth, Faith points out that God moved to a PLAN B (humans struggle against evil) because PLAN A (humans avoid forbidden fruit) failed. But wouldn't a perfect God have known how Adam and Eve would upset PLAN A? The traditional theodicy presents God as being stupid in not knowing such things.

I, Skepticus again, was impressed by Faith's answers; she's pretty smart for a believer. She added that her class would study a better theodicy, one inspired by Irenaeus (c. 130–202). She asked if I'd like to meet with her again to talk about it. I smiled and said, "Yes, we can destroy this view together." Faith frowned and said, "Hey, you need to be more open to God."

8.3 Skepticus: The Biblical Problem of Evil

This is Skepticus again. I found atheist thinkers who point out embarrassing biblical verses. These verses show that sometimes Jesus or God teach hatred, revenge, or genocide – or are just foolish. These verses provide further objections to religion from evil. Here are four examples:

1. *Luke 14:26.* "If any one comes to me [Jesus] and does not hate his own father and mother and wife and children and brothers and sisters, yes, and even his own life, he cannot be my disciple."
2. *Matthew 21:18–19.* "In the morning, as [Jesus] was returning to the city, he was hungry. And seeing a fig tree by the wayside he went to it, and found nothing on it but leaves only. And he said to it, 'May no fruit ever come from you again!' And the fig tree withered at once."
3. *Exodus 21:23–25.* "If any harm follows, then you shall give life for life, eye for eye, tooth for tooth, hand for hand, foot for foot, burn for burn, wound for wound, stripe for stripe."
4. *Deuteronomy 20:16–18.* "In the cities of these peoples that the Lord your God gives you for an inheritance, you shall save alive nothing that breathes, but you shall utterly destroy them, the Hittites and the Amorites, the Canaanites and the Perizzites, the Hivites and the Jebusites, as the Lord your God has commanded."

These are just four of many embarrassing biblical verses.

(1) Jesus tells us to hate our family members. I wonder if Faith knows about this and tries to follow it. This seems to contradict other Christian teachings, but maybe Jesus doesn't care about being consistent.
(2) Jesus curses a fig tree because it has no fruit (even though it's the wrong season for fruit), and the tree miraculously withers up. Jesus here is

irritable, strange, and not wise. Bertrand Russell (1930) argues that Jesus was morally inferior to Socrates. Russell doubts whether Jesus even existed or whether, if he did, we know anything about him, but here he's just analyzing Jesus as described in the Gospels.

(3) God in the Bible *accepts the law of revenge* (*"An eye for an eye"*); if someone harms you (by knocking out your eye or your tooth, or by killing your daughter), you're to harm that person in the same way. The Bible (Matthew 5:38–39) also *rejects the law of revenge*. So, if we assume that the Bible is God's will, then God's will has contradictions.

(4) God in the Bible often commands *genocide*. Everyone in another enemy group – men, women, children, and even animals – is to be killed. Based on many similar biblical passages, Richard Dawkins (2006) says:

> The God of the Old Testament is arguably the most unpleasant character in all fiction: jealous and proud of it; a petty, unjust, unforgiving control-freak; a vindictive, bloodthirsty ethnic cleanser; a misogynistic, homophobic, racist, infanticidal, genocidal, filicidal, pestilential, megalomaniacal, sadomasochistic, capriciously malevolent bully.

This general objection, based on many embarrassing biblical passages, is called the *biblical problem of evil*. It shows how foolish Christianity is.

Before going on, reflect on your reaction to Skepticus's passage. Do you see any problems with it?

8.4 Analysis: How Irenaeus Explains Evil

St. Irenaeus (c. 120–200) was Bishop of Lyons, in present-day France. He defended Christianity against Gnosticism, which taught that a good God created good in the world, while an evil god created evil. As a Christian, Irenaeus believed in just one God, who is supremely good and perfect, and created the whole world. But then why does the world have evil? His answer is that *struggle against evil* is valuable and important in God's plan.

Irenaeus is featured in many discussions of the problem of evil, such as John Hick's *Evil and the God of Love* (1978). Followers of *traditional theodicy* think evil comes from the sin of Adam and Eve, who were created perfect. Followers of Irenaeus's *soul-making theodicy* think differently and see their view as better and as also very "traditional" (in view of its early origin).

Irenaean theodicy makes three basic claims:

1. God is all good and all powerful. An important part of God's goodness is that he loves his creatures: he cares about their good.
2. God's creation plan has two phases. In phase 1, God creates a world where imperfect, weak, free beings can choose to care for one another in an epic struggle against evil. In phase 2, these beings attain eternal happiness.
3. God permits evil because it's required for the significance of the epic human struggle against evil.

John Hick contributed much to what is called "Irenaean theodicy."

(1) The Irenaean and traditional theodicies both affirm that God is all good and all powerful. Some other approaches limit God's goodness or power.
(2) God created us *imperfect* and intends that we, by *freely struggling against evil*, grow into greater perfection toward *eternal life*. Irenaeus says (Swindal 2005: 54–57):

God made man a free agent from the beginning, possessing his own power, even as he does his own soul, to obey the commands of God voluntarily, and not by compulsion. . . . But if some had been made by nature bad, and others good, these latter would not be deserving of praise for being good, for such were they created; nor would the former be reprehensible. . .

Paul the Apostle says to the Corinthians, "Know you not, that they who run in a racecourse, do all indeed run, but one receives the prize? . . . And the harder we strive, so much is it the more valuable; while so much the more valuable it is, so much the more should we esteem it. And indeed those things are not esteemed so highly which come spontaneously, as those which are reached by much anxious care. . .

If, however, anyone say, "What then? Could not God have exhibited man as perfect from beginning?" let him know that . . . all things are possible to Him. But created things must be inferior to Him who created them. . . . Now it was necessary that man should in the first instance be created; and having been created, should receive growth; and . . . see his Lord.

In *traditional theodicy*, the first humans, Adam and Eve, were created *perfect*; disease and death entered the world after their sin. This clashes with evolution, where disease and death exist long before the first humans. In *Irenaean theodicy*, the first humans were *imperfect*, weak, fragile – and developed from weak beginnings by struggling against evils like disease and death. This fits evolution better.

For Irenaeus, eternal life and perfection come at the end of the process, not the beginning. The path to get there is difficult and involves struggling against evil, which makes the process much more valuable and significant. So evils like disease and death – and the struggle against them – are an essential part of the plan, and not there as punishment for sin.

In the beginning, God decided to share his life with others by creating rational creatures in his image and likeness. But how would he create them? God rejected a quick solution: to create rational creatures fully formed and morally perfect and share his life with them immediately in heaven. He thought, instead, that virtue and happiness reached after a struggle against evil are much more valuable. So God decided that his rational creatures would struggle against evil, grow through free choices, and travel a long journey toward eternal life. A long, epic struggle toward the final fulfillment would ultimately be more meaningful.

God started phase 1 of creation with the Big Bang. After 14 billion years, the finely tuned universe brought forth at least one planet with intelligent life. Earthly humans then developed over perhaps millions of years.

God causes natural evils, like diseases and death. It would be wrong for humans to cause such evils; it's justified for God to do this, given that these are needed for phase 1 (which requires struggling against such evils) and the two-phase plan is justified.

God doesn't cause moral evils, as when we hurt others. God gave us free will – which makes us able, in an indeterministic way, to do good or to do evil, but God doesn't *cause* us to do evil.

This struggle against evil was God's plan for us from the beginning. It wasn't a backup PLAN B that God switched to because of unexpected fruit eating. God's plan requires that we grow by struggling against natural evils like disease and death, and so God's plan requires that there be natural evils.

(3) God permits natural evils because the significance of the human epic requires that we struggle against such evils. In traditional theodicy, all evil in God's world is either (a) a consequence of creaturely sin or (b) a punishment for creaturely sin. Irenaeus adds a third category: (c) natural evils, like disease and death, are needed to set the stage for the great and valuable epic struggle against evil.

God's plan requires *evils* for humans to struggle against, *free will* (which Hick rightly thinks requires an "epistemic distance" from God, whose existence can't be so clear that it destroys our free will), and a *middle degree of moral strength* (we're not so strong that we can always do the right thing easily and without a struggle). All three factors are present in our lives.

God made us "in his image and likeness" (Genesis 1:27). At first, it's a very faint image and likeness. We need to grow in love and knowledge as we travel a long epic journey back to God. Our lives are like the way of the cross (a struggle against evil) leading to the resurrection (eternal life).

8.5 Analysis: What Kind of World Would God Create?

Let's explore this question: "Suppose you were a perfect God; what sort of world would you create?" A perfect God would create (pick one):

1. *Pleasure*. A hedonistic paradise.
2. *Best possible*. The best of all possible worlds.
3. *Immediate heaven*. Immediate eternal life with God; this comes with great enjoyment, knowledge, and love but no suffering, ignorance, or hatred.
4. *Struggle*. A world where free beings can struggle meaningfully and lovingly against evil.
5. *Struggle+heaven*. Struggle (world-4) leading to heaven (world-3).

(1) *Pleasure*. If I were a perfect God, I'd create a hedonistic paradise for humans. They'd experience maximal pleasure and no pain. – This sounds nice, but superficial; higher values are neglected, and free will has no role.

(2) *Best possible*. If I were a perfect God, I'd create the best of all possible worlds. – But maybe there's no "best" possible world, just as there's no highest number; maybe for each finite world, there could be a better one. And maybe any really valuable world requires free beings whose choices could make the world better or worse, but then these free beings could, and likely would, bring about evil, which would make the world less good.

(3) *Immediate heaven*. If I were a perfect God, I'd create rational creatures fully formed and morally perfect, and share my life with them immediately in heaven (with great enjoyment, knowledge, and love but no suffering, ignorance, or hatred). – But virtue and happiness reached after a significant struggle against evil are much more valuable, and this option (3) has no use for free will. So (3) isn't the best option.

(4) *Struggle*. If I were a perfect God, I'd create a world where free beings can struggle meaningfully and lovingly against evil. I see the value of this. The news had a story about a single mother with three dying children; the woman could give up and drink away her problems or struggle lovingly to make life bearable for her family. There's a chance for something of great value and beauty in a world where the freedom to love can make a difference. – And yet, while we value the free struggle against evil, we also value having evil overcome; it would be disappointing for our lives to be all struggle but no final conquest.

(5) *Struggle+heaven*. If I were a perfect God, I'd create a world with two phases: heroic struggle (this present life) and evil overcome (heaven). Each phase has values lacking in the other, but the two together are complete. – This answer makes the most sense, and it fits *Irenaean*

theodicy. While phase 1 (struggle) fits our present experience of the world, phase 2 (heaven) fits the hope provided by world religions and near-death experiences.

Sometimes atheists (as in §8.1) argue this way: "If a perfect God created the world, then the world be such-and-such, but the world isn't such-and-such ∴ A perfect God didn't create the world." In evaluating this, examine the first premise carefully. We should complain when atheists assume that a perfect God would be a hedonist and create for us a pleasure palace with no pain. This would be a very superficial God, not a God who challenges us to be the greatest that we can be.

8.6 Analysis: Further Questions About Evil

Question 1. Is each evil required for a greater good (so the total good wouldn't be as great if the evil hadn't occurred) – so in the end everything happens for the best?

No. If each evil is required for a greater good, why fight evils? And why not cause evils ourselves (since then these will promote the greater good)?

If each evil is required for a greater good, it doesn't matter whether we fight evil or cause evil. It's important for God's plan that our actions can make a difference, that the world can be genuinely better or worse depending on how we act. Only then can our actions be significant.

Question 2. Why doesn't God let us freely choose what to do and then *always* block the bad consequences of our wrong actions?

Suppose that God allowed us to freely choose to hurt others, but then, always and in a predictable way, blocked the bad consequences of our actions. This would bring two bad results. (1) It again would make our actions less significant. It's important for God's plan that our actions can make a difference, that the world can be genuinely better or worse depending on how we act. (2) Evildoers could manipulate God if he acted in such a regular, predictable way – they could rely on God blocking evil consequences. This too is undesirable in terms of God's plan.

God might *sometimes* block bad consequences of individual wrong actions – especially if his interventions don't form a regular, predictable pattern. God might *miraculously* (violating laws of nature) cause an evildoer to have a heart attack just before exploding an atomic bomb in a city, might *miraculously* cause the police to see how to defuse a bomb, or might *miraculously* dull the pain of a tortured person. Or God might decide a *non-deterministic quantum event* – to stop a heart attack, bomb, or pain; this wouldn't violate laws of nature. It's unclear how often, if ever, God intervenes in this way. Maybe he'd intervene only in extreme cases – perhaps to avoid Earth's destruction or a Nazi world conquest. Or maybe he'd intervene more often.

> Question 3. Does God want us to be happy? If he does, and if he can make us happy, why are most people so miserable?
> (Hume 1779: part 10)

Pleasure differs from happiness. *Pleasure* is an enjoyable feeling; *happiness* is an overall contentment with our life and how it connects with higher purposes. We might have many pleasures but be unhappy, seeing our life of pleasures as ultimately meaningless. Or we might have few pleasures but be happy, seeing our life as deeply meaningful, as making a difference to people's lives. God wants us to be happy but cares little about whether we have a life of pleasure.

Why are so many people miserable? Mainly they look for happiness in wrong place, in self-interest and immediate pleasure. The real tragedy in life isn't to suffer pain but rather to live in a way that's selfish and without meaning.[4]

Why doesn't God *make* us happy? The key to happiness is to live properly, as God intended: *to care about others in a meaningful life*. In other words, we need love and faith; this gains us a hundredfold here and eternal life hereafter. Choosing love and faith, as God invites us to do, will tend to make us happy,[5] but God doesn't *make* us choose this way. We can choose otherwise, since God made us free. To be happy, we need to *cooperate* with God's plan.

> Question 4. Why do the good often suffer while the evil prosper?

Suppose it were clear to everyone that the good always prosper while the evil suffer. This would make impossible the struggle between doing something because it's right and doing it from self-interest; that would be a loss, since such struggles are important. Even though right actions may in the end always serve our self-interest, this shouldn't be too obvious in our present life.

> Question 5. Why did God make my mother suffer so much from rheumatoid arthritis [actual case]? Did God want her to suffer?

---

4 External circumstances have less to do with overall happiness than most people think. A famous study (Brickman 1978) compared million-dollar lottery winners with quadriplegic accident victims; a year later there was little difference in their happiness. Other research shows that the blind, retarded, and malformed aren't less happy than other people.
5 Much empirical data support the idea that religion promotes happiness (see Chapter 2).

God didn't cause or desire this specific evil. But he set up the world so that a percentage of people will get such diseases, and this so we can grow by responding in love. God gives us the ability to make such evils an occasion of love and growth (as it mostly was for my mother and family). If we instead respond with bitterness, that's our fault; God at least gave us the option to give a loving response of great value.

I had two students, Matt and Ally, who met in freshman biology and grew ever closer. After graduation, Matt got a rare cancer and almost died; this brought them even together more. When I performed their wedding ceremony, the key words, which both parties repeat, stood out: "I promise to be true to you in good times and in bad, *in sickness and in health*; I will love you and honor you all the days of my life." Matt and Ally had a beautiful love for each other, a love deepened by sickness and suffering. My homily mentioned Irenaeus, which they read in my class: "He wrote about the role of evil and suffering in a world created by a loving God; he saw life as a difficult but meaningful struggle against evil, by which we grow into greater faith and love." And so it was for Matt and Ally.

Our suffering is a gift from God that can deepen our lives. How we respond is up to us; if we reject it and become bitter, that's our fault, not God's. Matt and Ally could have responded to cancer with bitterness and despair (which would have been out of character). We're here, ultimately, to care for each other – in sickness and in health, in good times and in bad – with a love that mirrors God's love for us. God calls us to a life that can be difficult and painful, but also deeply meaningful.

> Question 6. Augustine (400) said that our lives are so jumbled and random that it's difficult to discern a divine plan behind them. But God's care for us is clear from *reason* (how well God designed our bodies) and *revelation* (how Christ suffered, died, and rose for us). So it's better to see God as having a plan for us that's inscrutable. Do you agree?

Not entirely. We can grasp at least part of God's plan. God intends that we struggle to grow in wisdom and love through difficult and chaotic situations. Our lives have ups and downs, setbacks and tragedies, and crazy events that confuse and challenge us. That's what God intended. Our lives' messiness is part of God's plan.

> Question 7. Will God punish sinners in the afterlife? Will some suffer hell's eternal torments?

God doesn't punish us; instead, we punish ourselves. If we separate ourselves from God, temporarily or forever, we keep ourselves from our supreme fulfillment and happiness. We're made for God, and without God we'll be miserable. The worst way to punish ourselves is to reject God permanently, forever; this would be eternal damnation. But while free creatures could choose this, does it ever happen? Maybe God keeps giving people a second chance (and third, and. . .) to change, and so all are saved eventually. Or maybe God destroys one who'd never convert, to prevent endless, needless suffering. A good God would likely do such things, so I doubt that anyone actually suffers eternal damnation (see Hick 1978: 337–52). I'm open to the idea of (eventual) universal salvation – an idea that goes back at least to Origen (c. 185–254) and seems to be growing in popularity.

I agree with Vatican II (1962–65), an ecumenical council of the Catholic Church, that those who are neither Christians nor believers of any other sort can also be saved. *Lumen Gentium* 16 says:

> Those also can attain to salvation who through no fault of their own do not know the Gospel of Christ or His Church, yet sincerely seek God and moved by grace strive by their deeds to do His will as it is known to them through the dictates of conscience. Nor does Divine Providence deny the helps necessary for salvation to those who, without blame on their part, have not yet arrived at an explicit knowledge of God and with His grace strive to live a good life.

> Question 8. Given that God's plan requires *some suffering*, doesn't the world have *excessive suffering*?

John Hick (1978: 327–36) thinks "excessive" is relative, so we could object the same way with less suffering. If the most horrible suffering was eliminated, lesser suffering would become the "most horrible" – and we could similarly argue that God should eliminate it. Eventually there'd be no suffering – which would frustrate God's goals. So Hick has doubts about the "excessive suffering" objection. But he's not entirely happy with this answer and later talks about the *mystery of evil*.

> Question 9. If God's plan is as you described it, and thus requires much suffering, should I still think his plan is good?

That's your choice. This theodicy requires some value commitments that not everyone may want to make (e.g., we have to reject hedonism and we have to accept that virtue and happiness reached after a significant struggle are more valuable).

> Question 10. Does God, in creating a world with so much evil to struggle against, satisfy Gensler's golden-rule consistency requirement? Is God treating suffering humans as he's willing to be treated (or allow someone close to him to be treated) in their place?

Some atheists doubt this, thinking that the world's pain and suffering are too much; the pain isn't worth the gain. So God, they think, would fail the golden-rule test: he wouldn't be willing that he himself (or someone he loves dearly) be subjected to so much pain and suffering for the sake of an heroically meaningful life.

Most believers think the gain *is* worth the pain from the view of eternity and that God *does* satisfy the golden rule. Christianity makes a strong point here: God sent his Son to struggle against physical pain and mental suffering on the cross, to express his supreme love for humanity in the most powerful way possible. So God *was* willing that he himself (or someone he loves dearly) endure severe pain and suffering for the sake of supremely meaningful love. So God satisfies the GR as he treats us in a loving but Irenaean way. That's part of the message of the cross and resurrection.

> Question 11. Irenaean theodicy seems plausible and consistent, but is there any proof that it's true?

Irenaean theodicy is a defensive strategy (Hick 1978). We don't prove it; instead, we give it as a plausible possibility to counter atheist arguments. We defend it in terms of logic, science, morality, and our religious tradition. I'm confident that Irenaean theodicy is at least roughly true, but it may be incomplete on details (e.g. how to explain animal pain).[6] Its goal isn't to completely account for evil in God's plan; there'll always be some mystery in evil and in everything else we seek to understand (like the weather). Instead, we need to account for evil well enough to defend against atheist arguments from evil. I think we can achieve this limited goal.

> Question 12. While God loves us in many ways, are there any special ways that go nicely with Irenaean theodicy?

Yes. First, God used his supreme love and wisdom in designing the world. He put us on a challenging journey toward eternal life, where we struggle against evil to grow in love and wisdom. In this way, God gave us the possibility of having intensely meaningful lives. For this we can be very thankful to God.

Second, God gives each of us special gifts. Since all we have is from God, we can see God's goodness in our talents, our health, or the beauty of a canyon. We can't say that God wouldn't have been good if he hadn't given

---

6 Swinburne (2004) makes a good beginning on animal pain. He thinks only higher animals (those with backbones) have significant pain, their pain is less than that of humans, and some of their pain leads to good (like avoiding injury and caring for suffering animals). He thinks a good God would ensure that *each animal on the whole has a good life* (so any pain is outweighed by good); this is the most difficult part to defend (especially since we don't want to posit an afterlife for animals).

us these gifts; he might instead have given us a challenge, perhaps sickness instead of health. God gives us such things at his discretion; he can rightly make different choices about them. Even challenges that God sends us, like sicknesses, are intended for our good; they too can be "special gifts" for us *if we respond properly*. Ignatius of Loyola (1524) suggested that we pray to be *indifferent* about whether God ultimately sends us gifts or challenges (like health or sickness), desiring only what helps us serve God better; this is a wise but challenging attitude for believers to have about personal evils. One of God's "special gifts" for Ignatius was a cannonball that shattered his leg; his recovery changed his life. Challenges can promote growth.

> Question 13. Isn't Irenaean theodicy too intellectual? Why doesn't it say how to have an *emotionally good attitude* toward God while suffering?

Remember what we're doing here; as the book's title says, we're *reasoning about God*. We're dealing with the *intellectual problem of evil* – defending belief in God from atheists who attack this belief.

There's also a *personal-faith problem of evil*, about being committed to God when we're discouraged and suffering cancer pain; we cry out to God and are tempted to curse him: "Why did you make my life so difficult and painful?" In reflective moments, our minds may see that God picked the best and most meaningful path for us (an epic struggle against evil leading to eternal life), and from eternity's view, God's plan wins easily. But we may still struggle emotionally. Two books by C.S. Lewis mark the difference: *The Problem of Pain* (1940) is about the intellectual problem, while *A Grief Observed* (1961) deals with personal struggles and coping with his wife's death.

There's also a *pastoral problem of evil*, about how to minister to suffering people. My book deals just with the intellectual problem; for help on the other problems, you need to look elsewhere. But understanding the intellectual problem may be a good start.

> Question 14. Does Skepticus's emotivism ruin his *problem of evil* arguments?

Yes. Since Skepticus is an emotivist (§§3.4–3.8), his premises with moral terms translate into exclamations instead of truth claims. "If God doesn't want to prevent *evil*, then he isn't all *good*" would be perhaps "If God doesn't want to prevent boo!, then he isn't all hurrah!" This doesn't make sense, but I challenge you to translate it better. His *problem of evil* arguments can't have their premises all true, in his view, because some of them are just exclamations.

One way to avoid this problem is to move to a consistency attack. J.L. Mackie (1955) argues that theism is *inconsistent* in combining three beliefs: "God is omnipotent; God is wholly good; and evil exists." Deriving a contradiction, he says, requires two further principles based on the meaning of "omnipotent" and "wholly good." Alvin Plantinga (1974a: 7–64) argues that his further principles are misworded and that a correct wording blocks the contradiction. Plantinga's *free-will defense* argues for the consistency of these three beliefs by giving a possible situation where all three are true. (See Gensler 2017a: 226 prob. 20–21 and 239 prob. 4–6.) After Plantinga's work, atheist thinkers have mostly given up trying to show that theism is inconsistent about evil – except for Sterba (2019), and I don't think his attack works.

Emotivist atheists could also avoid the problem by formulating their arguments without moral terms. They might argue that the world's *pain* shows that an all-powerful God creator must be *cruel*.[7] Irenaean theodicy works against all these approaches.

8.7 Analysis: The Biblical Problem of Evil

The sacred texts of Christianity or other religions seem at times to have immoral or unwise teachings. We'll here consider four examples from Skepticus (§8.3).

> *Luke 14:26*. If any one comes to me [Jesus] and does not hate his own father and mother and wife and children and brothers and sisters, yes, and even his own life, he cannot be my disciple.

My friends who are Bible scholars would answer this way:

> This verse really means that we shouldn't follow family members when they lead us to do the wrong thing – to be racist, for example. The Greek word here can mean "love less" instead of "hate" (and so "hate" is a misleading translation). In addition, people in the ancient world (as many today) often express things in exaggerated ways they don't mean literally, as when we speak of "totally killing" the other side's football team. A good sign that we shouldn't take "hate" here literally is that this goes against Jesus's main message in the gospels, which teaches love instead of hate.

A good rule for interpreting another's ideas is "Understand before you criticize." It's poor scholarship to criticize another's ideas without understanding

---

7 Differing views about the nature of value may also heavily influence how we view the *problem of evil* argument. Some believers see "good" and "bad" as claims about God's will (see DCT §§10.1–10.2), so any premise about these (even in a *problem of evil* argument) affirms and presupposes a belief in God. For more on this, see Gensler (2016: §8.2) and Thomas Carson (2007).

what these ideas mean. Atheists who point out shocking verses seldom bother to research how biblical experts understand these verses.

An Iranian philosophy grad student at the University of Tehran, Mohammad Kamiri, e-mailed me about a similar problem in Islam. Muslim scriptures, like Christian ones, have passages that convey golden-rule or love-neighbor, as well as ones that seem cruel and divisive; which should we follow? I answered like the previous answer and emphasized that we should interpret difficult passages using the religion's central teachings, which for both Christianity and Islam include loving God and loving neighbor.[8] As some atheists unfairly criticize Christian verses without trying to understand them, so too some Christians criticize Muslim verses this same unfair way; I condemn both.[9]

> *Matthew 21:18–19.* In the morning, as [Jesus] was returning to the city, he was hungry. And seeing a fig tree by the wayside he went to it, and found nothing on it but leaves only. And he said to it, 'May no fruit ever come from you again!' And the fig tree withered at once.

Most biblical scholars think this action was symbolic, teaching that our faith must bear fruit in action instead of being just for show. A faith that doesn't express itself in how we live is like a fig tree that produces no fruit. Matthew 7:19 says "Every tree that does not bear good fruit is cut down and thrown into the fire" and is similarly about faith that doesn't express itself in action.

> *Exodus 21:23–25.* If any harm follows, then you shall give life for life, eye for eye, tooth for tooth, hand for hand, foot for foot, burn for burn, wound for wound, stripe for stripe.

Paul Copan's *Is God a Moral Monster? Making Sense of the Old Testament God* (2011) can help to neutralize difficult passages. He follows earlier Christian thinkers (§6.3) about not taking the Bible all literally, and Augustine's advice about not taking literally what goes against central biblical teachings (like love-neighbor and God being loving). Copan adds that ancient Israelites

---

8 http://www.acommonword.com has a strong statement massively supported across Islam on the centrality of love of God and neighbor (the latter often expressed using the golden rule). The Iranian grad student claimed (and I'd agree) that the golden rule, being rational and global, has priority as we interpret difficult passages.

9 I got an anti-Islam e-mail criticizing Koran 48:29, about being "ruthless to unbelievers but merciful to one another." I suggested searching the Web to see how Muslim scholars take the passage (most translations are softer than "ruthless," using words like "forceful" and "firm of heart"). I added that Christianity too has verses that seem embarrassing at first, and we need to see how Christian scholars take these verses before drawing conclusions.

(including King David) were often morally crude. Some biblical rules that we see as crude were progressive by Near Eastern standards, motivated by all being created in "God's image and likeness" (Genesis 1:27). Many rules were meant not to hold forever but to lift a crude and barbaric people a little higher. So the "eye for an eye" rule was meant to move morality forward a little, by having us only knock out ONE eye (instead of TWO eyes) from someone who knocked out ONE of our eyes. Jesus later (Matthew 5:38–39) totally rejects "eye for an eye" (which Gandhi said would leave us all blind and toothless).

The most difficult passages are those that seem to command genocide:

> *Deuteronomy 20:16–18.* But in the cities of these peoples that the Lord your God gives you for an inheritance, you shall save alive nothing that breathes, but you shall utterly destroy them, the Hittites and the Amorites, the Canaanites and the Perizzites, the Hivites and the Jebusites, as the Lord your God has commanded.

Copan points out that ancient peoples often used exaggerated language which shouldn't be taken literally. The Bible says that the Israelites *killed all the Canaanites* – men, women, children, and animals – *complete genocide*; but years later, they're still fighting Canaanites, so evidently the language was exaggerated. We sometimes use such exaggerated language today, as when we say we "killed" our football opponents (but indeed we may play them again later, so they weren't really killed).

Copan often appeals to other factors, like the meaning of words, different ways to interpret a passage, and cultural background. It's poor thinking to pick random statements written thousands of years ago and, in ignorance of linguistic and historical context (which can often be easily researched), draw negative conclusions. Many who attack religion on the basis of the scriptural problem of evil do just that.

9
Why So Many Religions?

We'll begin by listening to the fictional student Skepticus describe negatively the diversity of religions across the world. As you read Skepticus's passage, first try to understand it in a sympathetic way, and then try to find problems with it. We'll later consider objections. And then we'll talk about the golden rule, which is important in all major world religions and most minor ones.

9.1 Skepticus: Chaotic Religious Diversity

This is Skepticus again. When I look at the huge religious diversity across the world, I see the sorry side of humanity.

Every groundless superstition abounds somewhere. There's just one God, or two (maybe a god and goddess), or a triple God, or several gods, or millions of gods. Maybe trees and frogs are gods, or each of us has a little god inside. Maybe the One, a Being beyond gods, produced the gods. Or maybe there's no god as such, but all the universe together is like a god. The theological diversity makes me dizzy.

Why are there so many religions? If there's a God, then he would have revealed himself more clearly and uniformly. If there's no God, then likely diverse humans just created wildly different make-believe supernatural beings.

Each religion thinks it's *the one, true religion* – all other religions are false. Since the various religions are all pairwise incompatible, at most one can be true (if even that); this is a matter of logic. So if you accept a religion, and there are thousands of different religions, then your chance of accepting the one, true religion is very small. In light of this, isn't it narrow minded to think your religion is *the true one*?

Religious practices vary, from universal love to castes, slavery, and human sacrifice. Alcohol can be forbidden as evil – or respected and used in sacred ceremonies. How about pork and caffeine? How many wives can you have? Do you sacrifice animals or virgins in your worship? Different cultures – some very ignorant or cruel – have created a bewilderingly diversity of religious practices and norms.

DOI: 10.4324/9781003320920-10

Despite some words about love, each religion tends to treat those of other religions badly. Believers think their own religion is special – *the true religion*, so other religions and their followers are evil. Thus religion divides people.

If you accept a religion, then you reject every religion besides your own as a FALSE religion. I also reject all the religions that you reject, but I reject yours, too.

> Before going on, reflect on your reaction to Skepticus's passage. Do you see any problems with it?

9.2 Analysis: Similarities and Differences

Despite what Skepticus says, religions aren't "true" or "false," except derivatively. Statements (or propositions, or beliefs that express these) are true or false.

We Christians believe many things. Our core, essential beliefs are in the ancient creeds, especially the Nicene and Apostles' Creed. The latter begins, "I believe in God, the Father almighty, the creator of heaven and earth." If you don't believe this, you aren't a Christian in any significant way. There are other authoritative beliefs, from church councils and (especially for Catholics) from the pope. Eventually, you get down to beliefs that are more a matter of opinion.

Skepticus says that any two religions are "pairwise incompatible"; this means that some essential beliefs of the first religion are logically incompatible with some essential beliefs of the second. I doubt that this is always true. I remember a talk from someone who claimed to be both Christian and Hindu, who said that the essential beliefs of his two faiths don't contradict each other. While this is perhaps an easy example (since Hinduism is light on essential beliefs), I'm sure that we could find many cases where the essential beliefs of a pair of different religions don't conflict.

My Catholic faith speaks positively about other faiths and how beliefs often overlap. Vatican II (1962–65) in *Nostra Aetate* says:

> The Catholic Church rejects nothing that is true and holy in these religions. She regards with sincere reverence those ways of conduct and of life, those precepts and teachings which, though differing in many aspects from the ones she holds and sets forth, nonetheless often reflect a ray of that Truth which enlightens all men.

I once tried to formulate briefly what were for me the most important Christian beliefs. I wanted a very short formula that had not all core beliefs but just a few really central ones. My result was "*Love God, love neighbor, Jesus is Lord"* – seven words, nine syllables, the "Gensler Creed." Each part can be unpacked further (§11.2):

1. *Love God.* Love the Lord your God with all your heart and mind and soul and strength, in this world and the next. This presupposes belief in God.
2. *Love neighbor.* Love your neighbor as yourself, in this world and the next. And live the golden rule, "Treat others as you want to be treated."
3. *Jesus is Lord.* This ancient creedal statement proclaims Jesus's divinity, as true God and true man and thus the bridge between God and man.

If we compare these with other world religions, we see similarities and differences.

(1) "Love God" is shared with other monotheistic religions, like Judaism and Islam, and presupposes "There's a God." Most people on the planet belong to a *monotheistic religion*, accept "Love God" and "There's a God," and thus share important truths about God with my religion.
(2) "Love neighbor" and golden-rule analogues are part of practically every religion. So when I meet someone of *any other religion*, I can *expect* that there's at least one key area that we share.[1] Since the golden rule is so widespread and important, we'll say much about it in the rest of this chapter.
(3) "Jesus is Lord" distinguishes Christianity from other religions (which, as in Judaism or Islam, may accept Jesus as a rabbi, holy man, or prophet – but not as God). So there are *differences and similarities* between religions, and we need to recognize both.

Not all Christians are so openminded about other faiths. If you search the Web for my "There are many paths to God" slogan, you'll find conservative Christians who think it violates Christianity, which says that *Jesus is the only path to God*. The issue is about a disputed gospel verse: "Jesus answered, 'I am the way, the truth, and the life; no one comes to the Father except through me'" (John 14:6).

There are three main ways to interpret this verse:

1. *Exclusivism.* Unless you have *explicit faith in Jesus in this life*, you won't be saved. So non-Christians all go to hell.
2. *Inclusivism.* Non-Christians and atheists can be saved, but the final Kingdom of God is brought about by Jesus, who has a unique status as true God and true man and the unique bridge between God and man.

---

1 When I meet those of other faiths, I *expect* them (given no contrary evidence) to follow a GR or love-neighbor approach, which is so universal across the world's religions. Unfortunately, some perverted religious factions teach hatred (§2.5), so my initial expectation may be wrong.

3. *Radical pluralism.* All religions have the exact same message, the fatherhood of God and the brotherhood of man. We should ignore apparent disagreements on other points.

(1) *exclusivism* is a bad interpretation. It makes God unjust and evil, since he eternally torments non-Christians who don't deserve it; this violates Augustine's idea (§6.3) that we shouldn't take a verse literally if doing so clashes with purity of life or soundness of doctrine – and (1) clearly clashes with God's justice and love. (1) also clashes with Jesus's openness toward other faiths; should Jesus have explained the Good Samaritan parable (Luke 10:24–37, §9.6) differently and said that the Samaritan is evil and going to hell because he didn't help the stranger *from explicit faith in Jesus*? And several verses clash with option (1)'s narrowness if you take them literally and without qualification: Lamentations 3:31–33, 1 Corinthians 15:22 & 15:28, 1 Timothy 4:10, and Colossians 1:17–20. Option (1) is biblical literalism at its worst.

(2) *inclusivism* is the mainstream Christian view; I accept it, as do C.S. Lewis (1952) and Vatican II of the Catholic Church (§8.6 Q7). It permits non-Christians to be saved and many paths to God. I reserve the term "bridge" for Jesus's special status and function as true God and true man.

(3) *radical pluralism* goes too far, since there are *differences and similarities* between religions, and we need to recognize both. It's arrogant and insulting to tell other religions that no, sorry, they don't really believe such-and-such, because this goes beyond the only two doctrines that a religion is permitted to have.

9.3 Analysis: Fellow GR Pilgrims, or Enemies?

Unfortunately, Skepticus is right when he thinks people often see those of other faiths as enemies. It's better to see those of other faiths, and nonbelievers too, as *fellow pilgrims* on the long journey to God. As fellow pilgrims, we can help each other as we travel. Nonbelievers can help by challenging our ideas about God's existence and pushing us to understand and defend them more deeply. All, or almost all,[2] on life's long pilgrimage share one important idea that will help greatly in our travels together: *the golden rule*, "Treat others as you want to be treated."

A few years ago, people from all over the world, representing more faiths than you ever knew existed, met at the Parliament of the World's Religions (1993). Together they overwhelmingly passed a *global ethics document*

---

2 "Almost all" provides for perverted religious factions that teach hatred (§2.5).

endorsing the golden rule as "the irrevocable, unconditional norm for all areas of life"; they also endorsed four commandments (against killing, stealing, lying, and adultery) that can be based on GR. So they together see GR as part of their own religious tradition.[3]

Anthropologists, too, after emphasizing cultural differences for so long, have come to accept *ethical universals*, present in the great majority of cultures. A summary of research says this (Kinnier et al. 2000: 5) about GR:

> Perhaps the most agreed-upon universal moral value is the Golden Rule. Several writers . . . have identified the many (only slight) variations of "Do unto others as you would have them do unto you" found within all of the major religions. The case for the universality of the Golden Rule is most impressive.

So there's evidence that GR is a *global norm*, present in many religions and cultures across the planet.

Despite GR being so universal, not all religious people follow it in their dealings with other religions. A few years ago, a Christian pastor celebrated a burn-a-Qur'an day; but he'd probably complain if Muslims celebrated a burn-a-Bible day.

I try to treat other religions as I want mine to be treated. But how do I want my faith to be treated? I want others, when they approach my Christian faith, to:[4]

- listen carefully, be fair, show respect, and not distort;
- not generalize from a few bad cases (don't say that *all* Christians are evil just because a *few* are);
- not compare the best of their faith with the worst of mine;
- give Christianity the benefit of the doubt (don't take verses about hating your parents like Luke 14:26 literally, when most Christians don't);
- neither deny nor exaggerate differences between their faith and mine;
- grant Christians *freedom of religion* – the right to choose their religion, without persecution, threats, or intimidation.

We likewise, following GR, ought to treat those of other religions fairly.

The shared GR also give us a common basis to criticize some flawed religious views, such as the perverted "Hate your enemies" idea that Jesus criticized (§2.5).

---

3 My GR chronology has much data about GR across history and across the world: http://harryhiker.com/chronology.htm or http://harrycola.com/chronology.htm.

4 Christian Troll (2008) (a Christian and Jesuit) and Sohaib Saeed (2010) (a Muslim) both apply GR to how we ought to treat those of other faith perspectives.

Why are there so many religions? People say things like:

- Religion results when a spark of divinity strikes a blob of humanity. It happens all over the world, in different cultures in widely separated areas, with blobs at different levels of development. Some think the early Israelites were polytheists (Yahweh was their local god), then henotheists (there were many gods, but Yahweh was the greatest), then monotheists (Yahweh is the one God) – all three having traces in the Old Testament.
- There are many paths to God. We don't all have to follow the same path.
- God is too big to fit into one religion. We struggle to worship him and picture him and never do so adequately. It's helpful to have different faiths that we can learn from.
- It can be difficult to decide between faiths (as some students who are brought up in two faiths may eventually have to do) on the basis of which faith better represents God's revelation and presence.
- Qur'an 5:48 suggests that God pushes different faiths to compete with each other in doing good.

Different religions often say different things about GR; usually these are additional insights that we can incorporate into our own understanding.

The rest of this chapter is about the golden rule, a common core value of the many religions of the world. We need to see how GR works and then connect it with religions and sciences. The basic rational ethical insight behind GR is that *we ought to be consistent in thought and action*, and this in light of understanding the situation and imagining ourselves in different places in the situation.

9.4 Analysis: The Golden Rule

The golden rule says "Treat others as you want to be treated."[5] The idea is global. It's common to all major world religions; Confucius, Hillel, Jesus, and many others used it to sum up how to live. For centuries across the planet, it's been important in families and professions and in thinkers and cultures, both religious and nonreligious. Today it's part of a growing global-ethics movement.

I'll start with a story (Grimm Brothers 1812). There once was a grandpa who lived with his family. As Grandpa grew older, he began to slobber and spill his food. So the family had him eat alone. When he dropped his bowl and broke it, they scolded him and got him a cheap wooden bowl. Grandpa was so unhappy. Now one day the young grandson was working with wood.

---

5 For more on GR, see Gensler (2017a: ch. 7–9) or Gensler (2013a). See also Wattles (1996).

"What are you doing?" Mom and Dad asked. "I'm making a wooden bowl," he said, "for when you two get old and must eat alone." Mom and Dad then looked sad and realized how they were mistreating Grandpa. So they decided to keep quiet when he spilled his food and let him eat with the family.

The heart of GR is *switching places*. You step into another's shoes. What you do to Grandpa, you imagine being done to you. You ask, "Am I willing that if I were in the same situation then I be treated that same way?"

GR seems simple. We want others to tell us the truth and not steal from us, so this is how we treat them. But GR's loose wording can be confusing to apply and can give strange results. We need to understand GR more clearly.

I put my attempt at a clearer wording on a t-shirt.[6] My shirt has symbols for eight major GR world religions arranged alphabetically (Bahá'í, Buddhism, Christianity, Confucianism, Hinduism, Islam, Judaism, and Taoism):

Many people nod in approval to my formula, which is intended to help us apply GR to difficult cases. Note the *same situation* clause: "Treat others only as you consent to being treated *in the same situation*."

My formula commands consistency. It demands a fit between my *act* toward another and my *desire* about how I'd be treated in the same situation. GR doesn't replace other moral norms or give all the answers. GR doesn't say specifically what to do (and so doesn't command bad actions if we have flawed desires). Instead, it forbids an inconsistent combination.

Don't combine these:

- I do something to another.
- I'm unwilling that this be done to me in the same situation.

---

6 Http://harryhiker.com/gr and http://harrycola.com/gr are my *golden rule* Web pages, with much information and many links. Scroll to the bottom to buy GR shirts.

GR, far from being a vague platitude, is a precise consistency test. Suppose I force Grandpa to eat alone. I switch places in my mind: I imagine that *I'm* forced to eat alone in the same situation. Do I condemn this same act done to me? Then I condemn how I treat Grandpa. *I condemn how I treat another if I condemn the same act when I imagine it done to me in the same situation.*

Switching places is a golden idea that's global and beautifully simple. It promotes justice, consideration, cooperation, and unity. But alas, there are ways to mess up the GR reasoning, and I call these "GR fallacies."

9.5 Analysis: Five GR Fallacies

I'll now present five GR fallacies and illustrate each with a story.

> (1) *The literal GR fallacy* assumes that everyone has the same likes, dislikes, and needs that we have.

There once lived a monkey and a fish. The monkey followed GR, always trying to treat others as he wanted to be treated. But he sometimes applied GR foolishly. Now one day a big flood came. As the threatening waters rose, the monkey climbed a tree to safety. He looked down and saw a fish struggling in the water. He thought, "I wanted to be lifted from the water." And so he reached down and lifted the fish from the water, to safety on a high branch. Of course that didn't work. The fish died.

The monkey applied GR literally: *treat others as you want to be treated*. He wanted to be lifted from the water, so he lifted the fish from the water. He didn't consider how monkeys and fish differ. Being lifted from the water saves a monkey but kills a fish. So the monkey applied GR foolishly.

Here's another example. I visit my sister Carol at her house. In the morning, I wake energized and like to chat. But Carol hates early chatting, since she needs to wake up before she can deal with others. Should I chat with Carol? The literal GR says yes: "If I want Carol to chat with me, then I'm to chat with her." But this is inconsiderate, since her needs differ from mine.

Or suppose I'm a waiter, and I hate broccoli (which I do). Becky orders broccoli (which she likes). Should I serve her broccoli? Not by the literal GR, which says: "If you want Becky not to serve you broccoli, then don't serve her broccoli." Becky would be upset, and I'd likely be fired.

So it may be wrong to treat others *in their situation* as I want to be treated *in my situation* – since their situation may be different. Does this show that GR is flawed? Many think so. They contend that GR wrongly assumes that everyone's the same (in likes, dislikes, needs, and so on). Since we're not all the same, they conclude, GR is simplistic and flawed. I think, rather, that this literal understanding of GR is flawed. Fortunately for us, the island with a foolish monkey also had a wise monkey.

Kita was a wise GR monkey. She learned that fish die when lifted from water. When the flood came, she considered lifting a fish from the water. But she imagined herself in his situation. She asked, "Am I now willing that if *I were in the same situation as the fish*, then I be lifted from the water?" She answered, "Gosh no: this would kill me!" So she left the fish in the water.

We are to treat others only as we consent to being treated *in the same situation*. We imagine ourselves having all the other's qualities – including likes, dislikes, needs, and so on. So Kita asks: "Am I now willing that if I were in the same situation as the fish, then I be lifted from the water?" And she says "No, that would kill me."

The *same situation* clause also helps our other cases. So I ask, "Am I willing that if I were in the same situation as Carol (who hates early morning chatting), then someone chat with me in the morning?" I answer no; so I won't chat with her. Or I ask, "Am I willing that if I were in the same situation as Becky (who loves and ordered broccoli) then I be served broccoli?" I answer yes; so I can serve her broccoli.

By a marvelous coincidence, "Kita" is also an acronym (Know-Imagine-Test-Act) for some main elements in using GR wisely:

- *Know*. "How would my action affect others?"
- *Imagine*. "What would it be like to have this done to me in the same situation?"
- *Test for consistency*. "Am now I willing that if I were in the same situation then this be done to me?"
- *Act toward others* only as you're willing to be treated in the same situation.

When Kita considered lifting the fish from the water, she tried to *know* how her action would affect the fish. She *imagined* being in the fish's exact place and having this same thing done to her. She *tested* her consistency by asking: "Am I now willing that if I were in the same situation as the fish, then I be lifted from the water?" Finally, she *acted* on GR (by leaving the fish in the water).

Memorize the wording of the GR question: *"Am I now willing that if I were in the same situation then this be done to me?"* The underlined "willing that if" is important.

My favorite historical GR example is President John Kennedy's (1963) civil rights speech during the first black enrollment at the University of Alabama. While Kennedy didn't know about GR monkeys, his speech followed Kita. He first got people to *know* how blacks were treated as second-class citizens in voting, schooling, and jobs. He had whites *imagine* themselves being treated as second-class citizens because of skin color. To *test* their consistency, he asked whether they'd be content to being treated that way. Finally, he urged *acting* on GR: "The heart of the question is whether all

Americans are to be afforded equal rights and equal opportunities, whether we are going to treat our fellow Americans as we want to be treated."

The heart of morality is GR. And the heart of GR is switching places. What we do to Grandpa (or blacks, gays, or whomever we mistreat), we imagine being done to ourselves. And to avoid the literal GR fallacy, we can imagine ourselves in the other's exact place (having their likes, dislikes, needs, and so on).

> (2) *The soft GR fallacy* assumes that we should never act against what others want.

There once was a baby squirrel named Willy. Being curious but ignorant of electricity, he wanted to put his fingers into electrical outlets. Momma Squirrel considered stopping him. She asked, "If I were in Willy's exact place, then would I want to be stopped?" She answered no; if she were in his exact place, then she too would be a curious baby squirrel, ignorant of electricity, wanting to put fingers into outlets, and she wouldn't want to be stopped. Following GR foolishly, she didn't stop him. So Willy put his fingers into an outlet and was electrocuted.

Foolish Momma Squirrel asked the GR question wrongly, in a way that forced her to follow Willy's desires. She should have asked about her *present reaction to a hypothetical case*: "Am I now willing that if I were in Willy's situation then I be stopped from putting my fingers into electrical outlets?" She would have answered yes. She's willing that if she were a baby squirrel in his exact place then she be stopped. And she's grateful (now) for when her parents, showing tough love, stopped her from doing this when she was young.

Sometimes we need to act against what others want. We may need to stop a baby who wants to put fingers into electrical outlets, refuse a salesperson who wants to sell overpriced products, fail a student who doesn't work, defend against an attacker, or jail a dangerous criminal. And yes, we're now willing that if we were in their situation then we be treated that way. GR lets us act against what others want, as long as we're now willing that if we were in their situation then we be treated similarly.

> (3) *The doormat GR fallacy* assumes that we should ignore our own interests.

There once was a woman named Frazzled Frannie. Frannie wanted to follow GR. But she thought GR makes us always do what others want (the previous fallacy). So she said yes whenever anyone asked a favor. People took advantage of her, asking "Please loan me $50,000" and "Could you watch my children while I vacation for three months?" Frannie always said yes; she thought saying no violates GR and makes you a bad person. Soon

Frannie had no life. She became a doormat for others, serving their every whim, ignoring her own interests. She shriveled up and became cranky.

For every Frannie, there are a dozen Frannie-wannabes, who sometimes say no but feel guilty about this. Both groups misunderstand GR. GR doesn't force us to do what others want or say yes to unreasonable requests. GR lets us say no, if we're willing that if we request such things then others say no to us.

GR should build on self-love and extend this to others; it isn't supposed to destroy self-love and make you a doormat. GR works best if you love yourself and care about how you're treated. If you lack a healthy self-love, you need to build this up. See your good points more positively, and don't fixate on your defects. Repeat to yourself, "As others have needs and rights that ought to be respected, so too do I." Most of us have the opposite problem: we treat others, not ourselves, as doormats.

> (4) *The third-parties GR fallacy* assumes that we should consider only ourselves and the other person.

There once was a student named Pre-law Lucy. Lucy realized that she needed good grades to get into law school; but she was lazy. Now one day Lucy had a bright idea. She'd plead her case to her professor: "Please give me an undeserved A in this course so I can get into law school! This will help me and not hurt you – so there's no GR objection to this."

Alas, Lucy ignored third parties. If she's accepted, then another student will be rejected. Imagine yourself being rejected because a less qualified student gets accepted dishonestly. And if Lucy becomes a lawyer, then we've likely added another lazy and dishonest lawyer; imagine having to deal with such a lawyer.

The *generalized GR* has us satisfy GR toward each affected party: "Act only as you're willing for anyone to act in the same situation, regardless of where or when you imagine yourself or others." If your action affects X, Y, and Z, you must be willing that it be done regardless of your place in the situation. The affected parties may include future generations. This leads to the *carbon rule*: "Keep the earth livable for future generations, as we want past generations to have done for us."

> (5) *The easy GR fallacy* assumes that GR gives an infallible test of right and wrong that takes only seconds to apply.

There once was a woman named Electra. Electra wanted to follow GR, but she got her facts wrong. She thought severe electrical shocks were pleasant. So she shocked others and, yes, she was willing that if she were in their place then she be shocked.

While Electra satisfied GR consistency, she didn't get her facts right. Applying GR wisely requires more than sitting down in ignorance and asking how we want to be treated. To lead reliably to right action, GR must build on *knowledge* and *imagination*. But even if we're misinformed, GR doesn't command specific wrong acts – because it doesn't command specific acts; instead, GR forbids inconsistent combinations.

Keep in mind how we expressed the core principle of moral rationality:

> We ought to be consistent in thought and action, and this in light of understanding the situation and imagining ourselves in different places in the situation.
>
> (§9.3)

In thinking morally and in applying GR, we need all three factors to work together: consistency, understanding (knowledge), and imagination. False beliefs (like thinking severe electrical shocks are pleasant) lead us in the wrong direction.

Here's another example. There once was a coal-mine owner named Rich. Rich was very rich, but paid his workers only a miserly $1 a day. He was asked if he's willing that if he were in their place then he be paid only $1 a day. He said yes, and so was consistent. But he said yes only because he thought (wrongly) that his workers could live well on this much; if he knew how little $1 buys, he wouldn't have answered that way. Rich needed to get his facts right; he might have tried going to the store to buy food for his family with only $1 in his pocket.

Now suppose that Rich decides to run his mine by the golden rule. What would he do? Following Kita, he'd do four things.

(K) Rich would gain *knowledge*. He'd ask, "How are my company policies affecting others – workers, neighbors, customers, and so on?" To know this, Rich would need to spend time talking with workers and others.

(I) Rich would apply *imagination*. He'd ask, "What would it be like to be in the place of those affected by these policies?" He'd imagine himself as a worker (laboring under bad conditions for a poor salary) or a neighbor (with black smoke coming into his house). Or he'd imagine his children living as poorly as the workers' children.

(T) Rich would *test* his consistency by asking: "Am I now willing that if I were in the same situation (as my workers, neighbors, or customers) then I be treated that same way?" If the answer is no, then his actions clash with his desires about how he'd be treated in a similar situation – and he must change something. Changing company policies requires creativity. GR doesn't tell Rich what policies to consider; instead, it gives a way to *test* proposed policies. Any acceptable policy must be one he can approve regardless of where he imagines himself in the situation: as owner, worker, neighbor, or customer. The final solution will likely be a compromise that's minimally acceptable (but not ideal) from everyone's perspective.

(A) Rich would *act* on GR: "Treat others only as you consent to being treated in the same situation." Yes, it's a simple formula. But applying it wisely requires *knowledge* and *imagination* – which may be difficult. Our knowing and imagining will never be perfect. But the fact that we'll never do something perfectly doesn't excuse us from trying to doing it as well as we reasonably can.

Why does consistency require that we follow GR? Suppose I make Grandpa eat alone but am not willing that if I were in the same situation then I be treated that way. Why is that inconsistent? GR is based on two consistency norms: that we be *impartial* (make similar evaluations about similar actions, regardless of the individuals involved) and *conscientious* (live in harmony with our moral beliefs). If I'm impartial and conscientious, I'll necessarily follow GR. The argument for this is difficult but gives a deeper insight into GR.

Suppose I'm consistent. Then I won't make Grandpa eat alone unless I believe that this act is all right – and thus believe that if I were in the same situation then it be all right to be done to me – and thus am willing that if I were in the same situation then it be done to me. Hence, if I'm consistent, then I won't do something to another unless I'm willing that if I were in the same situation then it be done to me.

Abstract consistency arguments can justify my GR formula and many variations. So we might imagine someone else we care about (maybe our daughter) on the receiving end of the action. Or we might give consistency conditions not for *doing* something but for *wanting* something or for *holding a moral belief*. GR can be, and historically has been, worded in many ways. GR is a family of related ideas.

GR also fits well into a wide range of religions, philosophies, and sciences. GR is a point of unity in a diverse world.

9.6 Analysis: GR in Christianity

Religions have been great teachers of the golden rule. We'll now look at GR in Christianity (my faith) and other world religions (the next section).

In Matthew's gospel (7:12), Jesus gave GR as the summary of the Bible: "So always treat others as you want to be treated, for this sums up the Law and the prophets." "The Law and the prophets" refers to the Jewish scriptures (which we Christians call the *Old Testament*), which contain the 10 commandments and 603 other rules. Jesus sums these up using GR.

This GR verse is from Jesus's inaugural Sermon on the Mount (Matthew 5–7), which is still a good introduction to Christianity. It starts with beatitudes. Blessed are the poor in spirit, the meek, promoters of justice, peacemakers, and the merciful – for all will be rewarded. Then there are radical demands. Don't just act well, but also have pure inner dispositions (for example, about anger and lust). Love your neighbors *and* your enemies: do good to those who hate you. Care about divine, not human, approval. Pray to our common Father, free yourself from worries, trust God. Don't be judgmental; evaluate yourself by the same standards that you evaluate others. As you treat others, so God will treat you. So treat others as you want to be treated, for this sums up the Law and the prophets. Finally, put all these teachings into practice.

Jesus suggests various motives for following GR. One is self-interest: we'll be blessed if we follow GR. Blessed are those who are merciful to others, for they themselves will be given mercy. God will forgive us if we forgive others, but he'll condemn us if we condemn others. The measure we give is the measure we'll get; God will do to us as we do to others. We're also called to a higher moral perfection, to be perfect as our heavenly Father is perfect, caring about others for their own sake. Jesus's example and our gratitude to God give further motives to treat others well (as we want to be treated).

Jesus was asked to give the greatest commandment of the Jewish law. He gave two: "Love God above all things" and "Love your neighbor as yourself" (Matthew 22:35–40). He added that these sum up the Law and the prophets. So GR and the love norms both summarize how we are to live.

Luke's gospel (10:25–37) adds a wonderful parable about the Good Samaritan. There once was a man traveling from Jerusalem to Jericho. He was robbed, beaten, and left to die. While several people saw him and just passed by, the one who stopped to help was a Samaritan – a member of a hated religious faith. So Jesus's great parable about loving your neighbor features helping someone of another faith.

St. Paul, in his letter to the Romans (2:14–15), says that the moral law is written on everyone's hearts and minds, including those outside the Judeo-Christian tradition. Building on this and ancient Greek philosophy, later Christian thinkers accepted a "natural moral law" that saw the basic rules of right and wrong as built into our reason and accessible to people of every religion and culture. They saw the golden rule as a key part of this natural moral law.

Christianity has a strong GR tradition. St. Augustine said that GR is part of every nation's wisdom and leads us to love God and neighbor (whom we want to love us). St. Francis of Assisi used perhaps the earliest *same situation* clause, in "Blessed is the person who supports his neighbor in his weakness as he would want to be supported were he *in a similar situation.*" St. Thomas Aquinas saw GR as common to the gospels and to human reason – and a way to analyze "Love your neighbor as yourself." Martin Luther and John Calvin saw GR as a practical way to learn how to live. Popes John Paul II and Benedict XVI emphasized GR's role in interfaith dialogue. And Pope Francis used GR in his 2015 talk to the US Congress about immigration.

How does GR ("Treat others as you want to be treated") relate to "Love your neighbor as yourself"? There are several plausible views here. The *equivalence* view says both mean the same thing: "Love your neighbor as yourself" = "Take your self-love as the model of how to treat others" = "Treat others only as you're willing to be treated in the same situation."

The *complementarity* view sees love as giving a *motivation* (to care about others for their own sake) and GR as giving a *procedure* to translate this into action.

- Love-neighbor (care for others for their own sake) is the *highest motivation* for following GR. Some may follow GR from lower motives, like social conformity or self-interest.
- GR (with KITA) gives a *procedure* to move this love motivation into action. To love your children in the GR way, get to know them (including their needs and desires), imagine yourself in their place, and treat them only as you're willing to be treated yourself by a parent in the same situation.

Ideally, we'd use both together – we'd follow GR toward others because we care about them for their own sake.

9.7 Analysis: GR in Other Faiths

World religions divide into two main groups. We'll first look at *Abrahamic religions*, ones that trace their origin through Abraham. These include Judaism, Christianity, Islam, Bahá'í, and others. Abrahamic religions accept a supreme personal God who created the world out of love for us and revealed himself and his will through sacred writings. And they endorse GR and concern for others.

Judaism was the original Abrahamic religion. The Jewish bible doesn't have a classic GR formula, but it has some related ideas: "Love your neighbor as yourself" (Leviticus 19:18) and "Don't oppress a foreigner, for you well know how it feels to be a foreigner, since you were foreigners yourselves in the land of Egypt" (Exodus 23:9 and Deuteronomy 10:19). The latter suggests that, when we apply GR to migrants, we recall that our ancestors were migrants.

Judaism's classic GR source is a popular story in the Talmud about the Rabbi Hillel. A Gentile came to see Hillel and said he'd convert to Judaism if the Rabbi explained the Jewish Law (Torah) while he (the Gentile) stood on one foot. Hillel responded: "What is hateful to yourself, don't do to another. That is the whole Torah. The rest is commentary. Go and learn." Hillel gave GR as summarizing the Torah, which, with 613 commandments, needed a summary. Some Jews call GR "the Torah on one foot."

In Islam, the Qur'an is the highest revelation; also important are Hadiths (sayings or actions of Muhammad or companions). While the Qur'an lacks the phrase "Love your neighbor as yourself," it (4:36) says this in different words: "Show kindness and do good to parents, relatives, and orphans – to the near neighbor and the distant neighbor who is a stranger – to the companion by your side and the traveler that you meet." Islam's classic GR occurs in Hadiths, which attribute it to Muhammad: "None of you has faith until you desire for your neighbor what you desire for yourself."

Islam has a long and rich GR tradition. Here are quotes from an article I wrote[7] for a journal in Iran (where six of my books are available in Persian):

- Imam Ali (c. 650), Muhammad's relative: "What you prefer for yourself, prefer for others; what you find objectionable for yourself, treat as such for others. Don't wrong anyone, just as you would not like to be wronged; do good to others just as you would like others to do good to you."
- Ibn Arabi (c. 1230): "All the commandments are summed up in this, that whatever you'd like the True One to do to you, that do to His creatures."
- The Persian poet Sa'di (1259) wrote this, as displayed at the United Nations: "Human beings are members of a whole, In creation of one essence and soul. If one member is afflicted with pain, Other members uneasy will remain. If you have no sympathy for human pain, The name of human you cannot retain."
- Hazrat Khan (1922): "Although different religions, in teaching man to act harmoniously and peacefully, have different laws, they all meet in one truth: do unto others as you would they should do unto you."
- Abdullah An-Na'im (2008): "My right to be myself requires me to accept and respect the right of others to be themselves too, on their own terms. The golden rule is the ultimate cross-cultural foundation of the universality of human rights."

Bahá'í, founded in Persia 200 years ago, believes in one God and just one religion; God revealed himself through prophets that include Abraham, Moses, Krishna, Buddha, Zoroaster, Christ, Muhammad, and Bahá'u'lláh. Humanity is one family. The classic Bahá'í GR says: "If your eyes be turned towards justice, choose for your neighbor that which you choose for yourself."

The Bahá'í have seven temples throughout the world, and I visited the one north of where I lived in Chicago. This beautiful temple is open to all faiths. The information center has a poster that says: "The children of men are all brothers, and the prerequisites of brotherhood are manifold. Among

---

7 Http://harryhiker.com/persia&gr.pdf or http://harrycola.com/persia&gr.pdf.

them is that one should wish for one's brother that which one wishes for oneself."

Non-Abrahamic religions, ones that didn't originate through Abraham, are more diverse. They may believe in one God, many gods, or no gods, so the theology varies. What is common is GR and concern for others.

Hinduism, India's traditional religion, is colorful and complex, with vast scriptures, complicated spiritualities, and many gods (but often taken to represent aspects of one supreme God). It believes in Karma, that the good or evil we do to others will come back to us, in this life or a future reincarnation. And it believes that we're all mystically identical to our neighbor and to God, so if I harm my neighbor, then I harm myself, for my neighbor *is* myself.

Of the many Hindu GR passages, my favorite is from the *Mahabharata*:

> One who practices the religion of universal compassion achieves his highest good. . . . One who regards all creatures as his own self, and behaves towards them as towards his own self . . . attains happiness. . . . One should never do to another what one regards as hurtful to one's own self. This, in brief, is the rule of righteousness. . . . In happiness and misery, in the agreeable and the disagreeable, one should judge of effects as if they came to one's own self. *Mahabharata*.
> (c. 400, bk. 13: Anusasana Parva, §113)

Buddhism, which started in India and spread to China, has many branches. Most don't believe in gods, but some believe in many gods or one supreme God. Buddhism talks about controlling desires, loving enemies, and having compassion for all. The classic Buddhist GR says "Hurt not others with what pains yourself."

GR fits Buddhist compassion and peace of mind. The peaceful serenity suggested by Buddha statues goes well with how to respond to evil done to us (c. 500 BC):

> "He insulted me, hit me, beat me, robbed me" – brooding on this increases violence; not brooding on this decreases violence. Violence increases through violence but decreases through non-violence. If a man foolishly does me wrong, I will return to him the protection of my ungrudging love; the more evil comes from him, the more good shall go from me.

Treating others as badly as they treat us (revenge) divides people; it brings violence and inner torment. Being forgiving and non-violent to others, as we want them to be to us, unites people; it brings inner peace and serenity. Hate is poison, love brings life.

Confucius's *Analects* teaches an elevated morality that sets the tone for ethical thinking in China. He writes as a sage – with proverbs, anecdotes, and brief dialogues. He focuses on how to live and says little about gods, karma, or the afterlife. When challenged to sum up his teaching, Confucius (c. 500 BC 15:23) uses GR:

> "Is there one word which can serve as the guiding principle for conduct throughout life?" Confucius said, "It is the word altruism (*shu*). Don't do to others what you don't want them to do to you."

Shu also translates as "reciprocity," "fellow-feeling," or "consideration for others."

I once taught an ethics course in China in English at the University of Wuhan. On my first day, I wore a Confucian golden rule shirt of my own design, with his GR saying 己所不欲勿施於人 in Chinese. I told my students that we'd study Western ethics, yes, but also *global ethics* – and that our course's central GR idea is as rooted in their culture as it is in mine. I could begin this same way (using a different local language) practically anywhere in the world.[8]

Taoism for centuries in China was the chief rival to Confucianism and Buddhism. Taoism accepts many gods, is mystical and poetic, and emphasizes meditation and worship. It gave us acupuncture, t'ai chi, and yin-yang. It teaches three great virtues: love, moderation, and modesty. And it says: "Regard your neighbor's gain as your own gain and your neighbor's loss as your own loss."

Many other religions endorse GR. Paul McKenna, a friend who got me interested in GR's interfaith side, created a best-selling GR poster that also has Aboriginal religions, Jainism, Sikhism, Unitarianism, and Zoroastrianism.[9] My GR book (Gensler 2013a) also has Deism, Mormonism, Christian Science, Unification, Mohism, Shintoism, Greco-Roman polytheism, Yoruba, and Scientology. Augustine, who experienced many religions and philosophies, said in about 400 AD that GR was part of practically every nation's wisdom; people today are rediscovering this same insight.

Many atheists accept GR. I got an e-mail from an atheist complaining (with levity) about the lack of an atheist symbol on my GR shirt: "Why not an atheist GR shirt? Same rule for us, same logic, yes, just without supernatural justifications. Any thoughtful atheist likely supports GR in some form." Yes, atheists can support GR too. They might see GR as a self-evident moral

---

8 See http://harryhiker.com/china or http://harrycola.com/china. I'm trying to create similar GR shirts for further languages and religions, see https://www.zazzle.com/store/harrygensler.
9 See http://harryhiker.com/poster or http://harrycola.com/poster on how to get the poster.

truth, a cultural convention, reflecting altruistic feelings, promoting self-interest, part of a social contract that we accept to further our self-interest, endorsed by ideal observers, or built into our moral language. Believers can accept GR on these grounds too, but they add a religious dimension. So GR can be a point of unity between believers of all types and nonbelievers.

9.8 Analysis: GR and Evolution

Charles Darwin's (1809–82, §6.2) *Descent of Man* (1871) described human evolution. He saw the moral sense (conscience) as rightfully supreme over humans and the most important difference between humans and other animals. Analogues of morality exist in other *social animals*, such as dogs, wolves, ants, and bees. Wolves work together in packs and help each other. Dogs sympathize with another's distress or danger and show fidelity and obedience. Baboons follow a leader and enjoy being with each other; this promotes their survival. Many social animals have concern for the welfare of their offspring or comrades, even risking their safety. With social animals, evolution encourages instincts and behaviors that benefit the group's survival.

Humans are social animals, living in families or groups. We evolved social instincts. We enjoy helping others and are distressed by another's misery. We often show concern for others, especially offspring and group members. We value the approval of others, internalize group values, and follow the leader. Opposing our social instincts are anti-social impulses, like lust, greed, and vengeance.

Primitive morality had arbitrary taboos, little discipline, and little concern for those outside one's clan or tribe. But we gradually developed intellectual powers through observation, language, and reasoning. Morality became more rational, disciplined, and about consequences. As human groups expanded, so did our circle of concern. As religion purified our social feelings and moral instincts, we moved toward a higher morality, supported by reason and directed to everyone's good, even the weak and animals. Our noblest attribute became a love for all living creatures. GR sums up this higher morality: "Treat others as you want to be treated."

Evolution gave us two great gifts to promote our survival: *social instincts* and *reason*. Any social animal with strong *social instincts* would develop a moral sense when its *reason* becomes well developed. And so humans, according to Darwin, over many centuries developed from a narrow, instinctive concern for offspring and tribal members toward a higher, rational GR morality of concern for everyone.

I'll mention some further GR scientific studies. Neuroscience explains what goes on in our brain as we apply GR (Pfaff 2007, 2008). Psychology gives transcultural stages of moral thinking that lead to GR (Kohlberg 1973, 1979, 1981–84, Kohlberg and Levine 1990). Cognitive dissonance describes our built-in motivation to avoid inconsistencies, like GR violations (Festinger 1957; Aronson 1969). Child psychology shows how infants at three months don't like GR-violating puppets who hit other puppets. Classical conditioning shows how we associate pain behavior with our inner distress and later experience distress from seeing another's pain behavior; this motivates us to prevent in another what would cause pain if done to us. Social learning theory shows how we teach GR by example. And sociology discusses GR's advantages for group happiness and survival. Yes, there are many scientific paths to GR.

GR is a big part of who we are as human beings. We've discussed three factors behind this. *Philosophy* sees GR as part of a consistency norm that's essential to us as rational beings, as we evaluate views and make decisions. *Religion* finds GR everywhere, suggesting that God gifted it to us through revelation, creation, or both. *Science* – a mix of sciences, starting with biology and evolution – also affirms GR's presence and importance in our lives.

Our main concern here, though, is religion – and how centrally important GR is in practically every religion of the world. The next chapter goes further into the ethics-religion connection. We'll start with the question: "Is ethics based on religion?"

10
Is Ethics Based on Religion?

We'll begin by listening to the fictional student Skepticus find objections to the two main forms of religious ethics: divine command theory (DCT) and natural law (NL).[1] As you read Skepticus's passage, first try to understand it in a sympathetic way, and then try to find problems with it. We'll later consider objections.

10.1 Skepticus: Divine Command Theory

This is Skepticus again. Many religious philosophers accept *divine command theory*, which holds that ethics is based on religion. While I reject the view, I was surprised to hear that my friend and fellow philosophy-major Faith, who believes in God, also rejects this view, although she used to find it attractive. I asked her if she'd like to talk to me about the view, and she graciously agreed.

Faith started with a definition:

> *Divine command theory*: Moral judgments describe God's will. Calling something "good" means that God desires it. So "X is good" means "God desires X." Ethics is based on religion, and we pick our moral principles by following God's will.
>
> What does "God" mean? The usual definition is "the all-good, all-powerful, all-knowing Creator of the world." But this makes my definitions circular (since I'd use "God" to define "good," and then "good" to define "God"). It also suggests that standards of goodness exist prior to God's will (instead of God's will creating the standards). So it's better to define "God" as simply "the all-powerful, all-knowing Creator of the world."

---

1 Gensler (2016: ch. 2–6) discusses these more thoroughly, including nonsemantic and modified DCTs and a combination of DCT with natural law. DCT is also controversial in Judaism and Islam. For Judaism, see Harris (2003) and Brody (1974). For Islam, see Al-Attar (2010) and Michel (2010: 197–99); Al-Attar (2010: 109) nicely asks: "Does God create or clarify morality?" See also Williams (1972), Frankena (1973a & 1973b), Helm (1981), and Carson (2012).

There are three arguments for DCT, and at first I found them attractive. These argue from the Bible, from God's sovereign power, and from the source of morality. The first two are based on prior religious beliefs and show how DCT flows from religion.

(1) *Bible*. Given a belief in the Bible, DCT has to be true – because the Bible teaches it. The Bible uses "good" interchangeably with "what God desires," and God's writing the ten commandments on stone tablets teaches DCT vividly. So if you believe in the Bible, then you'll accept DCT.

The problem here (even if we assume that what the Bible teaches must be true) is that the Bible doesn't really teach DCT; properly understood, it doesn't take a stand for or against DCT. Years ago, my Bible teacher cautioned against using the Bible to answer questions that its authors didn't ask and wouldn't have made immediate sense to them. The biblical authors weren't concerned with Socrates's technical question about DCT (which we'll see later). So we shouldn't use the Bible to prove DCT.

The Bible teaches that *we ought to obey God*, but this is compatible with other views about ethics. Maybe we ought to obey God because his commands reflect a deeper knowledge of an independent moral order. In this non-DCT view, stealing isn't bad because God forbids it; instead, God forbids it because it's already bad. This non-DCT approach is consistent with the Bible; nothing in the Bible contradicts it. If so, then believing in the Bible doesn't require DCT.

(2) *Sovereign power*. If you believe in God, then you believe that all laws of every sort depend on God's will. But then all moral laws must depend on God's will. So God created the moral order, and his will distinguishes right from wrong. So if you believe in God, then you'll accept DCT.

The problem here (even if we assume that there's a God) is that it's doubtful that all laws depend on God's will. Is "$x = x$" true because of God's will and would have been false had God willed otherwise? This law seems true of its very nature, not true because God made it true. Maybe moral laws are the same. Maybe hatred is evil in itself, not evil because God made it so.

(3) *Source*. If you accept objective moral duties that bind you, you must accept that these have a source – and the only workable source is God. The source of objective duties can't be a non-person (these are lower than persons and so can't impose duties on persons), you (then your duties wouldn't bind since you could cancel them), or other individuals or society (these have no moral authority over us if they tell us to do wrong). Thus belief in objective moral duties requires belief in God. This argument doesn't presume belief in God, but it might lead to God as the source of duties.[2]

---

2 Given DCT, there's a very simple argument for God's existence: Something is good ∴ God desires something ∴ There's a God. Gensler (2016: 27–28) formulates and criticizes two other moral arguments for God's existence, one from Immanuel Kant (based on the highest good being impossible without God) and one from John Newman (based on how we experience conscience).

The problem here (even if we accept objective moral duties) is that it's doubtful that such duties need a source. To say they need a source assumes that "A ought to be done" means something like "X legislates A." But why accept this? Maybe basic moral truths (like the logical truth "x = x") are true in themselves, not true because someone made them true. Then they wouldn't need a source.

How does believing in the divine origin of values influence people's lives? I see three main influences.

- DCT followers see morality as objective and so take it seriously. So racist actions are objectively wrong, since God forbids them. Many are prepared to die for their moral beliefs and can't see how we could take morality seriously if it were based only on personal feelings or social approval.
- DCT followers connect morality closely to religion. So they have a strong religious motivation to be moral, and they follow a religious approach to moral education. They think we can't teach morality without teaching religion; if we try, children will grow up without firm values.
- DCT followers see atheists as confused about morality. How can atheists accept morality and try to live moral lives? Atheists likely got their values from a religious source. They lost their religion but kept the values – even though the values make sense only on a religious basis. So atheists who accept morality are confused. Clearheaded atheists, like Jean-Paul Sartre, reject morality, saying that everything is permissible if there's no God.

I, Faith, liked much about divine command theory. DCT is popular among ordinary people; it's not a view that only a philosopher could love. It explains morality simply and clearly. It makes morality objective; human values have to conform to a higher law. It can appeal to higher motives (unselfish love and gratitude to God) or lower ones (punishments and rewards). It can give us community support in living a moral life. And it can make morality part of our personal relationship with God.

10.2 Skepticus: Divine Command Objections

But, alas, Faith continued, I later found two big problems with DCT: the *atheism problem* and *Socrates's question*. I concluded that ethics and morality don't connect as closely as DCT claims; "X is good" doesn't mean "God desires X," and moral beliefs don't require belief in God.

(1) One problem is that DCT makes it impossible for atheists, like Skepticus, to make positive moral judgments. Imagine that Skepticus says "*Kindness is good, but there's no God.*" If "X is good" means "God desires X," then

this claim is self-contradictory (since it means "God desires kindness, but there's no God"). But it *isn't* self-contradictory. So "X is good" doesn't mean "God desires X."

1 If DCT is true, then atheists can't consistently make positive moral judgments.
2 Atheists can consistently make positive moral judgments.
∴ DCT isn't true.

My argument doesn't assume any alternative view about what "good" means. But it does assume that my friend Skepticus isn't contradicting himself when he makes positive moral judgments.

Some believers think such atheists *are* contradicting themselves, since their moral beliefs assume God's existence. Such believers often add: "Atheists first got their values from religion; they lost religion but kept the values, even though the values make sense only on a religious basis." But not all atheists got their values from religion. Morality can grow up in an atheist society that's never taken God's existence seriously. It's difficult to believe that such atheists by "good" mean "desired by God."

It's also difficult to believe that my atheist friend Skepticus uses "good" this way. Imagine that I'm discussing a moral issue with him. I suggest that we both say "desired by God" instead of "good." This would likely *end* the discussion; Skepticus surely doesn't use the two expressions as equivalent in meaning.

Could it be that believers, by "good," mean "desired by God," while atheists mean something else? Then atheists can make moral judgments, even though they deny God. But then how can believers and atheists have fruitful moral discussions? If both sides mean something different by "good," then they can't really agree or disagree *morally* – but at most only *verbally*. I can have fruitful moral discussions with people even if I know nothing about their religion, and these will mostly go the same regardless of religious beliefs. So believers and atheists seem to mean the same thing by "good." But atheists surely don't use "good" to mean "desired by God." So, presumably, neither believers nor atheists mean this by "good."

Also, it would be better to base ethics on something less controversial than religion.

(2) Socrates, the first major philosopher of ancient Greece, was a religious person who tried to follow God's will. He connected ethics closely to religion. But he rejected DCT in Plato's *Euthyphro* dialogue, largely on the basis of a penetrating question. Let's suppose that there's a God and he desires all good things. Then:

> Is a good thing good *because* God desires it? Or does God desire it *because* it is good?

Let's assume that kindness is good and God desires it. Which is based on which? Is kindness good because God desires it? Or does God desire kindness because it's already good (and God knows that it's good)?

Socrates and most people prefer the second alternative: God desires kindness *because he knows that it's good*. His desires don't make it good. Instead, he wouldn't desire it if it weren't already good. But then kindness is good prior to and independently of God's will. It would presumably be good even if there were no God. This alternative requires giving up DCT.

DCT holds that kindness is good *because God desires it*. Kindness wouldn't be good if God didn't desire it. Prior to God's desires, kindness is neither good nor bad. This answer seems to make ethics arbitrary.

Let's assume that hatred is bad, and God forbids it. Is hatred bad because God forbids it (so if he didn't forbid it, then it wouldn't be bad)? Or does God forbid it because it's already bad? "Already bad" seems better, but it requires giving up DCT.

This point is subtle but important. If you don't get the point, I suggest that you reread the last few paragraphs a few times until the idea comes through.

This might surprise you, but relatively few Christian philosophers clearly favor DCT (that God's will *makes* things good or bad). William of Ockham (Swindal 2005: 220–22) of the late Middle Ages was DCT's most famous defender. Suppose we assume DCT (that God's will *makes* things good or bad). We ask, "What if God desired hatred; would hatred then be good?" Ockham would have shouted, "Yes, if God desired hatred, then hatred would be good!" But this is implausible.[3] Imagine that an all-powerful and all-knowing being created a world and desired that its people hate each other. Would hatred then be good? Surely not! Such a creator would have an evil will. But then we can't say that "good" by definition is what the creator desires.

Also, DCT trivializes "God is good." In DCT, this means only "God is (or does) what is desired by God." But even evil people can be (or do) what they desire.

And so I, Faith, told Skepticus that I now reject DCT and prefer the natural law approach, which connects religion to ethics but also holds that some things are good or bad independently of God's will. As with my Socrates example, kindness is good in itself and hate bad in itself; we know these things by moral intuition.

Skepticus thanked me for my contribution and said that it clarified things in his mind, especially about the major objections to DCT.

---

3 Some say God couldn't do this, because his *nature* is to love (and not to hate). But what about a creator with a different nature, to hate – would such a being impose obligations on us? And if God's nature is necessarily good – and this necessarily goes with loving and not hating – then aren't we again assuming moral standards independent of God's will.

10.3 Skepticus: An Objection to Natural Law

This is Skepticus again. Religious thinkers who reject DCT (like Socrates and Faith) tend toward a *natural law* ethics, which seems much like intuitionism. In NL, basic moral principles are objectively true or false, but we can't reason about them; instead, we know them by moral intuitions. But society heavily influences moral intuitions. So "We ought to treat black people badly" may be *intuitively true* to someone in a racist society but *intuitively false* to someone in an egalitarian society, and reason can't resolve the issue. Intuitionism is much like emotivism, which is my view; but where emotivism sees a clash in feelings, intuitionism sees a clash in intuitions. In both views, we often can't rationally resolve moral disputes.

Natural law fits badly with belief in God. Suppose your racist society teaches you to have moral intuitions in favor of "Black people ought to be treated badly." And suppose that God's will, on the contrary, is that we love everyone and not be racist. How can natural law, which has us follow our moral intuitions, lead us to God's will – since it just tells us to follow our moral intuitions, which may be racist?

> Before going on, reflect on your reaction to Skepticus's passage. Do you see any problems with it?

10.4 Analysis: Natural Law and Racism

I accept *natural law*, which claims that basic objective moral truths are "written on the human heart" (St. Paul, Romans 2:14–15) instead of depending on society, personal feelings, or revelation. Such moral truths are based on reason, authoritative over our actions, the same for everyone, and known by nearly everyone. I see the basic moral truth as about *consistency*: "We ought to be consistent in thought and action, and this in light of understanding the situation and imagining ourselves in different places in the situation." This is built into us by evolution and leads to the golden rule (often used to summarize the moral law); the previous chapter talked about such things.

Skepticus raised this question about natural law:

> How can natural law, which has us follow our moral intuitions, lead us to God's will – since it just tells us to follow our moral intuitions, which may be racist [and thus go against God's will]?

Natural law, as I understand it, tells us to *be consistent and follow the golden rule* – which gives us good ways to criticize inherited racist intuitions; it doesn't just tell us to follow our moral intuitions, which may be flawed. We can reason about basic moral principles by appealing to *consistency*.[4]

To see how this works, consider a *shortist* norm that says "Short people ought to be treated badly."[5] Suppose you enjoy treating short people badly; your society endorses shortism; and you have strong shortist moral beliefs, intuitions, and feelings. Can your shortism be rationally criticized? Yes, it can, on the basis of consistency. Are you consistent in your shortist *principles, arguments*, and *actions*?

1. *Shortist principle*. "Short people ought to be treated badly, just because they're short."
2. *Shortist argument*. "Short people ought to be treated badly, because all short people are such and such, and all who are such and such ought to be treated badly."
3. *Shortist action*. You treat X badly because he's short. (Chapter 9 would criticize such actions using GR: "Don't treat X badly because he's short without being willing that this be done to you in the same situation.")

Now please read lines 1–3 again, but substituting "racism" for "shortism" and "black" for "short"; the lines still make sense. This same consistency framework is useful for different sorts of discrimination (racial, religious, gender, sexual orientation, etc.).

(1) *Shortist principle*: "Short people ought to be treated badly, just because they're short." This gives shortism as a *basic moral principle*, not dependent on other facts. To criticize the idea, we'll appeal to this, which is at the heart of moral rationality:

> We ought to be consistent in thought and action, and this in light of understanding the situation and imagining ourselves in different places in the situation.
>
> (§9.3)

Suppose you accept the *shortism principle*. To be consistent, you'd have to *believe that if you were short then you ought to be treated badly* – and *desire that if you were short then you be treated badly*. Consistency forbids a combination:

Don't combine these:

- I believe "All short people ought to be treated badly, just because they're short."
- I don't desire that if I were short then I be treated badly.

---

4 Gensler (2008: ch. 9) and (2013: ch. 8 & 9) have more on racism and other areas of applied ethics.
5 Here "badly" in my racism and shortism examples could be spelled out in different ways. Maybe such people should be beat up, made fun of, kept in low-paying jobs, denied the vote, restricted in education, or so on.

You'd likely violate this and be inconsistent – especially if you *know* what it's like to be treated badly and *imagine* yourself, vividly and accurately, in the place of short people treated this way. So, against Skepticus and many other thinkers, *we can reason about basic moral principles – on the basis of consistency*.

In rare cases, you could be *consistent* in holding shortism, since you may *believe* that you ought to be treated badly if you were short and *desire* to be treated that way in their place. But why would you have such strange beliefs and desires about how YOU are to be treated? Perhaps you *lack knowledge* – maybe you think short people enjoy being mistreated; then you need to understand the facts better. Or perhaps you *lack imagination* – maybe you never vividly and accurately visualize yourself on the receiving end of the action; then you need to do this. Or perhaps you have *perverted desires* – maybe society programmed you to hate short people so much that you hate yourself when you imagine yourself short and so desire that you then be treated badly.

Perverted desires against groups are unfortunately fairly common. All over the world, people are taught to hate those of another group. We teach young children: "Be suspicious of *those other people*. They're of a different race (religion, ethnic background, sexual orientation, or caste). They aren't our kind. They have strange customs and do strange things. They're evil and inferior." *People often believe very negative things about other groups on the flimsiest of evidence*. But when we broaden our knowledge and personal experience, we conclude, "They're people too, much like us, with many of the same virtues and vices." Rational moral thinking requires that we try to neutralize perverted desires against other groups; this can be difficult, because we may need to work against years of lies and other negative social conditioning. It's important we be able to rationally criticize perverted desires against a group by broadening our knowledge and experience of the other group in an open way.

(2) *Shortism argument*: "Short people ought to be treated badly, because all short people are such and such, and all who are such and such ought to be treated badly." Here's a specific argument with this structure:

1 All short people are evil.
2 All evil people ought to be treated badly.
∴ All short people ought to be treated badly.

This is silly, since premise 1 is ludicrously false, and premise 2 would be difficult to hold consistently. Let's instead discuss a racist argument that used to be popular.

I recall from the 1950s hearing people say (and I hated the idea even then) that *blacks should be treated badly because they're inferior*. This is an argument, with a *premise* ("Blacks are inferior") and a *conclusion* ("Blacks ought to be treated badly"). How should we respond? Should we counter with our own ideas, like "All races are genetically equal" or "People of all races ought to be treated equally"? While these are fine ideas, our racist opponent will just reject them. And then we'll have an irresolvable dispute, where the racist has his premises and we have ours, and neither can convince the other. It's better to raise objections that are more decisive.

I suggest that we express the racist's argument clearly and then watch it explode in his face. His conclusion, presumably, is about how *all* blacks ought to be treated. Since the conclusion has "all," the premises also must have "all." So he needs to claim that *all* blacks are inferior – and to add that *all* inferior people ought to be treated badly. His argument then goes this way:

1   All blacks are inferior.
2   All who are inferior ought to be treated badly.
∴   All blacks ought to be treated badly.

To clarify this further, we can ask what the racist means by "inferior." What exactly puts someone into the "inferior" group? Is it IQ, education, wealth, physical strength, or what? Let's suppose that the racist decides on an IQ criterion: "inferior" = "of IQ below 80." Then his argument goes:

1   All blacks have an IQ of less than 80.
2   All who have an IQ of less than 80 ought to be treated badly.
∴   All blacks ought to be treated badly.

Once he assigns this or another clear meaning to "inferior," we see that his inferior/non-inferior division cuts across racial lines. Every race has some members with IQ less than 80, and some with IQ of greater than 80. So premise 1 is clearly false. And premise 2 ("All who have IQ of less than 80 ought to be treated badly") would apply to *whites* of low IQ. To be consistent, the racist must hold that such *whites* ought to be treated badly (as he treats blacks), and he must treat them this way himself and desire that others do so too. The racist won't be consistent on this.

The problem with using an intelligence criterion to justify treating blacks badly is this: It's very clear that *some blacks are smarter than some whites*; even the most twisted racist has to admit this. So any intelligence criterion for treating people badly would either (1) treat some whites badly (as the racist wants to treat blacks) or (2) treat some blacks well (as the racist wants to treat whites). Either result clashes with the racist's view: that all whites ought to be treated well and all blacks badly.

Our strategy for criticizing racist arguments has three steps:

1. Formulate the argument into clear premises and a conclusion, where the conclusion follows from the premises.

2. Criticize the factual premises, if necessary.
3. Test whether the racist applies his moral premise consistently, especially to his own race.

If the racist's conclusion is about how *all* blacks (or Jews, women, gays, or whatever) are to be treated, then he needs a criterion to separate the groups cleanly, so all blacks will be on one side and all whites on the other. An IQ number doesn't do this – and neither does any other plausible criterion. These considerations of logic and consistency can destroy most racist arguments.

(3) *Shortist action*: You treat X badly because he's short. (Chapter 9 would criticize such actions using GR: "Don't treat X badly because he's short without being willing that this be done to you in the same situation.")

Skepticus asked how natural law can help us find God's will. He wrongly thought that natural law just tells us to follow our moral intuitions; the problem here is that we may have flawed moral intuitions from society (like racist ones) that go against God's will. A better understanding is that natural law tells us to *be consistent and follow the golden rule*, and these help us to criticize racist intuitions. God's will (according to almost every religion that has ever existed) tells us to follow the golden rule. Natural law helps us to find God's will, as expressed in the golden rule, and put it into practice.

10.5 Analysis: Knowing God's Will

How can we know God's will? Religious thinkers propose that we can know God's will through (1) the Bible, (2) the church, (3) prayer, or (4) reason – or (5) we *can't* know God's will – or (6) we should *combine* these answers.

(1) *Bible*. Some were brought up to believe that the Bible teaches clear-cut answers to all moral issues. But there are gray areas where people interpret the Bible differently. During the Vietnam war, many Christian pacifists thought it wrong to kill a human for any reason, even self-defense; they took "Thou shalt not kill" and "Turn the other cheek" literally. Others thought it their duty to fight the "godless Communists"; they quoted passages urging the Israelites to conquer their enemies. Which side was right? Should a biblical Christian be a pacifist or a militarist? And how do we decide this? I think we need to understand individual passages in the light of the Bible's general message. People who try to do this may interpret things differently. So the Bible leaves us with gray areas. And the Bible doesn't directly address many issues.

Also, which religion and bible should we follow? Jews, Muslims, and Mormons have different scriptures. But nearly all religions have the same general message about God's will, that God wants us to have concern and love for each other and treat others as we want to be treated. The details vary, but the general message is the same.

(2) *Church*. Many see their church as a moral authority. Some think their church teaches an unchanging and infallibly true moral system, and we must accept everything it says. But history shows that church teaching has evolved over the years and sometimes has blind spots that need correction. Many look at their church as a wise teacher; they listen and try to learn – but in the end may disagree on some details. Perhaps the church's biggest moral role is to encourage people to think and act in a way that's based on love and knowledge.

(3) *Prayer*. Many pray to God for guidance, and then take their feelings as a sign of God's will. But our feelings can distort God's will. We've all seen religious fanatics who feel God wants things that in fact are crazy and hateful. So we need input from the Bible, church, and reason to help us to form our conscience.

(4) *Reason*. Our NL moral rationality follows the GR and love-neighbor message that's an important part of almost every religion that has ever existed. So moral rationality can be an excellent way to know God's will – and it has allies in other sources (the Bible, church, and prayer). Reason is especially useful in thinking about new cases, areas where other methods conflict, or moral controversies.

(5) *Can't know*. Some think God's will is completely unknowable, since God is above our little minds. Romans 11:34 asks, "Who has known the mind of the Lord?" – which suggests that we can't know God's will. But surely we know *some* things about God's will, even though we can't know all the details.

(6) *Combine*. I think religious people need to combine all four sources: the Bible, the church, prayer, and reason. Where the sources speak clearly and in unison, our belief is solid. So it's clear that God wants us to love each other and to treat others as we want to be treated. It's also clear that God opposes stealing, lying, adultery, and killing – and racism (which violates "Love your neighbor"). But there are gray areas, like pacifism. Here we follow our prayer and reason as best we can, while we gain insight from the Bible and the church. In these gray areas, we should be less confident of our beliefs and more tolerant of opposing views.

10.6 Analysis: Natural Law's Three Parts

Natural law is an ethical tradition that goes back to the medieval St. Thomas Aquinas (1224–74), or earlier. Natural law is multi-dimensional, emphasizing reason, biology, and our supernatural destiny. For religious thinkers, it's the main alternative to DCT, which bases ethics directly on *God's will*. Natural law instead bases ethics on *reason* – God's reason and our reason – and how God made us, for his purposes, with a specific three-part nature, which brings certain duties. While the full natural law approach is religious, atheists like Skepticus can accept a pared-down NL by ignoring any part that mentions God.

As noted earlier, the term *natural law* (or *natural moral law*) refers to objective moral principles that are "written on the human heart" (Romans 2:14–15). Such norms are based on reason, the same for everyone, authoritative over our actions, and known by nearly everyone. GR is often used to summarize the moral law.

In natural law, God is a supremely good being. Calling God "good" doesn't mean that he fulfills his own desires. Instead, it means that his life fits inherent truths about goodness – for example, that love is good in itself and hatred bad in itself. In natural law, basic moral truths are true in themselves. Both believers and atheists can use their God-given reason to know these truths. But some people are poor at moral thinking, so it's useful to have a second way to know the basic moral truths, through religion and the Bible. Believers also have additional motives for doing the right thing; an important motive is gratitude to God and love for his creatures. Doing the right thing thus links to our personal relationship to God. So religion can strengthen our commitment to morality.

Morality is possible for us because of how God created us, as rational animals with intellect and will. Through our God-given intellect, we can arrive at the basic principles of right and wrong; these needn't be based on divine revelation or human convention. Through our will, we can freely choose to follow or violate what we know to be right. We're naturally inclined toward altruism and good, to love God and our fellow human beings as God has loved us. But we're also inclined toward selfishness and laziness, so acting rightly can be a struggle. Morality's ultimate purpose is to lead us to happiness – a partial happiness on earth and a complete happiness with God in the afterlife.

My approach to natural law sees our duties as based on our God-given nature, as rational, biological, and spiritual beings. So my *natural law* ethics has three parts. (1) From our *rational nature*, there are norms of practical reason; these are logical or quasi-logical rules for thinking about right and wrong. (2) From our *biological nature*, we're social and rational animals and need certain goods to survive and prosper, so we need to apply practical reason to our specific biological nature and needs. (3) From our *spiritual nature*, we're called to eternal happiness with God; this gives a fuller framework for our duties and how they fit into God's plan for us.

Atheists could accept the *moral reasoning* and *biological nature* parts but reject the *spiritual nature* part about God. So, while theistic *natural law* ethics is fuller and more multi-dimensional, a pared-down atheist *natural law* ethics is fully possible.

10.7 Analysis: As Rational Beings

Natural law sees practical reason as "written on the human heart" – and as norms that, as *rational beings*, we ought to follow as far as practically possible. I see this as the central norm of practical reason:

We ought to be consistent in thought and action, and this in light of understanding the situation and imagining ourselves in different places in the situation.

(§9.3)

This leads to the *golden rule*, which I phrase in the previous chapter as "Treat others only as you consent to being treated in the same situation." The KITA procedure (know, imagine, test, act) shows how to apply GR. This current chapter showed how to use these ideas to criticize racism and other discrimination.

How are GR and practical reason "written on the human heart"? In §9.8, I began with Darwin's evolutionary explanation; humans, to promote group survival, evolved to be *social* (naturally helping each other and being distressed by another's misery) and *rational* (able to think things out, consider alternatives and consequences, imagine another's situation, avoid inconsistencies, and follow GR). A range of further scientific studies – like neuroscience (GR operating in the brain), psychology (moral thinking stages, cognitive dissonance, child psychology, classical conditioning), and social learning theory – showed further how GR and practical reason are "written on the human heart" (or "hard-coded into our genes").

Most humans are motivated to reconsider a decision if they believe any of these:

- "My decision is based on factual errors."
- "I'd decide differently if I had more information."
- "I'd decide differently if I better visualized my action's effects."
- "I'm inconsistent."
- "I'd complain if someone did that to me."

Such violations of practical reason are often felt as *cognitive dissonance*; we feel bad about ourselves and our rational failings. Cognitive dissonance is a feeling and motivation that supports our rational and moral side; evolution put this into us, and society reinforces it for its survival.

If we think of GR and practical reason as thus "written on the human heart" (Romans 2:14–15), we shouldn't think of these as always written in big, bold letters. Sometimes the message is obscured by other things written on the human heart – like selfishness, groupism, impulsiveness, stupidity, and cruelty. Morality can be a struggle. Despite this, the seeds of GR and practical reason are inside of us, as *natural law* ethics insists; we need to cultivate these seeds.

10.8 Analysis: As Biological Beings

As *biological beings* of a certain sort, we have further duties. These are based on applying practical reason (including GR) to the specific kind of biological life that we call *human*. But how should we describe this *human biological nature*? What are its central features? And what duties do beings of this sort have?

A few years ago, I camped alone at remote Boucher Creek in the Grand Canyon. I thought about human biological nature and how to describe it. A squirrel there, whom I called *Squirrel Boucher*, tried to get my food. I thought about how humans differ from squirrels and how this impacts morality. First, squirrels are far better adapted to nature than we are. If you drop a squirrel with nothing else (clothing, tools, or whatever) all by herself in a random part of the world, like Boucher Creek, she'll probably survive pretty well. This isn't so with humans. If you drop a human without possessions, clothing, or tools all by herself at Boucher Creek, she very well may die.

In this way, humans are more poorly adapted to nature than squirrels. Our survival depends on practical reason, on being intelligent and cooperative, where *cooperative* means we can mostly depend on people following GR toward each other. Yes, I camped alone; but I was still part of a web of human relationships. My trails, maps, food, water filter, tent, clothing, and so on – indeed my presence at Boucher Creek – was possible only because of human intelligence and cooperation.

My first conclusion was that, because humans are so weak and poorly adapted to nature, our survival and prospering requires that we cultivate *GR and practical reason* (including knowledge that informs action). This is a *biological imperative* for *Homo sapiens*: "If we want to survive and prosper (either as individuals or as a species), then we ought to develop GR and practical reason."

How else do humans differ from squirrels? *Possessions* are important for humans. To survive, we need shelter, clothing, shoes, and so on. If you camp at Boucher Creek and someone takes all your possessions, you might die. You're in trouble if you don't have maps, clothing, food, water containers, or shelter. Squirrels need none of this; they do well without possessions (but sometimes build nests).

Speech is important for humans. We work together and need speech for this. We depend on others to mostly tell the truth and do what they say they'll do. While speech is hugely important for humans, it's not so important for squirrels.

Family is also more important for humans. Squirrel sexuality is fairly simple. Squirrels of most species live alone but get together to copulate; then the male's job is over. A baby squirrel is born, needs brief mother care, and then lives alone. Humans are the opposite. A human baby is born helpless and needs years of intense love and upbringing – and it's difficult for one person to provide for this. So we evolved families that can work together, love each other, and bring up children. Our deepest life bonds are usually family ones, like husband-wife, mother-child, and brother-sister.

So humans, because of biology, have certain needs – especially possessions, speech, family, and (in common with squirrels) life. If we apply GR and practical reason to these areas, we generate four general duties widely accepted across the globe: against stealing, lying, adultery, and killing; these protect four key goods: possessions, speech, family, and life. While humans have many duties, these four are especially important and, with GR, were noted in the *global ethics* statement of the Parliament of the World's Religions (1993). This wide recognition of common norms – based on our rational and biological natures – supports the *natural law* moral framework.

10.9 Analysis: As Spiritual Beings

As *spiritual beings* called to eternal life with God, we ought, as far as practically possible, to love God with our entire being.

The duty to love God *with our entire being* is comprehensive, covering all aspects of our lives. It requires that we *obey* God, whose will flows from his supreme love and wisdom. Other duties, given that God wants us to follow them, are also obedience duties; thus obeying God fulfills all our duties. Religion personalizes morality. When we steal, lie, or break the golden rule, we do something that's wrong on non-religious grounds, but we also disobey God and sin against the one who created us and loves us. (Sin is an intentional violation of God's will; atheists can accept wrongdoing but not sin.) So morality connects to our personal relationship with God.

Loving God with our entire being requires loving our neighbor and following the golden rule. Since God's commandments include "Love your neighbor" and "Treat others as you want to be treated," this too follows from obedience.

Loving God with our entire being requires that we praise and love God in other aspects of our lives. If you're an artist, praise God through your art. If you do science, praise God through your science. If you're a parent, praise God through loving your family. If you hike the Grand Canyon, praise God through your hiking. If you struggle with faith, praise God in your struggles. If you suffer illness, pray that your suffering may bring you closer to God. Love, serve, and praise God with your entire being. For believers, morality is part of loving God. That's the biggest difference that theism makes to morality.

Religion gives a context for morality, a world-view that supports morality. We were created by a loving God to know right from wrong, have free will, and love one another. The core of right and wrong is caring for others, the golden rule, loving your neighbor, and growing toward God. This hugely motivates morality.

Bruce Sheiman's *An Atheist Defends Religion* (2009) claims that this religious dimension moves people. Religious people, he argues, tend to accept mostly the same moral norms as atheists, but they live them far better – in terms of volunteer work, caring for others, not stealing on the job, being honest, and so on. He bases these claims on much social studies research; science shows quite clearly that the spiritual dimension (which he, as an atheist, rejects) is a powerful force in living out the moral life.

In my approach to natural law, morality has three dimensions: rational, biological, and spiritual. Atheists can accept the first two but not the third. Atheists can agree about practical reason – including the importance of being informed, imaginative, and consistent (GR, ends-means, etc.). Atheists can agree on how morality relates to our biological nature – including how we evolved concern for others and a sense of right and wrong; how we ought to respect possessions, speech, family, and life; and how to use practical reason to explore ethical controversies. And atheists can be committed to morality and cooperate to make the world a better place.[6]

But atheists miss much of the story. Theistic ethics is more powerful because it appeals to the whole person. It sees GR not only as a rational consistency imperative and a biological imperative for individual and social well-being but also as a divine command and part of God's plan for us to grow in personhood toward eternal life (our final destiny and our fulfillment). And so we're motivated to follow GR by love of God, gratitude to God, and seeing that we're all children of one God, made in his image and likeness. GR and morality fit religion nicely. Atheists can accept morality, and it's genuine but incomplete; it omits the spiritual dimension, which is an important part of moral thinking.

---

6 While believers and nonbelievers will *mostly* come to the same moral beliefs (for example, that stealing is wrong), there may be some differences. Believers will recognize a duty to worship God, while nonbelievers won't. And there may be differences about issues like mercy killing, based on different beliefs about the origin and destiny of our lives.

11

The Meaning of Life

We'll begin by listening to the fictional student Skepticus explain why he thinks that life has no meaning. We'll later consider objections. This chapter is also a summary of the book and tries to show connections.

11.1 Skepticus: Life Has No Meaning

This is Skepticus, for the last time, and I'm asking "Does life have a meaning?" My answer is no: life has no meaning.

Let's get clearer on this. I'm really asking whether the force(s) that brought about us as living organisms in the universe had a purpose or plan in doing so. Those who believe in God say yes. They think God (a supreme personal being) created intelligent organisms "in his image and likeness" *in order to* (*purpose*) share his life and love with them. God's plan (purpose, meaning) for them then become their plan (purpose, meaning). So the *meaning of life* is from God and mirrors why God created us.

As an atheist, I reject this and accept the scientific explanation. Evolution brought about living organisms by *randomness* (random variation of inherited characteristics) and *physical laws* (survival of the fittest); no God, purpose, or plan was involved. In the scientific view, which I accept, life itself has no purpose or meaning; it just happened, but not from a mind with purpose and a plan.

How do we atheists personally react to life's having no meaning or purpose? Some get upset, think their lives aren't worth living, and consider suicide. Others complain about *"the absurdity of life"* (which needs to be spoken with a heavy French accent).

My atheist reaction is more moderate. Since there's no God to create purpose or meaningfulness for my life, I can and must create these myself. So I ask, "What sort of life am I to lead?" I study what others have said about this – for example, what leads to personal happiness, how relationships are important, and how we need to develop talents and help others. Yes, it's fully possible for atheists to lead a meaningful life. So even though life itself (its origins, how it came to be) has no meaning, still my life can have a meaning (since I choose to give it a meaning).

What's the difference here between believers and atheists? Believers follow a divine life-plan they see as built into the "fabric of the universe." God helps us along the way and leads us to eternal life at the end. The universe is a home that God made for us to lead us back to him. We atheists, on the other hand, see the universe as indifferent to our values and desires. We're accidents in a world with no purpose or meaning and shouldn't expect help along the way. Which side has the advantage? We atheists have the advantage, since believers' views about God and the universe are make-believe fantasy, as Freud pointed out. As the problem of evil shows, this is not the sort of universe that a loving and perfect God would create for his people.

Are humans especially important in the universe? Believers think so; God created the universe in order to create us, as beings "in his image and likeness." From the view of astronomy, this idea is really silly. The universe is super huge – and we humans are so small, in a tiny, tiny corner of something so big. Think of the huge, lifeless, super-hot or super-cold stars and planets – all so alien to human life. In the larger universe, we don't belong. The larger universe cares nothing about us.

> Before going on, reflect on your reaction to Skepticus's passage. Do you see any problems with it?

11.2 Analysis: Life Has a Meaning

Due to cancer struggles, I retired from Loyola University Chicago a year ago and now live in a Jesuit retirement community. I published two articles here so far (Gensler 2022, 2023). If you're reading this, I succeeded in publishing *Reasoning about God* (likely my last book). I also wrote prefaces for two of my books translated into other languages: *Introduction to Logic* (2017a) into Chinese as 逻辑学导论 and *Ethics and Religion* (2016) into Persian as اخلاق و دین. To celebrate the second, I had an international Zoom interview between the United States (me) and Iran (Saied Abdollahi, a Tehran University graduate student in philosophy of religion, who asked me questions and did an excellent job). We talked about ethics and religion in both our faiths, and I wore a shirt I made with a Muslim version of the golden rule in Persian:

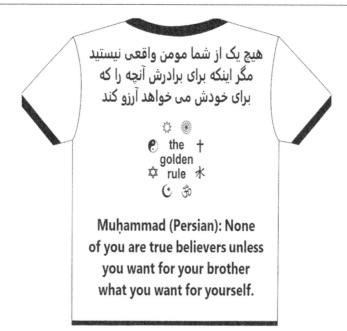

Saied's last question was about the meaning of life. This was my answer:

> I can express the meaning of life in simple terms, shared by Christianity and Islam. There's a wonderful [https://www.acommonword.com] "Common Word" Muslim Web site about the importance of something Christians and Muslims share: loving God above all things with your heart and mind and soul and strength (that's the Christian expression, Muslims use different words), and loving your neighbor as yourself (and the golden rule). Why were we created? What's our purpose in life? Most fundamentally, to love God and our neighbor. If we do that, we're happier, we have a better world, we have eternal life, we have fulfillment. Even facing cancer now, my attitude matters hugely. Does life have a meaning? Why are we here? Is life *meaningless*? No, it is not. We were created by a loving God to love God above all things and love our neighbor as ourself. Many religions share this, and I think it's the meaning of life.[1]

---

1 The video is on YouTube, https://youtu.be/IX6TE-Hjp9M ("Meaning of Life" starts at 1:03:20). Saied may post it with Persian subtitles and make it into an article. See http://harryhiker.com/persia or http://harrycola.com/persia and Common Word (2006 & 2009). For my Persian GR shirt, see https://www.zazzle.com/persian_golden_rule_shirt-235719983829125313.

To be more precise, I'd say that the meaning of life (the reason God created us) is *to love God above all things and our neighbor as ourselves, both in this life and in the next*.

Christianity is bold about the purpose of human life. In Catholic grade school, I memorized these answers from the *Baltimore Catechism* (1941: 12):

1. *Who made us?* God made us.
2. *Who is God?* God is the Supreme Being, infinitely perfect, who made all things and keeps them in existence.
3. *Why did God make us?* God made us to show forth His goodness and to share with us His everlasting happiness in heaven.
4. *What must we do to gain the happiness of heaven?* To gain the happiness of heaven we must know, love, and serve God in this world.

So what's the purpose of human life? It's to *show forth God's goodness and share everlasting life with God – which requires that we know, love, and serve God in this world*. Ignatius of Loyola (1524), wording it differently, said that man was created *to praise, reverence, and serve God our Lord, and by this means to save his soul*. While neither formula has "loving your neighbor," this is implicit, since loving God entails obeying God's commandments; but I much prefer to make love-neighbor explicit.

What I give as the purpose of human life is the same as the first two parts of my seven-word Christian "Gensler Creed" ("*Love God, love neighbor, Jesus is Lord*"), which I unpacked as follows (§9.2):

1. *Love God.* Love the Lord your God with all your heart and mind and soul and strength, in this world and the next. This presupposes belief in God.
2. *Love neighbor.* Love your neighbor as yourself, in this world and the next. And live the golden rule, "Treat others as you want to be treated."
3. *Jesus is Lord.* This ancient creedal statement proclaims Jesus's divinity, as true God and true man, and thus the bridge between God and man.

While we Christians share (1) and (2) with Islam and others, we likely share just (2) (except for the next-life part) with atheists and agnostics. But (3) is unique to Christianity and is based on revelation.

Revelation tends to intensify our religious experience. Augustine (Swindal 2005: 92–93) came to believe in God from studying Platonist philosophers, but he saw God as distant and struggled to get closer to him. Augustine also struggled with the Christian belief that Jesus was both God and man. Eventually, both struggles came together; Augustine, despite his intellectual problem, came to see Jesus – as both God and man – as his bridge to God, as the one that would bring God closer to him. It was like God was on a far off mountain, but now Jesus was the path that leads to God (as close and personal, not distant and theoretical). I earlier mentioned (§6.5) a similar example with Francis Collins (2006) and Antony Flew (2007), prominent atheists who came to God through the *fine tuning* argument; after that, they went in different directions – Collins accepting revelation (and becoming a firm Christian) but Flew hesitating to take this next step (and so his faith remained distant and theoretical).

Regarding divine revelation, I'd somewhat follow St. Thomas Aquinas. Once we believe in a personal God, we should think it likely that he'd reveal himself to us in more intimate terms. So we'd look for historical revelation (as in the Bible) and signs of its authenticity. Aquinas found revelation in Christianity and signs of its authenticity in Jesus's miracles. My view would be more complicated, since I think God can reveal himself through various religious traditions. I see miracle reports as weak evidence, since these reports are so common in different religions; and Jesus preferred that people believe from his words rather than from miracles (John 4:41 & 4:48). I'd put more weight on the miracle of Jesus's resurrection, which was attested to by many alleged first-hand witnesses who were prepared to die for their belief; several authors make an impressive case on these grounds for the special role of Jesus as the great bridge between God and humans (§4.2).

My main focus in this book is to defend what is common to the great monotheist religions (like Judaism, Christianity, and Islam). So please forgive me if I'm vague on how to decide between them (for example, whether we should favor the Jewish Bible, the Christian Bible, or the Islamic Koran). The latter issue would require a different book and maybe an author with different interests.

11.3 Analysis: Why Think That Life Has a Meaning?

Skepticus raised a common astronomy objection (§11.1):

> Are humans especially important in the universe? Believers think so; God created the universe in order to create us, as beings "in his image and likeness." From the view of astronomy, this idea is really silly. The universe is super huge – and we humans are so small, in a tiny, tiny corner of something so big. Think of the huge, lifeless, super-hot or super-cold stars and planets – all so alien to human life. In the larger universe, we don't belong. The larger universe cares nothing about us.

Pierre Teilhard de Chardin (1881–1955), a Jesuit scientist, looked at it differently and saw humans as central to the cosmic process. Teilhard (1966, see Swindal 2005: 326–29), thought everything in the universe has both material ("the outside") and mental ("the inside") properties; at low complexity (like an ice cube), mental properties are negligible. His *law of complexity-consciousness* says that the evolutionary cosmic process tends toward beings appearing of increasing material complexity ("the outside") and consciousness ("the inside"). This has stages from atoms, to complex molecules, to one-cell organisms, to multi-cell organisms, to humans (with the ultra-complex brain going with a greatly enhanced mind), to increasingly complex forms of human society, to eventually the final goal and culmination of the whole process, which he calls the Ω *omega point* and identifies in faith with the Christian *Kingdom of God*. Humans, as far as we know, seem to be at the cutting edge of the complexity-consciousness process. If we're more impressed with complexity and consciousness than size, we should be more impressed with the human brain and mind than a huge star or planet. In Teilhard's view, yes, we humans are especially important in the universe.

The *fine-tuning argument* (§6.5) gives further reasons for believing that intelligent life in the universe happened out of design and not just chance. There's much scientific evidence that our world is *fine-tuned*; this means that the physics laws and constants governing it – like the gravitational constant "g," the charge and mass of the proton, the density of water, and the world's total mass – are in the narrow range of what's required for life (and intelligent life) to be possible. I argued that the best explanation for this is that the world was created by an intelligent being *intending to create life (and intelligent life)*. God created the world to bring forth beings like us, made in his "image and likeness," and to be our earthly home, as we journey back to God. So the whole structure of the universe, down to the precise values of the individual physical constants, reveals to us that yes, there's a purpose behind the universe.

Near-death experiences (§§4.4–4.7) give further reasons for believing that the universe is part of God's plan and purpose for us and that a central part of this is to love God and our neighbor. That's what we experience in the afterlife.

Additional factors push us in the same direction, like the testimony of the world's religions, our inner urges for eternal life with God, and how we live better if we believe that life has a meaning and purpose.

As human beings, much of our interest in God comes from trying to understand ourselves: our origin, purpose, and destiny. Are we accidents in a meaningless universe? There are big signs that no, we're rather children of a loving God.

11.4 Analysis: Atheism's Dark Side

Suppose that, despite my efforts, you're still an atheist. I have a suggestion for you: *Please, please avoid atheism's dark side*.

What moved me to write this section was an unfair criticism of atheism that I read, which described atheists in very dark terms. What are atheists like? According to this criticism, atheists are miserably unhappy, suffer meaningless lives, don't care about others, and lack any moral compass. This is what atheists are like – or at least what they'd be like if they understood atheism and were consistent about it. So atheists are described in very dark terms.

Yes, a few atheists live very dark lives, but most don't – and I don't see why any of them should. So my advice to atheists, again, is: *Please, please avoid atheism's dark side*. There are better ways to live. If you're an atheist, you have alternatives.

Suppose you believe in God, and your belief is a deep part of your life. Then you become an atheist, and you have to live without God. Here are two challenges:

1. *Life's meaning*. Does life have a meaning?
2. *Ethics*. Are there objective ethical norms?

In my opinion, Skepticus does well on (1) but could do better at (2).

(1) Skepticus distinguishes two questions that (1) could be asking. First, "Did we and other living organisms come to be as the result of a design plan?" As an atheist, Skepticus says no, living organisms came from mutation-selection, there's no designer God or divine plan. Or (1) could be asking, "Is my own life meaningful?" As an atheist, Skepticus thinks his life has no meaning or purpose from God, but this leaves him free to create a meaning or purpose for his own life:

> So I ask, "What sort of life am I to lead?" I study what others have said about this – for example, what leads to personal happiness, how relationships are important, and how we need to develop talents and help others. Yes, it's fully possible for atheists to lead a meaningful life. So even though life itself (its origins, how it came to be) has no meaning, still my life can have a meaning (since I choose to give it a meaning).

The *dark side*, instead, is to wallow in despair about life's absurdity, spend your life in negativity, and perhaps contemplate suicide. Atheists have to decide how to *feel* about the situation.[2] There's no good argument that consistent atheists must pick the dark side; instead, atheists have to choose whether to be miserable or happy. And yes, helping others can be deeply satisfying even if we don't believe in God – and enjoying a sunny beach can

---

2 French atheists Albert Camus (1913–60) and Jean-Paul Sartre (1905–80) represent opposite choices: Camus (1942a, 1942b) taught "Endure dark despair" while Sartre (1946) taught "Create your own meaning." French Christian thinkers of the time, like Maurice Blondel (1861–1949, see Swindal 2005: 297–98), wrote about the meaning and destiny of our lives in more theistic terms.

bring pleasure even if we know that someday our existence will cease. Atheists who are positive about life can be happy.

(2) asks "Are there objective ethical norms?" Skepticus unfortunately says no and accepts emotivism: ethical norms express feelings instead of truth claims. He needs to appreciate emotivism's problems (§§3.4–3.8). While he regrets that emotivism is weak in arguing against racists with different feelings and intuitions (§§3.6 & 10.3), he thinks intuitionism isn't any better.

There are many views about ethics, some accepting objective ethical norms and some not; see Gensler (2018). *Divine command* theory is the only such view that *requires* belief in God, and this view has strong objections (§10.2). Atheists who want objective ethical norms have several choices, including *ideal observer* (good is what we'd desire if we were ideally informed, impartial, consistent, etc.), *social contract* (follow social norms that rational individuals agree to for mutual advantage), and *intuitionism* (basic moral norms are intuitively self-evident – the nonbeliever G.E. Moore [1873–1958] was the prominent intuitionist).

In my opinion, the best view of ethics for Skepticus to accept is a scaled-down version of my *natural law* view that drops all reference to God (see §§9.4–9.8 & 10.3–10.9). This view accepts one rational, objective, basic ethical norm ("We ought to be consistent in thought and action, and this in light of understanding the situation and imagining ourselves in different places in the situation") – and it leads to the golden rule. It gives strong ways to argue against bad ethical views, like racism (§10.4), so not just anything goes. And this view would let Skepticus join the world's religions and cultures in their overwhelming acceptance of the golden rule.

Why am I writing this section? Am I endorsing atheism? No, not at all, as should be clear from the rest of this book. Instead, I wrote this section to defend atheism from unfair criticisms (that atheists have to be unhappy people and moral nihilists) and to suggest how atheists can lead happy and moral lives.

11.5 Analysis: Skepticus Errors

As we reach the second-last section of this book, I'd like to thank our fictional student Skepticus for explaining his thinking so well and for giving us so many objections to belief in God and religion. To help us better respond to such objections, I'll here summarize them under various categories.

(1) Skepticus in criticizing religion appeals to several ideas that may sound good at first but turn out to be self-refuting:

- "We shouldn't accept what isn't proved." (Since this isn't proved, we shouldn't accept it.)
- "Science is the only path to knowledge." (This seems not to be knowable from science.)

- *Logical positivism.* "All genuine truth claims (claims that are true or false) are empirically testable or true by definition." (Since this isn't empirically testable or true by definition, it can't be a genuine truth claim.)

These violate the duty to be consistent, which I see as the first duty of a rational being.

(2) Skepticus often ignores recent empirical data relevant to the issue:

- Following Freud, Russell, and many atheist writers today, Skepticus claims that religion is very harmful. These critics all ignore massive empirical data showing that believers do much better than nonbelievers psychologically, medically, and ethically.
  Skepticus and Russell reject the *first cause* argument, saying "There's no reason to suppose that the world had a beginning." But today, based on new evidence, most scientists think the world had a Big Bang beginning 14 billion years ago. This leads to the Kalam *first cause* argument.
- Skepticus and many atheists reject the afterlife, but they often ignore (or dismiss too easily) near-death experiences.
- Skepticus and many atheists argue that evolution can explain life's origin without God, but they often ignore (or dismiss too easily) fine tuning.
- Skepticus and many atheists sometimes describe the religions across the world as having a chaotic diversity on moral issues, while in fact they're very united in supporting the golden rule.

Skepticus is poor at getting and using recent empirical data.

(3) Skepticus often claims that *science proves XYZ against religion*, but in fact science doesn't really prove this unless you add some assumed philosophical premise not itself based on science.

- Skepticus and many atheists say that evolution *proves* that life arose in the world due to random variation plus selection – and thus *proves* that divine purposes aren't part of life's cause. But it could be (and science can't show that this is false) that God set up evolution *in order to* bring about life; then divine purposes *are* part of life's cause.
- Skepticus and many atheists claim that biology *proves* that there can't be an afterlife. But many scientists accept mind-body views that permit an afterlife and that science can't disprove.

When atheists say that science *proves* something against religion, ask: "Could a believer accept the scientific data and yet dispute the negative conclusion? Is the critic making a hidden assumption here that can't itself be based on science?"

(4) Skepticus sometimes distorts views of religious thinkers. No, religious thinkers who use the *first cause* argument don't standardly have "Everything

has a cause" as a premise. No, Christian thinkers before recent times didn't take the Bible all literally.

(5) Skepticus sometimes uses anti-religion premises that can't be true in his emotivism (which sees evaluative statements as exclamations and not true-or-false). Here are examples: "Any view that's simpler and explains more is a *better* view," "We *shouldn't* accept what isn't proved," and "There's much *evil* in the world."

Skepticus is a fictional student who criticizes belief in God. Does his lowly student status explain why he's *sometimes* so poor at reasoning?[3] In part, it may explain this. But he often repeats the same flawed ideas that professional critics of God also use; much of *their* reasoning against belief in God is poor too.

I mentioned that intellectuals tend to be more skeptical about God and religion than other people. This has changed much in recent years, since roughly 1970. What has changed? Catholicism is more modern after the second Vatican Council (1962–65) and emphasizes more what faiths have in common. Freud declined in importance, and many studies show that religion benefits us – psychologically, medically, and ethically. Scientists came to believe that the universe had a beginning and that our physics laws and constants had to be finely tuned for life to emerge. Near-death experiences began to be studied in depth. The moral unity of the world's religions in the golden rule was rediscovered. Philosophy turned from logical positivism and became more open to belief in God. Many scientists and other intellectuals are returning to God and religion.

This book, *Reasoning about God*, would have been very different had I written it before 1970. Believers have reason to celebrate how things have changed since then. When critics of belief in God attack belief as "going against reason," the appropriate reaction now is to just laugh a little and say, "Do you really think so? Let's talk about specifics in a clear way." Criticisms of God and religion are often outdated.

11.6 Analysis: Your Favorite Paths to God?

There are many paths to God.[4]

My term "path to God" is rough and nontechnical. It points to various useful ways to gain true beliefs or knowledge about God. When I give my tentative list of "paths to God," I won't include items like "becoming

---

3 I shouldn't be too harsh on Skepticus. He's good at explaining things, as when he talks at the beginning of this chapter about atheist views on the meaning of life. But he does make mistakes in criticizing God and religion, and I point these out.
4 To solidify what you've learned, you might write a response to a question that early Skepticus struggled with (§§1.1–1.2): Why should we reject the tooth fairy and Santa Claus but accept God?

Catholic" (I'm looking for elements besides faith traditions) or "following reason" (not specific enough). And I won't see my list of such paths as final; we'll likely keep finding more paths to God if we look harder. Again, my term "path to God" is rough and nontechnical.

As last count, this book discusses roughly 15 different paths to God (poor St. Thomas Aquinas had only 5 ways). Here they are in alphabetical order – and if I omit ones important to you, please add them:

- *consistency* (useful to criticize anti-religious and racist ideas and to rationally ground the golden rule)
- *disease and suffering* (these can bring us closer to God and to a deeper sense of dependence on him)
- *fine-tuning argument* (God finely adjusting the universe to produce life)
- *following our feelings* (especially ones that, following Augustine, God put into us to encourage our search for God – like our desire for meaning in life and eternal happiness with God)
- *golden rule* (as strongly supported by the world's religions and defensible in many philosophical and scientific ways)
- *good skepticism* (critical thinking, objecting to flawed ideas, especially anti-religious ideas that may sound good at first)
- *instinctive ways to form religious beliefs* (as from experiencing nature, following reformed epistemology's "sense of divinity")
- *Kalam argument* (God starting the universe)
- *moral demands* (the GR natural law approach works better on a religious view of life, even though a reduced approach can work for atheists)
- *mystical experiences* (a special way to experience God)
- *near-death experiences* (a peek into the afterlife)
- *ontological argument* (both the reasoning and a perfect being's attraction)
- *preferring beliefs that help us to live better* (pragmatism; how believing in God empirically benefits us psychologically, medically, and ethically)
- *sufficient-reason argument* (why is there a world at all?)
- *Teilhard's complexity-consciousness law* (humans are important in the universe).

None of these paths to God give absolutely conclusive proofs, although some give strong arguments. All require at least some openness to God. The paths can combine and often work well together.

Different paths may be more important for different people. Maybe you prefer paths with subtle reasoning and complex scientific data – or maybe you prefer paths with instincts and feelings. God didn't make us all the same, so it's good that there are many paths to God. Which paths are the most important for you?

My two favorite paths are *fine tuning* and *near-death experiences*; both amaze me and involve much reasoning and empirical data. I've struggled with which is my absolute favorite; in the end, I'd give this honor to near-death experiences. NDEs better bring out God's love for us (through the bright red light and the afterlife's design) and the importance of love-neighbor and GR (in the non-judgmental life review). Jeffrey Long and Paul Perry (2009, 2016) did well in bringing the data together.

These two paths, so different, work well together. *Fine tuning* is about the beginning of the universe, alpha α, the Big Bang, 14 billion years ago, so distant and abstract and mathematical – Creation, the beginning of it all. *Near-death experiences* are about the end-goal of the universe, omega Ω, our soon-to-be future, a human life transformed – the Kingdom of Heaven, the fulfillment of it all. The two go together beautifully.

Let's now take a final look at the *meaning of life* and how it connects with various *paths to God*. The meaning of our lives, why God created us, is *to love God above all things and our neighbor as ourselves, both in this life and in the next*. To help on our life journey back to him, God has gifted us in many ways, for example:

- *being made in God's image and likeness* (at first with weak intellect and free will, including our grasp of GR morality, that's able to grow over time, with increasing consistency, knowledge, and imagination)
- *a very meaningful life* (of loving God and neighbor, toward eternal happiness, benefitting us even now – psychologically, medically, ethically)
- *a struggle against evils and difficulties* (to increase the significance of our earthly action and our eternal happiness)
- *desires inside us* (especially for meaning in life and eternal life with God) that lead us to search for God
- *an instinctive sense of divinity* (to form beliefs about God, as from nature, following reformed epistemology)
- *complex clues about God to exercise our reason* (Kalam and fine tuning)
- *near-death experiences* (a foretaste of our future eternal happiness with God).

God made us with a purpose: to love God and our neighbor, and in this way to reach our fulfillment. And he gave us many paths and gifts to help us on our journey back to him.

Bibliography[1]

Al-Attar, Mariam (2010) *Islamic Ethics: Divine Command Theory in Arabo-Islamic Thought*, New York: Routledge.
Altizer, Thomas (1966) *The Gospel of Christian Atheism*, New York: Westminster.
Anselm (1100) *Anselm's Proslogium; Monologium; An Appendix in Behalf of the Fool by Gaunilo; and Cur Deus Homo*, trans. Sidney Norton Deane, Chicago: Open Court, 1926.
Aquinas, Thomas (1265) *Summa Contra Gentiles*, 5 vols, trans. Anton C. Pegis, New York: Hanover House, 1955–57. https://isidore.co/aquinas/english/ContraGentiles.htm
——— (1274) *Summa Theologica*, 3 vols, trans. Fathers of the English Dominican Province, New York: Benziger Brothers, 1948. http://www.newadvent.org/summa
Archer, Maria (2017) "The positive effects of religion on mental illness." https://ifstudies.org/blog/the-positive-effects-of-religion-on-mental-illness
Aronson, Eliot (1969) "The theory of cognitive dissonance," in *Advances in Experimental Social Psychology*, ed. Leonard Berkowitz, vol. 4, London: Academic Press, 1–34.
Augustine (400) "God's providence," in Swindal and Gensler 2005: 107–11.
Ayer, A.J. (1946) *Language, Truth and Logic*, New York: Dover, 1952.
——— (1988a) "What I saw when I was dead," *Sunday Telegraph* (London Newspaper), August 28. http://www.philosopher.eu/others-writings/a-j-ayer-what-i-saw-when-i-was-dead
——— (1988b) http://danb.altervista.org/ayer-nde.htm (with more information)
Ayer, A.J., and Frederick Copleston (1949) "Radio debate on the logical positivism," in Edwards and Pap 1965: 726–56.
Ayer, A.J., and Bryan Magee (1976) "Logical positivism," a BBC interview. https://youtu.be/S6_Vy-Uzwzc; https://www.basicincome.com/bp/ratherlike.htm
Baltimore Catechism (1941) *A Catechism of Christian Doctrine*, revised ed., No. 2 (for grades 6–8), Paterson, NJ: St. Anthony Guild Press, 1954. http://www.catholicity.com/baltimore-catechism
Brickman, Philip, Don Coates, and Ronnie Janoff-Bulman (1978) "Lottery winners and accident victims: Is happiness relative?" *Journal of Personality and Social Psychology* 36: 917–27.
Brody, Baruch (1974) "Morality and religion reconsidered," in Helm 1981: 141–53.

---

1 All Web addresses in this book were checked out to work in January 2022.

Buddha (c. 500 BC). The quotes in the text are from Dhammapada Nikaya 1:3–5 and the "Sermon on abuse." http://www.accesstoinsight.org/tipitaka/kn/dhp/dhp.01.than.html; http://www.sacred-texts.com/bud/btg/btg58.htm

Camus, Albert (1942a) *The Myth of Sisyphus*, New York: Knopf Doubleday, 2018.

——— (1942b) *The Stranger*, New York: Pegasus, 2016.

Carson, Thomas (2007) "Axiology, realism, and the problem of evil," *Philosophy and Phenomenological Research* 75: 349–68.

——— (2012) "Divine will/divine command moral theories and the problem of arbitrariness," *Religious Studies* 48: 445–68.

Carter, Brandon (1974) "Large number coincidences and the anthropic principle in cosmology," in *Confrontation of Cosmological Theories with Observational Data* (Symposium in Krakow, Poland), Dordrecht: D. Reidel, 291–98. http://adsabs.harvard.edu/abs/1974IAUS...63..291C

Collins, Francis (2006) *The Language of God*, New York: Free Press.

Collins, Robin (1999) "A scientific argument for the existence of God: The fine-tuning design argument," in Michael Murray (ed), *Reason for the Hope Within*, Grand Rapids, MI: William B. Eerdmans, 47–75.

Common Word (2006) "Open letter to Pope Benedict XVI," signed by 38 Islamic leaders. http://ammanmessage.com/media/openLetter/english.pdf

——— (2009) *A Common Word Between Us and You*, Jordan: Royal Aal al-Bayt Islamic Institute. http://acommonword.com/index.php?lang=en&page=downloads

Confucius (c. 500 BC). *Analects*. https://www.sacred-texts.com/cfu/conf1.htm

Copan, Paul (2008) "Is Yahweh a moral monster?" *Philosophia Christi* 10: 7–37. http://www.epsociety.org/library/printable/45.pdf

——— (2011) *Is God a Moral Monster? Making Sense of the Old Testament God*, Grand Rapids, MI: Baker Books.

Copleston, Frederick, and A.J. Ayer (1949) "Radio debate on the logical positivism," in Edwards and Pap 1965: 726–56.

Copleston, Frederick, and Bertrand Russell (1948) "Radio debate on the existence of God," in Swindal and Gensler 2005: 390–99 and in Russell 1957: 125–52. https://www.youtube.com/watch?v=9t-oME07OVI has an audio version (a reading).

Craig, William L. (1979) *The Kalām Cosmological Argument*, London: Macmillan.

——— (1981) *The Son Rises: Historical Evidence for the Resurrection of Jesus*, Chicago, IL: Moody.

——— (1994) *Reasonable Faith*, rev. ed., Wheaton, IL: Crossway.

——— (2010) *On Guard*, Colorado Springs, CO: David Cook.

Darwin, Charles (1871) *The Descent of Man*, 2 vols., London: John Murray.

Dawkins, Richard (1995) *River out of Eden: A Darwinian View of Life*, New York: Basic Books.

——— (2006) *The God Delusion*, Great Britain, London.

Douglass, Frederick (1855) *My Bondage and My Freedom*, New York: Miller, Orton, & Mulligan.

Eccles, John (1989) *Evolution of the Brain: Creation of the Self*, New York: Routledge.

Eccles, John, and Karl Popper (1984) *The Self and Its Brain: An Argument for Interactionism*, New York: Routledge.

Edwards, Paul, and Arthur Pap (eds) (1965) *A Modern Introduction to Philosophy*, 2nd ed., New York: Free Press.

Epstein, Greg (2009) *Good Without God: What a Billion Nonreligious People Do Believe*, New York: William Morrow.
Felix, Minucius (c. 200) "The Octavius of Minucius Felix," in *The Ante-Nicene Fathers*, vol. 4, ed. A. Cleveland Coxe, Buffalo, NY: Christian Literature, 1895, 173–98. Swindal and Gensler 2005: 63–70, has a shorter version. https://www.ccel.org/ccel/schaff/anf04.toc.html
Festinger, Leon (1957) *A Theory of Cognitive Dissonance*, Stanford, CA: Stanford University Press.
Flew, Antony (1955) "Theology and falsification," in Flew and Macintyre (eds), *New Essays in Philosophical Theology*, New York: Macmillan, 96–99. https://www.qcc.cuny.edu/socialsciences/ppecorino/phil_of_religion_text/CHAPTER_8_LANGUAGE/Theology-and-Falsification.htm; https://www.stephenhicks.org/wp-content/uploads/2015/06/FlewHareMitchell-What-Faith-Is.pdf
——— (2007) *There Is a God*, New York: HarperCollins.
Flew, Antony, and Gary Habermas. (2004) "My pilgrimage from atheism to theism: A discussion between Antony Flew and Gary Habermas." LBTS Faculty Publications and Presentations. 333. https://digitalcommons.liberty.edu/lts_fac_pubs/333
Frankena, William (1973a) *Ethics*, 2nd ed., Englewood Cliffs, NJ: Prentice Hall.
——— (1973b) "Is morality logically dependent on religion?" in Outka 1973: 295–317 (also in Helm 1981).
Freud, Sigmund (1927) *The Future of an Illusion*, Garden City, NJ: Doubleday, 1957.
Fulwiler, Jennifer (2014) *Something Other Than God*, San Francisco: Ignatius Press.
Gensler, Harry (1996) *Formal Ethics*, New York: Routledge.
——— (2013a) *Ethics and the Golden Rule*, New York: Routledge.
——— (2013b) *The Golden Rule*, Rockville, MD: Learn25 Media. 12 audio/video talks. https://www.learn25.com/product/do-unto-others-the-golden-rules-moral-and-ethical-ideal-for-the-world
——— (2016) *Ethics and Religion*, New York: Cambridge.
——— (2017a) *Introduction to Logic*, 3rd ed., New York: Routledge.
——— (2017b) *Great Catholic Philosophers*, Rockville, MD: Learn25 Media. 24 audio talks. https://www.learn25.com/product/great-catholic-philosophers-meet-christianitys-greatest-minds-and-understand-their-best-ideas
——— (2018) *Ethics: A Contemporary Introduction*, 3rd ed., New York: Routledge.
——— (2022) "Formal ethical principles," *Filosofiska Notiser*, Årgång 9, Nr. 1: 3–48.
——— (2023) "Values and culture," in Sanjit Chakraborty (ed), *Human Minds and Cultures*, New York: Routledge.
Glynn, Patrick (1997) *God: The Evidence*, Rocklin, CA: Prima.
Grimm Brothers (1812) "The old man and his grandson." http://www.gutenberg.org/ebooks/2591
Harris, Michael (2003) *Divine Command Ethics: Jewish and Christian Perspectives*, New York: Routledge.
Hawking, Stephen (1998) *A Brief History of Time*, 2nd ed., New York: Bantam Books.
Helm, Paul (ed) (1981) *Divine Commands and Morality*, New York: Oxford University Press.
Hempel, Carl G. (1950) "Problems and changes in the empiricist criterion of meaning," *Revue Internationale de Philosophie* 41: 41–68. https://people.duke.edu/~lc190/hempel_rip1950.pdf
Hick, John (1978) *Evil and the God of Love*, 2nd ed., New York: Harper & Row.
——— (1990) *Philosophy of Religion*, 4th ed., Englewood Cliffs, NJ: Prentice Hall.

Hume, David (1735) "A treatise of human nature." https://www.gutenberg.org/ebooks/4705
——— (1748) "An enquiry concerning human understanding." https://www.gutenberg.org/ebooks/9662
——— (1779) "Dialogues concerning natural religion." https://www.gutenberg.org/ebooks/4583
Huxley, Thomas (1866) *Selected Essays and Addresses of Thomas Henry Huxley*, ed. Philo Buck, New York: Macmillan, 1910.
Iannaccone, Lawrence (1998) "Introduction to the economics of religion," *Journal of Economic Literature* 36: 1465–95.
Idziak, Janine (ed) (1979) *Divine Command Morality: Historical and Contemporary Readings*, New York: Edwin Mellen.
James, William (1896) *The Will to Believe*, New York: Longmans, Green & Company. http://www.gutenberg.org/files/26659
——— (1902) *Varieties of Religious Experience*, New York: Longmans, Green & Company. https://www.gutenberg.org/ebooks/621
Kinnier, Richard, Jerry Kernes, and Therese Dautheribes (2000) "A short list of universal moral values," *Counseling and Values* 45: 4–16.
Kohlberg, L. (1973) "The claim to moral adequacy of the highest stage of moral judgment," *Journal of Philosophy* 70: 630–48.
——— (1979) "Justice as reversibility," in P. Laslett and J. Fishkin (eds), *Philosophy, Politics and Society*, 5th series, New Haven, CT: Yale University Press, 257–72.
——— (1981-4) *Essays on Moral Development*, 2 vols., San Francisco: Harper & Row.
Kohlberg, L., D. Boyd, and C. Levine (1990) "The return of stage 6: Its principle and moral point of view," in T. Wren (ed), *The Moral Domain*, Cambridge: MIT, 151–81.
Kohlberg, L., C. Levine, and A. Hewer (1983) *Moral Stages*, Basel: Karger.
Kübler-Ross, Elisabeth (1969) *On Death and Dying*, New York: Macmillan.
——— (1985) *On Children and Death*, New York: Collier.
Lewis, C.S. (1940) *The Problem of Pain*, New York: HarperCollins, 2009.
——— (1952) *Mere Christianity*, New York: HarperCollins, 2001.
——— (1961) *A Grief Observed*, New York: HarperCollins, 2015.
Long, Jeffrey, and Paul Perry (2009) *Evidence of the Afterlife: The Science of Near-Death Experiences*, New York: HarperOne.
——— (2016) *God and the Afterlife: The Groundbreaking New Evidence for God and Near-Death Experience*, New York: HarperOne.
Loyola, Ignatius (1524) "The spiritual exercises." http://www.ccel.org/ccel/ignatius/exercises.html
MacIntyre, Alasdair (2009) *God, Philosophy, Universities*, Lanham, MD: Rowman & Littlefield.
Mackie, J.L. (1955) "Evil and Omnipotence," *Mind* 64: 200–12.
——— (1977) *Ethics: Inventing Right and Wrong*, London: Penguin.
——— (1982) *The Miracle of Theism*, New York: Oxford University Press.
Mahabharata (c. 400) "Ancient Hindu scripture." https://www.sacred-texts.com/hin/maha/mahatxt.zip
Manson, Neil (ed) (2003) *God and Design*, New York: Routledge.
McGowan, Dale (2013) *Atheism for Dummies*, Mississauga, Ont.: Wiley.
Michel, Thomas (2010) *A Christian View of Islam*, ed. Irfan Omar, Maryknoll, NY: Orbis.
Miller, J. Steve (2012) *Near-Death Experiences as Evidence for the Existence of God and Heaven: A Brief Introduction in Plain Language*, Acworth, GA: Wisdom Creek.

Moody, Raymond (1975) *Life After Life*, Atlanta: Mockingbird.
Moser, Paul (2008) *The Elusive God*, New York: Cambridge University Press.
Olson, Carl E. (2016) *Did Jesus Really Rise from the Dead?* San Francisco: Ignatius.
Outka, Gene, and John P. Reeder (eds) (1973) *Religion and Morality: A Collection of Essays*, Garden City, NY: Anchor.
Pannenberg, Wolfhart (1968) *Jesus – God and Man*, Louisville, KY: Westminster.
Parnia, Sam, and others (2014) "AWARE – AWAreness during resuscitation – A prospective study," *Resuscitation* 85: 1799–1805. https://www.resuscitationjournal.com/article/S0300-9572(14)00739-4/fulltext; https://doi.org/10.1016/j.resuscitation.2014.09.004
—— (2017) "Brain function does not die immediately after the heart stops finds study," with Dr. Aranya Mandal, *News Medical Life Sciences*, October 19, 2017. https://www.news-medical.net/news/20171019/Brain-function-does-not-die-immediately-after-the-heart-stops-finds-study.aspx
—— (2019) "Life after life: Does consciousness continue after the heart stops?" *Sudden Cardiac Arrest Foundation*, April 18, 2019. https://www.sca-aware.org/sca-news/life-after-life-does-consciousness-continue-after-the-heart-stops
Pfaff, D. (2007) *The Neuroscience of Fair Play: Why We (Usually) Follow the Golden Rule*, New York: Dana, ch. 5.
Pfaff, D., E. Choleris, and M. Kavaliers (2008) "Brain mechanisms theoretically underlying extremes of social behaviors," in D. Pfaff (ed), *Hormones and Social Behavior*, Berlin: Springer, 13–25.
Plantinga, Alvin (1967) *God and Other Minds*, Ithaca, NY: Cornell.
—— (1974a) *God, Freedom, and Evil*, New York: Harper & Row.
—— (1974b) *The Nature of Necessity*, New York: Oxford University Press.
—— (1983) "Advice to Christian philosophers," in Swindal and Gensler 2005: 478–87.
—— (1993a) *Warrant: The Current Debate*, New York: Oxford University Press.
—— (1993b) *Warrant and Proper Function*, New York: Oxford University Press.
—— (2000) *Warranted Christian Belief*, New York: Oxford University Press.
—— (2006a) "Evolution and design," in James Beilby (ed), *For Faith and Clarity*, Grand Rapids, MI: Baker Academic, 201–18.
—— (2006b) "Two dozen (or so) theistic arguments." https://appearedtoblogly.files.wordpress.com/2011/05/plantinga-alvin-22two-dozen-or-so-theistic-arguments221.pdf
—— (2011) *Where the Conflict Really Lies: Science, Religion, and Naturalism*, New York: Oxford University Press.
—— (2015) *Knowledge and Christian Belief*, Grand Rapids, MI: Eerdmans.
Russell, Bertrand (1927) "Why I am not a Christian," in Russell 1957. https://users.drew.edu/~jlenz/whynot.html
—— (1930) "Has religion made useful contributions to civilization?" in Russell 1957. https://www.update.uu.se/~fbendz/library/has_reli.htm
—— (1957) *Why I Am Not a Christian*, ed. Paul Edwards, New York: Simon and Schuster.
Russell, Bertrand, and Frederick Copleston (1948) "Radio debate on the existence of God," in Swindal and Gensler 2005: 390–99, in Russell 1957: 125–52, and in Edwards and Pap 1965: 473–90. https://www.youtube.com/watch?v=9t-oME07OVI has an audio version (a reading).
Saeed, Sohaib (2010) "The golden rule: An Islamic-dialogic perspective," paper at Edinburgh Festival of Spirituality of Peace. http://dialogicws.files.wordpress.com/2010/07/goldenrule_saeed1.pdf

Sartre, Jean-Paul (1946) *Existentialism Is a Humanism*, New York: Methuen, 1965.
Sheiman, Bruce (2009) *An Atheist Defends Religion*, New York: Penguin.
Sober, Elliott (2009) "Absence of evidence and evidence of absence," *Philosophical Studies* 143: 63–90.
Spitzer, Robert (2010) *New Proofs for the Existence of God*, Grand Rapids, MI: Eerdmans.
—— (2020) *Near Death Experiences*. https://www.youtube.com/watch?v=Ry0ETecH14w
Sterba, James (2019) *Is a Good God Logically Possible?* New York: Palgrave Macmillan.
Swinburne, Richard (2003) *The Resurrection of God Incarnate*, New York: Oxford University Press.
—— (2004) *The Existence of God*, 2nd ed., New York: Oxford University Press.
—— (2005) *Faith and Reason*, 2nd ed., New York: Oxford University Press.
—— (2010) *Is There a God?* 2nd ed., New York: Oxford University Press.
—— (2016) *The Coherence of Theism*, 2nd ed., New York: Oxford University Press.
Swindal, James, and Harry Gensler (eds) (2005) *The Sheed & Ward Anthology of Catholic Philosophy*, Lanham, MD: Rowman & Littlefield.
Tait, Katharine (1975) *My Father, Bertrand Russell*, New York: Harcourt, Brace, Jovanovich.
Taylor, Richard (1991) *Metaphysics*, 4th ed., Englewood Cliffs, NJ: Prentice Hall.
Teilhard de Chardin, Pierre (1966) *Man's Place in Nature*, New York: Harper & Row.
Troll, Christian (2008) "Future Christian-Muslim engagement," paper at a Cambridge meeting between Christians and Muslims. http://chiesa.espresso.repubblica.it/articolo/208895?eng=y
Vahanian, Gianni (1961) *The Death of God*, New York: George Braziller.
Van Buren, Paul (1963) *The Secular Meaning of the Gospel*, New York: Macmillan.
Vatican (2009) *In Search of a Universal Ethic: A New Look at the Natural Law*, a report of the Vatican International Theological Commission. https://www.vatican.va/roman_curia/congregations/cfaith/cti_documents/rc_con_cfaith_doc_20090520_legge-naturale_en.html
Vatican II (1962–65) All documents are online. http://www.vatican.va/archive/hist_councils/ii_vatican_council/index.htm
Wattles, Jeffrey (1996) *The Golden Rule*, New York: Oxford University Press.
Williams, Bernard (1972) "God, morality, and prudence," in Helm 1981: 135–40.
Wine, Sherwin (1985) *Judaism Beyond God*, Farmington Hills, MI: Society for Humanistic Humanism.
Wright, N.T. (2003) *The Resurrection of the Son of God*, Minneapolis, MN: Fortress.

Index

Abraham 4, 130–2
Abrahamic religions 4, 29, 130; believers 29; non- 132
absurdity 2; of life 152, 158
Adam and Eve 73, 100–4; sin of 95, 100–2
adultery 95, 120, 146, 150
afterlife 24, 32, 36–7, 44–8, 91, 109, 111n6, 133, 147, 157, 160, 162–3; and body-soul 39–42; myths 37, 48; and religion 37–9
agnosticism 4–5, 16, 70, 155
Al-Attar, Mariam 136n1
Ali, Imam 131
Altizer, Thomas 23–4n3
altruism 133–4, 147
Analects 133
analytic 22; philosophy 29, 30n5, 35, 89
animals 14, 101, 103, 111n6, 115–16, 134; plants-and-animals argument 69–74, 70n1; rational 70, 147; social 134
animism 12, 92n5
An-Na'im, Abdullah 131
Anselm, St. 23, 84–6
Anselm's argument 85–6; *see also* ontological argument
anthropic principle 76n7, 77, 81
Aphrodite 92
Apostles' Creed 117
Aquinas, Thomas 4n5, 29, 48n9, 50, 50n2, 52, 59, 59n11, 61–2, 65, 68, 71–2, 98, 129, 146, 156, 162; Five Ways 52–6, 52n4, 55–6n7, 61, 65, 72; *Summa Contra Gentiles* 29; *Summa Theologica* 4n5
Arabi, Ibn 131

Archer, Maria 17
argument(s) 2–4, 14, 23, 25–6, 38n1, 50n1, 54, 54n6, 80n11, 84n1; atheist 111, 113; consistency 101, 128; for DCT 137; deductive 87; direct 58–60, 59n10; for God's existence 54n6, 58–61, 59n10, 65, 68, 82, 89, 91, 137n2; inductive 87; medieval Muslim 64; racist 143–5; Shortism 142–3; sound 2; strong 61, 67, 79, 162; true premises 2, 50; valid 2; *see also* Anselm's argument; consistency argument; cosmological argument; design argument; fine-tuning argument; first cause argument; first mover argument; greatest being argument; Kalam argument; moral argument; near-death experience (NDE) argument; necessary being argument; ontological argument; orderly-things argument; plants-and-animals argument; problem of evil argument; simplicity argument; sufficient-reason argument; teleological argument; wager argument; world's designer argument
Aristotle 52, 55–6n7, 57, 95
Aronson, Eliot 135
astronomy 153, 156
atheism 13, 23, 38, 58, 65, 71n2, 88, 157–9; classical 61–2, 65; problem 138; *see also* Big Bang atheism; new atheism
atheists 5, 13, 16n1, 18n2, 24, 38, 60, 62, 65, 69–70, 76, 78–9, 88, 107, 111–12, 114, 119, 133, 138–9, 146–7, 150–1, 152–3, 155–60, 158n2, 162; emotivist 113; Marxist 18n2; militant 18–19; new 16–17; older (traditional) 16

Augustine, St. 12–13, 34, 59, 61, 70, 74, 79, 83, 87, 89, 97, 100n3, 101, 109, 114, 119, 129, 133, 155, 162
AWARE medical trial 44, 46
Ayer, A.J. 16, 21, 25, 30–2, 31n7, 35; near-death experience of 43–5

Bahá'í 38
Bahá'u'lláh 131
Baltimore Catechism 155
belief(s): basic 87; in Bible 137; Christian 93, 117, 155; core 48, 117; essential 117; ethical benefits of 18; false 11, 127; about God 34, 58, 88–9, 151n6, 163; in God 1–2, 6, 12–13, 27, 29, 32, 44, 61, 79, 88–90, 98–100, 112–13, 112n7, 118, 137–8, 141, 159, 161; happiness benefits of 18; medical benefits of 18; moral 25–6, 28, 32, 128, 138–9, 142, 151n6; mystical 90; non- 89; in objective moral duties 137; in one God 92, 95; psychic benefits of 18; psychological benefits of 17–18; rational 58; religious 8–9, 12, 22, 38, 58, 97, 137, 162; true 11, 161; in Yahweh 92
Benedict XVI, Pope 129
best explanation 45–6, 70–2, 78, 82, 82n13, 157
Bible 54, 61, 72–4, 101, 103, 113–15, 120, 128, 137, 145–7, 156, 161; belief in 137; Jewish 130, 156
biblical interpretation 72–4
biblical literalism 74, 101, 119
Big Bang 52–3, 63–5, 76–7, 105, 160, 163; *see also* Big Bang atheism
Big Bang atheism 61, 65; Big-gamble 79; Observation-selection 81–2; Parallel-worlds 79
bigotry 16
biological laws 36
biology 36, 71, 75, 109, 135, 146, 150, 160
body 4n6, 38–9, 41–3, 70, 90, 94, 160; animal 37, 48; human 37, 48; material 38–9, 41; *see also* epiphenomenalism; interactive dualism; occasionalism
body-mind problem *see* body-soul problem
body-soul: and afterlife 39–42; dualistic views 41; monistic views 39; problem 37, 39

Bonaventure 62
Brickman, Philip 108n4
Brody, Baruch 136n1
Buddha 131–2
Buddhism 122, 132–3

Calvin, John 12, 87, 89, 129
Camus, Albert 158–9n2
carbon rule 126
Carson, Thomas 113n7, 136n1
Carter, Brandon 76
Catholicism 4, 161
chance 22, 62, 69–71, 77–9, 81, 106, 116, 157; explanation 79
child psychology 135, 148
China 92, 132–3
Christ 15, 90–1, 109–10, 131
Christian 3–4, 4n5, 6, 11–12, 14, 23–4n3, 34–5, 40, 73–4, 80, 93–7, 101–3, 114, 114n9, 117, 119–20, 120n4, 129, 140, 145, 154–7, 158n2, 161; beliefs 93, 117, 155; philosophers 3, 35, 140; practices 96; scholars 114n9; schools 11; thinkers 23–4n3, 73–4, 101, 129, 158n2, 161
Christianity 4, 19–20, 19n3, 29, 38–40, 93, 96–7, 103, 111, 113–14, 114n9, 118, 120, 122, 128–30, 154–6; atheist 23–4n3
Christians 11, 13, 34, 37–9, 43, 48, 59n11, 62, 73, 92, 94–7, 110, 114, 117–20, 128, 154–5; non- 118–19
Christian Science 133
Church 15, 29, 145–6; Catholic 110, 117, 119
classical conditioning 148
cognitive dissonance 134, 148
Collins, Francis 71n3, 77n8, 80, 83, 156
Collins, R. 77n8
Common Word 154, 154n1
complexity-consciousness, law of 40, 157, 162
Confucianism 122, 133
Confucius 121, 133
conscience *see* moral sense
consistency 46–7, 74, 110, 112–13, 122–4, 127–8, 135, 141–3, 145, 151, 162–3; imperative 151; in- 16; norms 128, 135; requirement 110; test 123; *see also* consistency argument
consistency argument 101, 128

Index 171

contingent: being 54–7; fact 65–6
Copan, Paul 114–15
Copernicus 74
Copleston, Frederick 4, 32, 45, 65, 80, 90
cosmological argument 59
Craig, William 38n1, 65n15
Creation 62, 63n13, 73–5, 76n7, 77, 81n12, 90, 101, 104–5, 131, 135, 163; *see also* creation hypothesis
creation hypothesis 70
creationism (intelligent design) 81n12
creed 24, 46, 117–18, 155; *see also* Apostles' Creed; "Gensler Creed"; Nicene Creed
critical thinking 5–6n8, 9, 9–10n1, 162
cultural relativism 25
Curie, Marie 40n4
Cybele 96
cyber immortality 37

Darwin, Charles 69–72, 94, 134, 148; *Descent of Man* 134
David, King 115
Dawkins, Richard 16, 71, 103
death 5, 8, 24, 32, 94, 98–102, 104–5, 112; *see also* life after death; near-death experience (NDE)
death-of-God movement 23–4n3
deism 48, 48n10, 80, 133
Dennett, Daniel 16
Descartes, René 84n1, 87
design 68–83, 88, 157–8; *see also* design argument; Intelligent Design (ID); intelligent designer; world's designer
design argument 68–72, 94; biblical interpretation 72–4; evolution and purpose 74–6; *see also* fine-tuning argument; orderly-things argument; plants-and-animals argument; world's designer argument
discrimination 97, 142, 148
disease 15, 18, 98–102, 104–5, 109, 162; mental 9, 12; religion as 9, 15, 17
divine command theory (DCT) 26, 113n7, 136–41, 136n1, 146, 159
divine life-plan 153
divine plan 109, 158
divine revelation 48n10, 156; *see also* religious revelation; revelation
divinity 22n1, 121; Jesus's 118, 155; sense of 88–9, 162–3
dogmatism 15, 18n2

Doppler effect 63–4
double-aspect theory 39–41
Douglass, Frederick 19
dualism 39, 41–2

Eastern Orthodoxy 4
Eccles, John 41
efficient cause 50n2, 57
emotivism 25–6, 112–13, 141, 159, 161; ethics 25–7; moral reasoning on 28–9; problems with 32–4; simplicity argument for 27–8
empirically testable 21–3, 25–6, 30–2, 30n6, 160
Empiricus 99
Epicurus 38
epiphenomenalism 41, 46
Epstein, Greg 23–4n3
essential beliefs 117
eternal damnation 110
eternal life 13, 48n8, 104–6, 108, 111, 150–1, 153–4, 157, 163
ethical intuitionism 26
ethical universals 120
ethics 9–10n1, 28, 133, 158–9; applied 142n4; emotivist 25–7; global 119, 121, 133, 150; golden rule 16; and religion 4, 136–51, 153; *see also* ethics-religion connection
ethics-religion connection 135
evil 2, 8, 18n2, 19, 24, 71, 73, 75, 93–7, 106–13, 116–17, 119–20, 132, 137, 140, 143, 161, 163; biblical problem of 102–3, 113–15; intellectual problem of 112; Irenaeus on 103–5; moral 99, 99n1, 101, 105; mystery of 110; natural 99, 101, 105; pastoral problem of 112; personal-faith problem of 112; problem of 2, 15, 64, 89, 98–100, 103, 113n7, 153; scriptural problem of 115; *see also* problem of evil argument
evolution 13, 40, 58, 68–72, 73n5, 74, 76, 79, 81n12, 88, 101, 104, 141, 148, 152, 157, 160; golden rule and 134–5; and purpose 74–6
exclusivism 118–19

faith 3–7, 9, 12–13, 14, 17, 19n3, 23, 34, 40, 43, 50, 54n6, 59–60, 59n11, 64, 80, 87, 100, 108–9, 112, 114, 117–20, 120n4, 121, 129, 131, 150, 156–7, 162; *see also* interfaith

family 7, 14, 20, 43, 45, 47, 91, 102, 106, 109, 113, 121–2, 127–8, 131, 149–51; issues 13, 45
father figure 8, 12–13, 84, 96
Felix, Minucius 93, 95, 97
Festinger, Leon 135
fideists 59, 59n11
fine tuning 32, 35, 77–83, 80n11, 89, 94, 156, 160, 162–3; *see also* fine-tuning argument
fine-tuning argument 59, 72n4, 75–83, 77n8, 81n12, 157, 162
first cause 3, 14, 49–67; *see also* first cause argument
first cause argument 14, 49–50, 52, 54, 65, 160
first mover 52–4, 59
first mover argument 53–3, 54n6
Flatliners 42
Flew, Antony 16, 22–3, 31n7, 35, 79–80, 83, 156; gardener metaphor 22–3, 22n2
Foundationalism, classical 87
Francis I, Pope 11
Francis of Assisi, St. 129
Frankena, William 136n1
free choice 66, 99, 105
freedom of religion 120
free will 18, 41, 64, 101, 105–6
free-will defense 113
Freud, Sigmund 3, 7–13, 14, 16–17, 35, 37–8, 84, 89, 153, 160–1; and science 8–9
Fulwiler, Jennifer 13
fundamentalism 15, 18–19, 72, 74, 81n12

Galileo Galilei 74
Gandhi, Mahatma 16, 115
Ganymede 96
Garden of Eden 73, 100
Genesis 61–2, 64, 72–4, 77, 79, 81–2, 101, 105, 115
genetics 71n3, 80
genocide 102–3, 115
Gensler, Harry J. 2n1, 2n2, 5, 9n1, 25, 30n5, 50, 50n1, 52n3, 52n4, 55n7, 60, 69–71, 82n13, 84n1, 86, 86n2, 99, 100n2, 110, 113, 113n7, 121n5, 133, 133n8, 136n1, 137n2, 142n4, 153, 159; *Ethics and Religion* 153; *Introduction to Logic* 153; *see also* "Gensler Creed"
"Gensler Creed" 118, 155

global ethics document 119–20
Glynn, Patrick 17, 77n8
Gnosticism 103
God: all-powerful 93, 98, 113; belief in 1–2, 6, 12–13, 27, 29, 32, 44, 61, 79, 88–90, 98–100, 112–13, 112n7, 118, 137–8, 141, 159, 161; beliefs about 34, 58, 88–9, 151n6, 163; definition 4; eternal 20, 64; evil 103; as first cause 14; good 103, 110, 111n6; loving 19, 96, 109, 150, 153–4, 157; nature of 89, 140n3, 146; paths to 3, 61, 72n4, 80, 84, 89, 118–19, 121, 161–3; perfect 93–4, 99–102, 100n2, 106–7, 153; personal 57, 130, 156; supreme 4, 11, 95, 132; *see also* God's existence; God's love; God's plan; God's will; God-talk; One God; Yahweh
godless religion 23–5, 34–5
God's existence 44, 50, 52, 58, 59n10, 60, 64, 68, 71–2, 86, 89, 95, 98, 119, 139; arguments for 4n5, 54n6, 58–9, 59n10, 61, 82, 87, 89, 137n2; evidence for 60
God's love 20, 38, 80, 88, 99, 104, 109, 111, 163
God's plan 13, 18, 103, 105, 107–12, 147, 151, 152, 157
God's will 29, 103, 113n7, 136–7, 139–41, 140n3, 145–6, 150
God-talk 21–3
Golden Rule 4, 16, 111, 114n8, 118–19, 121–3, 122n6, 141, 145, 148, 150, 153–5, 159–62; in Christianity 128–30; and evolution 134–5; fallacies 123–8; fellow pilgrims or enemies? 119–21; in non-Christian faiths 130–4; *see also* golden-rule consistency requirement
golden-rule consistency requirement 110–11
Gospel of Christ 110
greatest being argument 57–8
Great Mind idea 82
Greek myth 44; river Styx 44
Grimm Brothers 121–2

Habermas, Gary 35, 38n1, 80
Hadiths 131
hallucinations 11, 42–3, 47, 90–1
happiness 12, 17–19, 29, 37–8, 104–6, 108–10, 108n4, 108n5, 132, 135, 147, 152, 155, 158, 162–3; religion and 17–19, 37, 108n5

harmfulness of religion 3, 9, 12, 14–20, 58, 160
Harris, Sam 16
hatred 5n7, 19, 28, 99, 102, 106, 118n1, 119n2, 137, 140, 147; racial 25–6, 32
Hawking, Steven 64n14, 76–8, 80
heaven 13, 32, 37, 43, 61, 64, 74, 79, 90, 92, 94–5, 105–7, 117, 129, 155; Kingdom of 163
hedonism 110
Helm, Paul 136n1
Hempel, Carl G. 32
henotheism 92, 95
Hick, John 35, 100n3, 103–5, 110–11
Hillel, Rabbi 121, 130
Hinduism 5, 19n3, 37, 43, 48, 92, 117, 122, 132
Hitchens, Christopher 16
Hitler 27
hope 11, 13, 17, 24, 40n4, 107
human genome 71n3, 80
Humanistic Judaism 13, 23, 34–5
human life 81–2, 153, 155–6, 163
human rights 24, 131
Hume, David 16, 22n1, 108
Huxley, Thomas 70

Iannaccone, Lawrence 12, 35n9
idealism 39–40
ideal observer 26, 134, 159; *see also* ideal-observer view
ideal-observer view 26
identity theory 40
Ignatius of Loyola 91, 91n4, 112, 155
ignosticism 23
illusion 8, 22n1, 100
inclusivism 119
India 92, 132
inductive reasoning 69
inference to the best explanation 70–1, 78, 82
infinite-regress problem 10
instinct 12, 32, 58, 61, 83, 87–9, 134, 162–3
Intelligent Design (ID) 81
intelligent designer 69
intelligent life 32, 76, 79, 157
interactive dualism 41
interfaith 5, 5n7, 129, 133
intuitionism 28, 141, 159; *see also* ethical intuitionism
intuitions (moral) 28, 140–2, 145, 159
Iran 114, 114n8, 131, 153

Irenaean theodicy 104, 111–13
Irenaeus 95, 102, 109; on evil 103–5
Islam 4, 19n3, 29, 114, 114n8, 114n9, 118, 122, 130–1, 136n1, 154–6
Israelites 114–15, 121, 145

Jainism 133
James, William 10–12, 18, 91; *Varieties of Religious Experience* 91
Jefferson, Thomas 48n10
Jesuits 3, 29, 91
Jesus 5, 16, 18–19, 35, 38, 38n1, 43, 97, 102–3, 113–15, 117–21, 128–9, 155–6; as bridge between God and humans 118–19, 155–6; divinity of 118, 155
Jewish: Bible 130, 156; congregation 23; identity 23; law 129–30; people 92; scriptures 128; synagogue 23
John Paul II, Pope 129
Judaism 4, 19n3, 23, 23–4n3, 29, 118, 122, 130, 136n1, 156; *see also* Humanistic Judaism
Judeo-Christian tradition 5
judgments: ethical 25; evaluative 27, 33; moral 26–9, 32–3, 136, 138–9
Jupiter 92, 95–6

Kalam argument 4n5, 59, 61–5, 65n15, 67, 80n11, 82–3, 160, 162–3
Kant, Immanuel 137n2
Karma 132–3
Kennedy, John 124–5
Khan, Hazrat 131
killing 27, 97, 103, 113, 120, 146, 150; mercy 151n6; *see also* murder
King, Martin Luther 16
Kingdom of Heaven 163
Kinnier, Richard 120
Kohlberg, L. 134
Koran 114n9, 156; *see also* Qur'an
Krishna 43, 92–3, 131
Kübler-Ross, Elisabeth 45, 47; and life after death 45–6

Leibniz, Gottfried 65
Lemaître, Georges 63n13
Lewis, C.S. 4, 22n2, 62–3, 63n12, 76, 112, 119; *A Grief Observed* 112; *Mere Christianity* 4; *The Problem of Pain* 112
life after death 1, 3, 4n4, 12, 35, 36–48, 39n2, 45n6
Locke, John 55–6n7

logic 2, 2n2, 22, 50n1, 52n4, 84n1, 86, 111, 116, 133, 145; advanced modal 86; propositional 51, 53, 69, 85, 99; quantificational 50; relational 55n7; symbolic 50
logical positivism 3, 21–35, 30n5, 30n6, 43, 58, 89, 160–1; problems with 29–32
Long, Jeffrey 46–8, 163; *Evidence of the Afterlife* 46; and life after death 46–8
love 9, 13, 17, 19–20, 19n3, 39, 43, 48, 55n7, 91–2, 104–6, 108–9, 111, 113, 117, 132–4, 140n3, 141, 146–7, 149–50, 152, 154; Christian 97; of God 18, 35, 74, 91, 114n8, 117–18, 129, 147, 150–1, 154–5, 157, 163; of neighbor 74, 91, 114n8, 129, 163; of science 8; self- 126, 130; tough 125; universal 19, 116; unselfish 29, 138; your neighbor 24, 101, 114, 117–18, 129–31, 145–6, 149–50, 154–5, 157, 163; *see also* God's love
Loyola, Ignatius 91, 91n4, 112, 155
Lumen Gentium 110
Luther, Martin 129
lying 28, 46n7, 88, 99, 120, 146, 150

MacIntyre, Alasdair 13
Mackie, J.L. 16, 64–6, 80–1, 112
Mahabharata 132
Mandela, Nelson 16
Manson, Neil 77n8
Mars 96
materialism 27, 38–42, 46
materialist view 42, 62–3
mathematics 21–2, 64, 163
McGowan 23–4n3
meaning of life 1, 4, 152–63, 161n3
mechanical laws 71, 75
medicine 18
Mendel, Gregor 71n3
mental health 17
Michel, Thomas 136n1
Middle Ages 54n6, 140
militarists 145
Mill, John Stuart 14, 49
Miller 48
miracles 39, 156
Mohism 133
monotheism 4–5, 4n5, 92–3, 96, 118, 121, 156
Moody, Raymond 42–3; *Life After Life* 42
moral argument 59, 63n12

moral authority 137, 146
moral duties 59; objective 137
moral education 28, 138
moral evils 99, 99n1, 101, 105
moral goodness 101
moral intuitions 140–2, 145
moral issues 28, 139, 145, 160
morality 15, 19, 21, 27n1, 27–8n2, 28–9, 34, 111, 115, 125, 133–4, 136n1, 137–9, 147–51, 163
moral knowledge 25–6, 34
moral law 129, 137, 141, 147
moral life 29, 138, 151
moral order 8, 137
moral principles 26, 28, 141–3, 147
moral rationality 127, 142, 146
moral sense (conscience) 14, 110, 134, 137n2, 146
moral system 146
moral thinking 134, 143, 147–8, 151; stages 148
moral truth(s) 25–6, 34, 138, 141, 147
Mormonism 133
Moser, Paul 60
Moses 131
Moses Maimonides 52
Moslem *see* Muslim
Muhammad 131
murder 1, 99, 101
Muslim 4, 4n5, 62, 64, 114, 114n9, 120, 120n4, 145, 153–4
mutation 71, 75, 158
mystical experiences 12, 89–91, 162
mysticism 3, 84, 89–92

names 16, 95
natural evils 99, 101, 105
natural law (NL) 34, 136, 136n1, 140, 146, 159, 162; as biological beings 148–50; and racism 141–5; as rational beings 147–8; as spiritual beings 150–1; three parts 146–7
natural moral law 129, 147; *see also* natural law (NL)
nature 12, 41, 47, 54, 72, 94–5, 104, 137, 149, 162–3; beauty of 45, 88; biological 147, 149–51; of cause 50; God's 89, 140n3, 146; laws of 107–8; rational 147; religious 12; sexual 12; spiritual 147; of value 113n7
near-death experience (NDE) 35, 40n4, 42–8, 46n7, 48n9, 58–9, 59n10, 61, 80, 91–2, 107, 157, 160–3

near-death experience (NDE) argument 46, 59n10
necessary being 4n6, 52, 52n4, 54, 56–7, 59, 65–6
necessary being argument 52n4, 54, 57
necessary fact 65
neuroscience 134, 148
neurosis 8–9, 12, 17
new atheism 16
Newman, John 137n2
Nicene Creed 117
nihilism 159
norms 10–11, 19, 28, 33–4, 147, 150; basic moral 159; consistency 128; ethical 159; global 120; ideal observer 159; intuitionism 159; love 129; moral 101, 122, 150; objective ethical 158–9; religious 116; of scientific method 33–4; shortist 142; social 37, 159; social contract 159
Nostra Aetate 117

obedience duties 150
objective standards 29
observational selection effect 81
Occam's razor 27, 33, 79
occasionalism 41
Ockham, William of 54n6, 140
Old Testament 4, 14, 103, 114, 121, 128
Olson, Carl E. 38n1
Ω omega point 40, 157
omnipotence 4n6, 86, 98, 112–13
omniscience 4n6, 86, 98
One God 3, 84, 92–3, 103, 116, 121, 131–2, 151
ontological argument 3, 59, 84–7, 162
orderly-things argument 68–9
organized religion 34
Origen 73–4, 101, 110
Otto 12

pacifists 145
pagan: gods 92; *see also* Pagan-Christian debate
Pagan-Christian debate 3, 84, 93–7, 97n7
Pannenberg, Wolfhart 38n1
parallel worlds 77–9, 81–2
Parliament of the World's Religions 119–20, 150
Parnia, Sam 44, 468–7
Pascal, Blaise 59n10; *see also* wager argument
path 58n9, 61, 83, 105, 112; to Golden Rule 135; to knowledge 1, 8–11, 159; to truth 31; *see also* paths to God
paths to God 3, 59, 61, 72n4, 80, 84, 89, 118–19, 121, 156, 161–3
Paul, St. 48n9, 90, 91n4, 104, 129, 141
Perry, Paul 163
Persian 4n5, 131, 153, 154n1
personal commitment 3; *see also* faith
perverted desires 143
perverted religion 19, 19n3
Pfaff, D. 134
philosophy 1–3, 5–6, 9–10, 13, 21, 22n2, 27, 29–30, 33, 42, 50, 58, 80, 89, 93, 100, 114, 135, 136, 161; analytic 29, 30n5, 35, 89; ancient Greek 129; contemporary philosophy 29; continental philosophy 29; of religion 1–2, 65, 153; religious 16; scholastic 86
physical laws 152
Plantinga, Alvin 12, 35, 59n10, 77n8, 84–9, 84n1, 86n2, 113
plants-and-animals argument 69–74, 70n1
Plato 38, 52, 91n4, 95, 155; *Euthyphro* 139; *Republic* 43
pleasure 88, 106–8, 159
polytheism 3, 12, 84–97; Greco-Roman 133
poverty 96, 98
pragmatic method 11
pragmatism 18, 58n9, 162
prayer 18, 87, 95, 145–6; colloquial 18; individual 24; meditative 18; non-theist 24; petitional 18; ritual 18
problem of evil argument 2, 98–100, 112, 113n7
proof 8, 10–11, 54n6, 60, 72, 86, 90, 111, 162
Protestantism 4
psychoanalysis 12
psychology 12, 35, 43, 58, 134, 148; *see also* child psychology; psychoanalysis
purpose 13, 32, 58–9, 62, 69–71, 93, 108, 147, 152–5, 157–8, 160, 163; divine 75, 77, 160; evolution and 74–6; God's 100, 146; human 75; of human life 154–5; moral 19

quantifier-shift fallacy 55–6n7
Qur'an 120–1, 131

Index

rabbi 23, 34, 118, 130
racism 15, 18, 32, 34, 103, 113, 138, 141, 143–6, 148, 159, 162; natural law and 141–5
radical pluralism 119
random variation/randomness 71, 74, 152, 160
rationalists 59
reasoning 1, 3, 17, 51, 52n3, 55, 57, 61, 83, 85, 88, 134, 161–2; abstract 22n1; experimental 22n1; about God 112; Golden Rule 123; inductive 69; logical 1–4; moral 28–9, 147
redshift 63–4
reductionism 30; materialistic 41; scientific 41
reformed epistemology 3, 84, 87–9, 162–3
reincarnation 37, 48, 132
religion: and afterlife 37–9; anti- 42, 74, 161; atheist 23–4n3, 24; attacks on 58; attraction to 38; benefits of 16–20, 35, 37, 59, 161; critics of 79; as disease 9, 15; and ethics 4, 136–51, 153; false 117; freedom of 120; genuine 19n3; and happiness 17–19, 37, 108n5; as illusion 8; as neurosis 8, 12, 17; nontraditional 23; organized 34; of our ancestors 93, 95; philosophy of 1–2, 65, 153; science and 11, 72, 80, 89; traditional 132; true 116–17; *see also* godless religion; harmfulness of religion; perverted religion
religions 4, 32, 35, 38, 90, 113, 116–35, 133n8, 145, 154, 156; Aboriginal 133; godless 23–5; monotheist(ic) 4, 118, 156; theist 38; *see also* Abrahamic religions; animism; Bahá'í; Buddhism; Catholicism; Christianity; Christian Science; Confucianism; deism; Eastern Orthodoxy; henotheism; Hinduism; Islam; Jainism; Judaism; Mohism; monotheism; Mormonism; polytheism; Protestantism; religions of the world; Scientology; Shintoism; Sikhism; Taoism; theism; Unification; Unitarianism; Unitarian Universalism; world religions; Yoruba; Zoroastrianism
religions of the world 121, 157, 159–62
religious beliefs 8–9, 12, 22, 38, 58, 97, 137, 162

religious communities 24, 34
religious diversity 116–35
religious knowledge 89
religious revelation 3
religious tradition 1, 3, 111, 120, 156
religious view 37, 62, 63n12, 120
revelation 62, 74, 80, 109, 121, 131, 135, 141, 155–6
revenge 99, 102–3, 132
Roman Empire 92, 95–6
Rushd, Ibn (Averroes) 4n5
Russell, Bertrand 4, 14–17, 16n1, 37, 44, 49–50, 52, 59, 62, 65–6, 79–80, 90, 97n7, 98, 103, 160; daughter 20

Sadducees 38
Sa'di 131
Saeed, Sohaib 120n4
Sartre, Jean-Paul 138, 158n2
scholastic philosophy and theology 86
science 1, 3, 7, 9–12, 14–19, 18n2, 21–2, 27, 30–5, 36–7, 40n4, 42, 44, 58, 61–6, 63n12, 70n1, 71–2, 72n4, 74, 76, 82–3, 111, 121, 128, 135, 150–1, 159–60; -fiction 79; Freud and 8–9; laws of 76–7; pseudo- 45; and religion 11, 72, 80, 89
scientific knowledge 34
scientific method 9–10, 21; norms of 33–4
Scientology 133
selection 71, 75, 160; mutation- 158
self-evident moral norms/truths 87, 133–4, 159
Sermon on the Mount 128
Sheiman, Bruce 19, 150–1
Shintoism 133
shortism 142–3, 142n5
Sikhism 133
simplicity argument 27–8, 33
sin 95, 101, 103–5, 150
Sina, Ibn (Avicenna) 4n5
skepticism 9–12, 9–10n1, 162
Sober, Elliot 81
social conditioning 143
social instincts 134
social learning theory 135, 148
sociology 25, 135
Socrates 15, 93–5, 97, 103, 137–41
Soul 19, 36–8, 41–2, 44, 48, 70, 95, 103–4, 118, 131, 154–5; *see also* body-soul; body-soul problem

sound 23, 63
Spitzer, Robert 13, 48, 65n15, 77n8
stealing 99, 120, 137, 146, 150–1, 151n6
"stepping stone" analogy 2–3n2, 3, 59
Sterba, James 113
struggle 13, 14, 44, 60–1, 69–70, 75, 82–3, 100, 102–12, 121, 147–8, 150, 153, 155, 161n4, 162–3
subjectivism 25–7, 33
suffering 3, 15, 18, 37, 39, 75, 94–5, 98–115, 111n6, 150, 162
sufficient reason 59; principle of 65–6; see also sufficient reason argument
sufficient reason argument 65–7
supernatural beings 32, 38
supernaturalism 26
survival of the fittest 71, 74, 152
Swinburne, Richard 4n6, 35, 38n1, 75, 77n8, 111n6
Swindal, James 29, 40, 50n2, 52n4, 54n6, 59n10, 59n11, 68, 70–1, 73–4, 84n1, 87, 87n3, 91n4, 104, 140, 155–6, 158n2

Tait, Katharine 20
Talmud 130
Taoism 122, 133
Taylor, Richard 65
Teilhard de Chardin, Pierre 40, 40n3, 40n4, 75, 91n4, 156–7, 162; see also complexity-consciousness, law of
teleological argument (argument from design) 32, 59, 68
ten commandments 137
Tertullian 59n11
theism 4, 19, 32, 38–9, 58, 112, 147, 150–1, 158n2; classical 61–2, 82; eternal-world 61–2
theodicy 100, 100n2, 100n3, 102, 110; Adam-and-Eve 100; Augustinian 100n3; Irenaean 100n3, 104, 106–7, 111–13; soul-making 103; traditional 98, 100n3, 101–2, 104–5
theology 3, 86, 132
Theresa, Mother 16
Thomism 29
Torah 130
traditional theodicy 98, 100n3, 101–2, 104–5

transcendental meditation 18
trialism 41
Trinity 93
Troll, Christian 120n4
true by definition (analytic) statements 21–3, 25–6, 30, 30n6, 32, 86, 160
truth claims 21–3, 25–7, 30, 30n6, 32–3, 112, 160

uncaused cause see first cause
Unification 133
Unitarianism 133
Unitarian Universalism 23–4n3
United Nations 131
United States 29, 153
unity 90, 95, 123, 128, 134, 161
universal salvation 110
unmoved mover see first mover
unnecessary hypothesis 71

Vahanian, Gianni 23–4n3
valid 50–1, 53, 85; argument 2; in- 55–6, 55n7
values 24, 29, 76–8, 81, 106, 134, 138–9, 153, 157
Van Buren, Paul 23–4n3, 35
Vatican II Council 29, 110, 117, 119, 161
Venus 92, 96
Vietnam war 145

wager argument 59n10
warrant 88–9
Wattles, Jeffrey 121n5
William of Ockham see Ockham, William of
Williams, Bernard 136n1
Wine, Rabbi Sherman 23, 34
wisdom 109, 111, 129, 133, 150
world religions 107, 116, 118, 121–2, 128, 130
world's designer 52, 58–9
world's designer argument 58
Wright, N. T. 38n1

Yahweh 23, 92, 121
Yoruba 133

Zeus 92
Zoroaster 131
Zoroastrianism 133